THROUGH NAVAJO EYES
An Exploration in Film Communication and Anthropology

THROUGH NAVAJO EYES

An Exploration in Film Communication and Anthropology

SOL WORTH
JOHN ADAIR

Indiana University Press

Bloomington / *London*

This book is dedicated
to
JACK AND IDA WISHNEPOLSKY
and to
CASEY

Contents

Acknowledgments

Although it is usual to say in a section acknowledging the contributions of others that the work reported could not have been done without the help of many people, in this case it is literally and exactly so. What we shall be writing about in the following pages is not only our own work but also that of a group of Navajo who patiently consented to be our students. They not only worked throughout a summer making films, which is a difficult creative task, but they also allowed us to observe, question, and write about them while they did it. Indeed, they encouraged us. They felt that producing knowledge about communication, how people in different cultures make films, was something they wanted to participate in.

This book, therefore, could not have come about without our Navajo students, Mr. Mike Anderson, Mrs. Susie Benally, Mr. Al Clah, Mrs. Alta Kahn, Mr. Johnny Nelson, Miss Mary Jane Tsosie, and Miss Maxine Tsosie.

The community of Pine Springs agreed to allow us to live with them while we were working. We wish we could thank each one individually, but since they acted as a community to welcome us, we must thank them as a community for their help and friendship.

Mr. and Mrs. Clarence Birch were the schoolteachers in the Bureau of Indian Affairs school at Pine Springs. Not only did they welcome us and help us in every possible way, but Clarence

Birch offered us the school's dormitories for our sleeping, teaching and work quarters. We used his school as our own and we want to thank him for allowing it.

Mr. Russell Griswold, the owner of the trading post at Pine Springs, gave us an office behind the post which we used for interviews and for our own personal notetaking and conferences. He was one of the most knowledgeable men in the area about the community and its members, and he and his family helped us in ways, both large and small, too many to be enumerated here.

Many other people helped to smooth our way. The Navajo tribal leaders at Window Rock supported and often encouraged us when it seemed as if bureaucracy would overcome us. To all those, and in particular to Mr. Maurice McCabe and Mr. Ned Hatathli, our thanks. Mr. Graham Holmes, Navajo area director, Mr. Walter Olsen, director of the Albuquerque area office, Mr. Ernest Magnuson, and Mr. Buck Benham, all of the Bureau of Indian Affairs, gave us invaluable help and support while on the Navajo reservation.

Our colleagues in anthropology and communication with whom we discussed our plans were unusually patient and encouraging. Some, however, gave their time and experience so generously that we want to take this opportunity to acknowledge their help. Ward Goodenough was one of the first anthropologists to recognize the possible contribution of the bio-documentary method to ethnographic research. He encouraged our plans and helped clarify our ideas in discussing the project with us. When we came to analyze our experience, Dell Hymes proved one of the intellectual rocks we leaned on most heavily. His detailed criticism of the first draft of this manuscript enabled us to correct many unclear passages. Margaret Mead stuck with us all the way. She helped us to work out many newly-formed ideas in hours of conversation with her. The day we spent with her when we returned from the field with the Navajo films, looking at the films over and over again, was probably the finest lesson in visual ethnographic method we ever had. Gene Weltfish was enormously helpful before we went into the field, reviewing problems of field method with a camera.

Our work was supported by the National Science Foundation under grants number GS 1038 and GS 1759, and by the Annenberg School of Communications, University of Pennsylvania. Allan Smith and then Richard Lieban, who were successively head of the anthropology section of the Foundation, not only helped us to solve problems of budget and red tape, but became valued friends with whom we could discuss our findings, research problems, and plans at any time. Their help and encouragement made the research much easier. Edward Hall and John Collier, Jr., visited us in the field and gave us an opportunity to review our findings and methods with them. We found these occasions both helpful and stimulating.

Last but not least, we want to thank George Gerbner, Dean of the Annenberg School, who allowed one of us, at least, to spend almost four years talking about nothing but Navajo making movies. He found space when space was hard to find, he allowed us to monopolize secretaries when there were almost none to go around. He made the cameras, projectors, and editing equipment available whenever they were needed. He criticized and questioned, with great sensitivity, our papers and the colloquia at which we first began to formulate our analyses. He was in the deepest sense a valued colleague. And so was the late Dr. Adan Treganzo, Chairman of the Department of Anthropology, San Francisco State College, for the other of us.

Miss Terry Zaroff not only was responsible for typing this manuscript, but she kept her cool during at least five successive rewrites. She checked every reference and helped to organize us so that the work could go on despite teaching, meetings, and numerous other distractions. She deeply deserves our thanks.

Murdoch Matthew of the Indiana University Press was our editor. He cut, questioned, rewrote, and made contributions on almost every page. As with a film, a book is made in the editing room. Murdoch Matthew is that kind of editor. We thank him.

We want to say something about Richard Chalfen in these acknowledgments, but it is difficult to thank someone whom we consider to be one of us. He started as our graduate assistant in the field and has continued working in visual communication and the ethnography of communication. Although his name appears on only one chapter, we would like to say here that the work reported in the following pages was done by the three of us.

SOL WORTH

JOHN ADAIR

Philadelphia, Pennsylvania
Gallup, New Mexico

THROUGH NAVAJO EYES
An Exploration in Film Communication and Anthropology

Introduction

We wish to tell how we went about answering the question, What would happen if someone with a culture that makes and uses motion pictures taught people who had never made or used motion pictures to do so for the first time? Would they use the cameras and editing equipment at all? If they did, what would they make movies about and how would they go about it? This book reports the outcome of such an endeavor among some Navajo Indians living in the Southwestern United States.

One of the places we visited in a preliminary trip was Pine Springs, Arizona, where, twenty-five years before, John Adair had done one of his first studies on Navajo silversmiths.

When we arrived in Pine Springs, Adair sought out an old friend, Sam Yazzie, who was one of the leading medicine men in the area. We wanted to tell Sam about our plan to teach Navajos to use motion picture cameras and to enlist his support for the project. Sam was, at the time of our visit, about eighty years old and had just returned from a government hospital after a severe bout with chronic tuberculosis.

We were told that Sam was in his hogan, and after wandering through several muddy tracks that proved to be wrong turns, we found his house. It was an apparently new square log cabin in a clearing next to a more traditional hogan, which we found out later he used only for sings (the traditional Navajo curing ceremonies). As we entered the dim interior and waited a moment for our eyes to adjust, we saw Husky Burnsides, one of Yazzie's relatives by marriage who had interpreted for Adair years before and who was ready to do so again.

The cabin had a dirt floor, like the traditional hogans. It was furnished with three cots, some old wooden chairs, and several stacks of heavily used suitcases, which served as storage and dresser facilities. Sam was lying on one of the cots, his hair braided in the old style, a colorful bandanna around his forehead. As he got up to greet us, he glanced at Worth, but reserved his greetings for Adair. He said, "Grandson" (in Navajo), and Adair replied, "Grandfather" (in Navajo). We seated ourselves in a circle around Yazzie, we on the other cots and Burnsides on a wooden chair next to Yazzie. Adair and Sam spent about twenty minutes catching up on the news since their last visit, Sam being particularly graphic about his hospital visit. His black eyes flashed as he described the horrors of being away from home and subject to alien authority.

Although Sam was old, tired, and still coughing a great deal, there was no mistaking the authority in his manner. Finally Adair felt that it was time to bring up the subject of our visit. Adair explained that we wanted to teach some Navajo to make movies and mentioned Worth's part in the process several times. By the time Adair had finished, Yazzie was looking at Worth frequently, seeming for the first time to acknowledge his presence as legitimate. When Adair finished, Sam thought for a while, and then turned to Worth and asked a lengthy question which was interpreted as, "Will making movies do the sheep any harm?"

Worth was happy to explain that as far as he knew, there was no chance that making movies would harm the sheep.

Sam thought this over and then asked, "Will making movies do the sheep good?" Worth was forced to reply that as far as he knew making movies wouldn't do the sheep any good.

Sam thought this over, then, looking around at us he said, "Then why make movies?"

Sam Yazzie's question keeps haunting us. We did not answer it then and it is not directly answered in this book, but we want to place it squarely before our readers. Research is designed to formulate and solve problems, to ask and to answer questions. All of us doing research, and our students working with us and being trained to become researchers on their own, are concerned about the kinds of questions and answers we provide. We have constantly before us the certainty that our colleagues will question and criticize our theories, hypotheses, methods, and conclusions. All too often we forget about the questions that people like Sam Yazzie ask. What will they think about what we did? How will they benefit from our research and findings?

There is an implicit and perhaps justifiable assumption behind much work of the kind we will be describing. It is that the proper study of mankind is man—that knowing more about how we live in our rich diversity, how we interact and become social through our manipulations of a variety of symbols and symbol forms, enables us to communicate more fully and fruitfully with each other and with ourselves.

We assume that "better communication" has a positive value, that the more channels of communication available to a group the better off they will be. We assume that knowing how people imply meaning through symbolic events will automatically benefit all of us. We assume that studying how people present themselves through the images they make will be beneficial and certainly will harm no one.

Perhaps.

Perhaps we ought to have the courage to say at the outset that we do not know the effect of such a study as ours. We have therefore tried to describe in great detail not only what the Navajos did when they learned to use the camera, make movies, and look at movies, but also what we the researchers did and felt as we were teaching, observing, and analyzing.

There has recently been much discussion in anthropological

and sociological circles about the need for a reflexive attitude (Scholte 1970) in ethnographic theory and description. We are aware that our own ways of seeing are mediated through our culture. We have attempted, by describing ourselves—our preconceptions, attitudes and actions in the field—to allow the reader room for comparing us with our Navajo students.

Perhaps we ought also to have the courage to say at the outset that we do not know whether this work will help Sam Yazzie's sheep, or help him to attain any of the other things he holds dear. We can say that Sam helped us. He cooperated to the extent of letting his granddaughters make a film about him, called "The Spirit of the Navajo." He said he thought that what we were doing was good. He said that he liked the films that were made during the project.

Incidentally, as far as we could learn, Sam Yazzie and his family owned no sheep at the time we were in Pine Springs. The sheep he asked about, we suspect, were a symbolic possession for him, as they have become a symbolic problem for us. Sam's concern was how the new method of communication that we were to teach his people could help the Navajo. How would making films support their values and their way of life?

In some way, then, Sam Yazzie's symbolic question leads us into our study of how one small group of Navajo learned to manipulate and to use a novel symbolic form. As with many symbolic events, this one also yields useful generalizations. In a time in which much of the world is deeply concerned about how people with varying cultures will learn to live with one another, a method by which one group can show another what it sees and how it feels must assume proportions larger perhaps than the specific research described here was meant to do. We feel that this study is relevant beyond the Navajo, that some of the methods and findings reported here can be applied in other countries with people of other cultures and might perhaps prove helpful in our own country at a time when we are particularly feeling the strain of differing groups struggling to know and to live with one another.

Since the work described here was started, scores of projects of a similar nature have been undertaken. Thousands of high school and even grade school students have been learning to use motion picture cameras and to make movies about events and subjects of their own choosing (Larson and Meade 1969, Laybourne 1968). Canada has started a project designed to teach Canadian Indians to use motion picture cameras (Challenge for Change 1969). Boards of Education in cities throughout this country and in Europe (particularly in England) are preparing or conducting experimental programs with this new mode of communication integrated within the standard curriculum.

Mt. Sinai Hospital in New York City has through its Department of Community Medicine begun a program of teaching doctors, medical students, patients and ghetto high school students in their area to make movies of events and problems of their own choosing. The medical staff believes that only by making new forms of communication available to all the participants in the health care field can a true sense of community develop.

Clearly, then, people of various kinds, with major differences in culture, technological training, and formal education, can use motion picture cameras. What is not quite as clear is what we are to say or think or feel about the resultant movies. How do we deal with these movies? Of what value are they? To whom? How shall we use them? How shall we allocate resources to produce them?

There is little research in this area today and there was none only five years ago. It is hoped that this study, by examining and analyzing one such project in detail, can clarify and lend impetus to the entire area of visual communication research.

In this sense this is not a study of the Navajo Indian. It is a study of how a group of people structure their view of the world —their reality—through film. In that sense the results may be generalized.

Many people today are seeking not only new ways in which they can know one another but new ways to present themselves to one another. Anthropology has always had as one of its aims the description of man. It has sometimes been forgotten that a corollary to that is the presentation of man. It is in that spirit, not only as a study of a small group of men, but as a study of how man can present himself, that this work is offered.

One other notion needs to be introduced. We are writing a book about motion pictures. We are trying in it to describe a visual process of communication in a verbal code, an intrinsically difficult task. Johnny Nelson, one of our Navajo students, said, "You make a movie about it and then it's moving around where you can actually see what is being done, how it moves. If you write a whole book about it, then it's still. You give it to somebody and he reads it and he does not get the picture in his mind. . . . What I want to see is something that can move in front of my eyes. . . ."

We have not succeeded in providing a book that enables one to "see something that can move in front of (his) eyes" and "where you can actually see what is being done—how it moves." We have not succeeded in translating images into words. The reader of this book will not be able to know completely what we are writing about without seeing the films that the Navajo made at least once.

We have explained in words what happened, how and why it happened, what we and the Navajos said and thought about what happened, and how we analyzed what they did. We have not been able to *show* what they did in words.

Although in some sense we are unhappy about this, in another sense we welcome our own failure. If we could have accomplished the translation of film into words the entire project we are reporting would have been redundant.

The films mentioned in this book are available from the Center for Mass Communication, Columbia University Press. They can be rented for classroom viewing at special prices, making it simple for students and teachers to *see* what they will be reading about and discussing. For those interested in a fuller examination of the materials described in the book, copies of all the film materials made by the Navajo and all the notes and interview transcriptions are on deposit at the Library of Congress and can be viewed there.

We have, however, included photographs in the book. Some of the scenes analyzed in depth are represented by still photographs made from one of the frames in the movie scene. This is not a substitute for seeing the scene on the screen in motion, but it may give you a feel for what is being written.

Scientific studies rarely concern themselves with such nonobjective things as atmosphere, or the "look of things." Wherever possible we have tried to do so. We must explain that we faced some self-imposed restrictions. We didn't want to use cameras ourselves until such time as we felt our students would be minimally influenced by our way of making pictures. We felt that walking around competing with our students as filmmakers or photographers would first impose a burden on us—we would look for "good shots" rather than at what was happening—and second, would provide a model of how use of the camera was organized and, most important, *what* was to be photographed. Some events that took place before the project started, such as the community meeting at which permission to work in Pine Springs was debated, were of such importance that we asked and were given permission to record them. We emphasize that the photographs in the book are not meant to be definitive about the Navajo or their culture or to take the place of motion pictures.

We have also attempted in the Appendix to describe briefly all the films. Obviously we face a danger in that, because we must abstract from the film and describe those events that seem significant to us in a way that we think will make the reader visualize what *we saw* on the screen. But we do it in our terms—in themes and stories, cuts, close-ups and so on. As you will note in the body of the book all those things have special and often different meanings for the Navajo.

We have accepted the obvious: that pretending we are not part of our culture, that we have no preconceived ways of viewing the world or of viewing a film, is impossible. Dismissing culture is no answer to the problem of cultural relativity. What we have tried to do is describe what we saw as honestly as possible, putting as much light upon ourselves as we could and hoping that the reader can make judgments within his framework, sometimes recognizing that we organize the world the way he does and sometimes recognizing differences. We hope that whatever issues develop will aid rather than hinder clarity and understanding.

Although we have done our best to describe the films in the Appendix, there is no particular point in time when we suggest that you familiarize yourself with them or their descriptions. Some people will feel more comfortable reading the synopses of the films and viewing the films before they start the book. Others will want to do it after finishing the book.

We know of no rules for learning to understand how a people present themselves. We hope that this book will add to all our abilities to do just that.

PART ONE

Chapter

1

How Do People Structure Reality Through Film? Some Problems in Communication, Anthropology, and Film

Our object in the summer of 1966 was to determine whether we could teach people with a culture different from ours to make motion pictures depicting their culture and themselves as *they* saw fit. We assumed that if such people would use motion pictures in their own way, they would use them in a patterned rather than a random fashion, and that the particular patterns they used would reflect their culture and their particular cognitive style.

   In this book, we report on three areas of this research. First, we describe some of the communications and anthropological problems underlying our work; second, we describe some of the

methods we used, both to teach the Navajo to make films and to
collect our data on the filmmaking process; and third, we describe
briefly some of the films and relate some of our observations and
analyses concerning them.

Malinowski (1922) wrote many years ago that: "The final goal,
of which an Ethnographer should never lose sight . . . is, briefly,
to grasp the natives' point of view, his relation to life, to realize
his vision of *his* world." This clearly formulated objective has
created a methodological problem that has been partially solved
by collecting life histories with nondirective techniques. These
materials not only reveal things about the dynamics of personality but also help us to understand how the individual relates
himself to the outer world through the terms provided by his
particular language. Myths and linguistic texts have likewise
given us extensive verbal records for analysis.

Another—nonverbal[1]—approach that has helped to bring anthropology part of the way toward Malinowski's goal has been
the endeavor to understand the way people use visual modes of
expression and communication to orient themselves, and to express their relationship with their environment. We have some

---

1. The term *nonverbal* is ambiguous. It has been used to refer to almost anything
expressive or communicative that falls outside the strict definitions of language
proposed by professional linguists. Thus *nonverbal* has been used to describe such
diverse acts as handwriting, painting, movies, and graphics; gesture, facial expression, and hand–body movement; music in its written form; as well as such language connected acts as pauses, shouting and whispering, and speech rhythm.
Many of the above activities are directly connected by correlation or transforma-
tion to speech and are more properly referred to as metaverbal. What we shall
be discussing are those acts that are not commonly believed to be speech or
language connected, and which might be more accurately described by such
words as *picture, image, pictorial* or *visual,* as opposed to the ambiguous *nonverbal.*
We will use the term *nonverbal* when we wish to make a point of separating what
we are talking about from speech or spoken language in general, but it is important to understand that we do not want to imply by *nonverbal* that nonverbal
events are not language related. That, in fact, is one of the important questions
discussed in this book. At all other times we will refer to the picture, image,
visual, movie, or film, whichever seems to connote the event most accurately.

slight idea based on our own experiences within our own culture of the uses of such pictorial modes, but information is sadly lacking in the area that might be called cross-cultural visual communication.

There has, to be sure, been some significant work in recent years. Collier (1967) and Leighton and Leighton (1944) have photographed the environment of their informants as a sensitive means for eliciting data often missed by other methods of investigation. Spindler (1955), Goldschmidt and Edgerton (1961), Mills (1959) and others (Bouman 1954) have used drawings of the environment made by native artists as a means of stimulating a verbal response from the informant. But to our knowledge, no one has yet devised a method of eliciting a visual response in any way comparable to statements obtained through the use of verbal linguistic techniques. Of course, pictures and particularly motion pictures have been used to communicate anthropological data, mainly when the anthropologist uses visual means to send messages concerning another society to his own colleagues. Here visual phenomena (images of other people and their environment recorded in movies, drawings, diagrams, photos, charts, etc.) are used primarily as a means of keeping visual records to enable other researchers and outsiders to see and learn something about the society under the view of the anthropologist's or filmmaker's camera. These records may be used to satisfy simple curiosity or for sophisticated analysis of specific social, personal, and physiological behavior. Excellent and informative film work has been done by such people as Paul Fejos, who, with a professional background in cinema, filmed the Yagua; Margaret Mead and Gregory Bateson, who have provided valuable research films from Bali and New Guinea; and Robert Gardner, Asen Balikci, Timothy Asch, and others, who have made beautiful films of various aspects of cultures and societies quite different from our own. These films range from the poetic analogy of Gardner, who related the mutual warfare of the Dani in New Guinea to his own attitudes toward war, to the straightforward works of Balikci on the Eskimo, which are single-concept teaching-films for use in grade schools.

Researchers such as Birdwhistell (1952, 1970), Osgood (1966), Ekman (1965), Sorenson and Gajdusek (1966), Harrison (1964) and others have also used film to study gesture, facial expression, and the coding systems of visual modes of communication.

Of course, making such films required the closest cooperation of the subjects being photographed. But the native's eye was not at the eye piece nor did his hand direct the lens or edit the filmed material, and seldom did he see the finished product. Some ethnofilmmakers have recently asked their native informants to view the finished films or selected sequences from them, to comment upon the "rightness" of the presentation, or to suggest comments for the sound track. Several anthropologists in recent years have proposed making movies of particular events in an alien culture and using these movies to elicit responses from native informants, asking them what certain events "mean to them" and how they are valued. At this writing we have not seen any of the completed studies done in this way. In any case, we know of no one before our experiments who taught the "native" to use the camera and to do his own editing of the material he gathered.

Worth and his students had had considerable success in teaching the use of the motion picture camera to young adults in Philadelphia and New York City. In the early sixties, when these attempts among black teenagers were still novel, he was asked how beginners, untrained technically and new to filmmaking, were able to produce such revealing films. He replied, "Adolescents and young adults who are unable to talk about themselves or write about themselves are frequently willing and even eager to reveal themselves and their world on film."

We reasoned that if a member of the culture being studied could be trained to use the medium so that with his hand on the camera and editing equipment he could choose what interested him, we would come closer to capturing *his* vision of *his* world.

Our current investigations derive largely from our anthropological-visual-aesthetic interests and from unanswered questions about pictures and visual communication in general that drove Worth, a practicing painter, photographer, and filmmaker, into the field of communications research.

The questions are global ones, however partially they are taken up in the work we are reporting. How do the pictures one makes —the paintings, the photographs, the films—work? How does a filmmaker know how, for example, to sequence a set of visual events recorded on strips of film so that when the viewer sees them, he knows what the filmmaker meant? What processes in human beings allow them to communicate visually? What happens when the filmmaker and the viewer do not share the same culture? Are there things we can understand in pictures or film no matter how different our cultures happen to be? Can we compare the structure of visual events such as paintings or photographs to structures of verbal events such as words and languages? Can we learn something about how we know our world by studying how we know things that others communicate to us visually?

Can anyone make movies? Can anyone understand a movie? How do you learn? What do you learn?

We will be discussing two things that are inseparable but nevertheless slightly different. One is the study of images themselves in their cultural context, under the variety of constraints that a culture and its technology impose. The other is the study of the way the human mind in general—panculturally—deals with images. The first would ask why a particular person, in a particular culture, in a particular situation, made a particular image or interpreted it in a particular way. The second would seek to learn how these particular ways are related to ways that all men use when they try to make sense of pictures.

Some Questions About Film

Most of us know, or confidently assume, that communication through film takes place. That is, we assume that film can "work," although it doesn't always work, or sometimes works only partially. Given that deep underlying assumption, however, it seems all the more remarkable that we do not know more about the generalities of film; we do not know much about the patterns of its use, the context both verbal and socio-cultural within which it occurs, and we have no idea of the possible rules of inference and implication that govern that improbable moment when someone sees a film and says, "I know exactly what he meant."

When we started thinking about tackling some of these problems, we were not so much concerned with exploring the aesthetic or normative questions like "What makes a film good?" but rather the substantive questions involved in how a person who sees a film determines what it means, and how a person who makes a film determines what to shoot, how to shoot it, and how to put it together in a sequence so that a viewer will get from the film the meaning the filmmaker wants him to.

It was clear to us that the normative question is not completely separable from the substantive one. We felt rather a difference in emphasis, which would determine the direction of questions we would ask in interviews, observations we would make of filmmakers and viewers, and ways in which we would analyze our data. A great deal of normative and evaluative information turned up in our data and wherever possible we have included it in our analyses.

In studying the process of filmmaking and trying to determine the patterns and perhaps even the rules by which people communicate through film, Worth wondered if the study of speech offered an analogy. That is, if he could observe the process of learning to use a film "language"—if he could observe someone becoming a "film speaker"—he might learn something about the process of being a speaker, a speaker of film.

Such a thing is worth doing, because surprisingly little is known about language and language acquisition. What is certain is that most human beings, without direct instruction, learn to speak their native language during their first five years of life. It is easy to take that fact for granted, or to gloss over it because of preoccupation with conformity to arbitrary rules of grammar or prevailing literary usage, but its importance should not be obscured. Human children learn to speak; and the universality of the achievement suggests to many that the ability to learn language is innate. Just what aspect is innate is a matter of controversy among linguistic scholars. Chomsky (1965) and others hypothesize that what actually happens when one learns to speak a particular language is that one learns the relations between the innate deep structure of language in general and the particular surface structure or grammar of his language.

But, of course, what we do with sound—learn to perceive it, to interpret it as evidence of a reality outside ourselves, and to make symbolic use of it—we also do with visual events. A baby must analyze what he sees as clues to distance, texture, weight, and motion. That virtually everyone with eyes learns to do so successfully, even precisely, suggests the possibility that there is an innate pattern for interpreting images. Perhaps what filmmakers in various cultures do is to learn to make relations between innate patterns for organizing knowledge obtained visually and the conventionalized set of regularities, or rules, prevalent in their own language, tradition, and culture. Perhaps the same structure underlies both the method of organizing sound through language and the method of organizing images through film, and thus helps to create a communicative deep structure that can be transformed to generate many surface structures for varying modes of communication.

While this study will not attempt to formulate the rules of

innate universal film communication, we have tried to search for pattern in the use of film by a specific group in a specific culture and context. By examining many different groups, by finding regularities and patterns common to each group or context, and by cross comparison of groups and contexts, we will suggest possible universal patterns by which film attains meaning. In the concluding chapter we will mention several other studies done with disparate groups and point out several areas of difference and similarity.

Worth has suggested that it is important to study film as an ongoing communication process consisting of at least three inter-related parts. First, there are one or more filmmakers. Second, there is the piece of celluloid called a film. And third, there are one or more viewers. Each of the three units, or parameters of study, exists within a specific context. The three parameters of the process of filmmaking can be called variously (depending on the model and the discipline of the analyst) sender, message, and receiver; or speaker, utterance, and listener; or creator, work of art, and re-creator. It seems clear that research in this area must be concerned with the total process and with the social, cultural, and institutional contexts surrounding it.

Some aspects of these relationships have, of course, been considered in the past. There is an extensive literature on film and film analysis, and there has been a fairly large body of research on the effects of specific films on audiences. Recently Worth, Kessler (1970), and Zillmann have been studying changes in the meaning inferred from a film when various aspects of its structure, such as time and sequence, are changed. Others have begun to study the general psychological and physiological responses of individuals in determining meaning from a film sequence. But in general little attention has been paid to the process of constructing (organizing, patterning, coding) visual communications. In the main, studies on the visual arts have been philosophical (aesthetic), historical (history of art, painters, or movements), or introspective (reports about how one goes about writing a poem or painting a painting). Work such as Panofsky's (1939) or Gombrich's (1961) has dealt with the symbolic and psychological aspects of painting and related them to the actual events and historical context of composition. The process of coding, however, the process by which meanings are put together from specific parts of a visual communication, has been neglected, even in the older fine arts. In the study of film, there has been almost no such research at all.

In some earlier investigations of what he had come to call the bio-documentary film, Worth found not only the obvious—that different groups respond differently to the same films on both emotional and cognitive levels—but that films could be classified in a crude way according to differences in the *structure* of the response of different audiences to specific film *structures*. That is, aspects of the structure or pattern in a film seemed relevant to the cognitive processes employed in dealing not only with film, but with other modes or media of communication as well.

The way one organized his visual utterances as a sender as well as a receiver seemed to be related to the way one organized his verbal utterances. When data on the context of the film experience (who made the film, how and when was it shown, who looked at it, with whom, when) was collected along with the inferences and interpretations of the films, it became apparent that a complex relationship existed between the way in which the subjects dealt with other communication forms (writing, speech, dance, etc.) and the way in which they made inferences from a film.

Within the first few years of teaching film in the northeastern United States, we decided that almost any student could be taught to use a movie camera and with it would make something that could be called a movie. This mode of communication seemed a more universal form of communication than drawing or painting, skills which, although taught and encouraged from kindergarten on, seemed to present special difficulties for most Americans past the age of twelve. Our culture seems to presuppose a special talent to be a painter or to paint pictures. Making movies, on the other hand, seemed to bypass painting's demand for specialized hand–eye coordination, which takes years to develop. Although folklore had it that making movies is technically difficult, the northeastern Americans in our classes seemed not to be discouraged by that. Anyone who could drive a car or wind a watch seemed to feel able to make a movie. Why and how a culture develops special and preferred methods of communication for specific and differing purposes and how these preferences change over time is a problem that has only just been recognized, and one that the methods and observations in this study are meant to illuminate.

Chapter

2

A Look at Film As If It Were a Language

The next aspect in our research plan intruded itself almost insidiously. If people can communicate through film—if people of varying cultures can use it widely as both makers and viewers—it becomes necessary, in order to understand this form of human interaction, to find or formulate some of the patterns, codes, rules, conventions or even laws by which such communication takes place.

Through most of the literature on the visual arts, and particularly in film, aesthetics, psychology and anthropology, one notion kept cropping up. "Film is a language," said Sergei Eisenstein (1949). The literature echoed this metaphor constantly, in statements asserting the "syntax of film," the "grammar of film," the "structure of pictures," and the "language of art" (Goodman 1968).

We became intrigued by the sheer multitude of statements linking film and language without any verification or reference to notions or theories of language. It seemed clear that the frequent use of linguistic terms was more poetic than scientific. Although pictures and film as language had not been studied extensively or productively, the study of verbal language and of pictures as an aspect of culture has been. These approaches as developed in anthropology, communication and linguistics, seemed to offer a fruitful paradigm for the study of culture through films produced by members of a culture *themselves.*

Once one begins to look at a film within a linguistic framework —and here we would like to emphasize that we mean to look for structures analogous to those of language and not to claim that film actually is a language in a linguistic sense—many questions of interest to anthropologists, communication researchers, and film theorists arise. It becomes necessary to formulate and consider questions such as: If film is like language, are there different languages of film? Are there native groups of hearer-speakers of film—could one community of persons produce and understand a film utterance that would not be understandable or makeable by persons of other groups? If such different languages of film exist, and if people acquire them natively, do the divisions follow the normal linguistic divisions? That is, do French speakers make films that only French-speaking people understand? Could linguistic families be grouped, so that speakers of Athabaskan-related languages would make films that their fellow speakers could all understand but that would not be understood by speakers of Romance languages?[1]

Or are we perhaps talking about such languages as surrealism or abstractionism which cut across linguistic groups and refer to deeper and more complex ways of conceptualizing? Or to patterns or conventions, which have diffused only within limited areas and act as a barrier between those areas and others?

---

1. Lomax (1968), in studying the music of different groups, reports that different codes and styles of music exist with different cultures. Meyer (1956), also referring to music, thinks that inferences from musical forms are different for people with different cultures.

We would then be proposing that the language of film is correlated with cultural patterns—values, myths, rituals, and world views. One might also ask whether the native speaker concept applies differentially to makers and viewers—do people understand films of different cultures or groups more or less easily than they can produce them?

These questions lead one to ask further whether the very concept, *grammatical,* so common to verbal language, has any counterpart in film communication.

The concept of grammaticality is a difficult one. In general we mean the notions implied by a native speaker of a language when he says "That is (or is not) a correct sentence" or "That's a sentence that nobody would say." The first level of correctness might correspond to our more conventional forms of grammar: every native speaker of English knows that "The boy went into the" or "Hit the John ball was" are not English. In the second level, everyone knows that if a stranger walks up to you on Fifth Avenue and says, "Excuse me, my name is John Jones, could you direct me to Times Square?" he is not saying what is normally said. It is correct in one sense, but it is a sentence that nobody uses. Grammaticality, then, as used here in relation to film, implies (1) correctness of form; that is, all the right elements are present in the right order, and (2) correctness of use, or appropriateness.

If languages have lexicons (dictionaries) which list synonyms of words and paraphrases of ideas, could we find evidence of such units in film communication—filmic synonyms or paraphrases within specific cultures or across cultures?

It became clear that many of these answers would depend upon research among "native" speakers of different cultures. We would first need to know who "spoke" film, or who *could* speak film, whether in our culture or in others. It would be only *after* we learned who could produce film utterances and under what conditions that we could begin to compare them. Even more precisely, only after we had (in a film can) *a variety* of utterances produced under known circumstances could we begin to test some of these questions. To look for rules or patterns in the use of a mode of communication, one must know the rule input and be able to subtract it from the patterned and analyzed output. In a sense the resultant pattern would represent the pattern imposed on this mode by cognitive processes native to the culture in question.

It was such questions that led us to specific research we will now discuss.

First, we proposed to determine the feasibility of teaching people in another culture to use film. Worth had already done so among eleven- to fourteen-year-old Negro dropouts in Philadelphia and college students in a school of communication. Since then many others have worked with a variety of subgroups such as middle-class whites, unwed mothers, grade-school children (some as young as eight years), Puerto Ricans, Mexicans, and Negroes. The methods and aims of the film teaching projects varied tremendously, but in all of them it was found that almost everyone could be taught to use motion picture cameras.

This method of filmmaking was designated as the bio-documentary film as opposed to the standard documentary. In 1964, before we had fully conceived the research method which is the subject of this book, Worth presented the first report of the bio-documentary method at a meeting of the Society for Applied Anthropology in Puerto Rico. He had at that time worked only with college students and black teenagers in Harlem, but the advantages of the method seemed to call for further exploration. The report stressed:

> The motion picture is no more than a recently invented and mechanically sophisticated tool to aid men in their desire to make pictures. Its development probably stems from the same needs that have motivated men for thousands of years to depict themselves, their fellows, and the world around them.
>
> Describing the cultural function of a picture, or its newest mani-

festation—the motion picture—is an extremely difficult task. It is difficult, I think, because its use is so very basic to man. Of all the acts of communication that man has learned to perform pictures seem to take a special place.

The picture made by the cave man is still recognizable as a picture. We know what it is, and feel quite close to it. The picture as a basic form of communication—as a device for one man to *show* another —has probably changed less in terms of our ability to recognize the image referent than almost any other communicative mode.

The anthropologist and other researchers in the social sciences use film as an aid to memory, a way to remember the look of a complex action or object, or as a way to describe it. . . . For whatever purpose the anthropologist uses his film—as an aid to memory or description, as a teaching tool or as a training device—he is primarily concerned with presenting, preserving, or documenting the facts about something he has observed. . . . The documentary filmmaker in this role is a reporter who, functioning at his best, observes, comments, and interprets the object of his observation and study. There is, however, another way the film can be used. And it is this new way of using film that I would like to describe. . . . For lack of a more precise name I am calling this kind of film Bio-Documentary as distinguished from the Documentary.

A Bio-Documentary is a film made by a person to show how he feels about himself and his world. It is a subjective way of showing what the objective world that a person sees is "really" like. In part, this kind of film bears the same relation to documentary film that a self-portrait has to a portrait or a [biography to an] autobiography. In addition, because of the specific way that this kind of film is made, it often captures feelings and reveals values, attitudes, and concerns that lie beyond conscious control of the maker.

In the chapter analyzing some of the films made by the Navajo, we will describe how one of the filmmakers explained the function of his film in almost the same way used above—as a "self-portrait" rather than an objective report, as a description of how it is "inside" rather than "out there."

The 1964 report continued:

The Bio-Documentary is a film that can be made by a person who is not a professional filmmaker or by someone who has never made a film before. It is a film that can be made by anyone with enough skill, let's say, to drive a car, by a person of a different culture or of a different age group, who has been taught in a specific way to make a film that helps him to communicate to us the world as *he* sees it and his concerns as he sees them.

It is the difference of intent between Documentary and Bio-Documentary that separates and defines them. Operationally, a film is a film. Both kinds of filmmaking require cameras, editing, sensitized emulsions, and lenses. Both need the same equipment. The distinction between the two forms is not only operational but intentional. The intent of the Bio-Documentary filmmaker is to present the subjective, the phenomenological, rather than the objective. The intent of the viewer of Bio-Documentary must also be different.

When one looks at a documentary, one expects to see an image of the world that can be accepted as 'real.' In a documentary film about the Navaho, for example, you would look for an objective presentation of how they live. . . .

Of course no view of one man by another is entirely objective. The most objective documentary film or report includes the view and values of the maker. The standard documentary film tries, however, to exclude as much as possible of this personal value system. The Bio-Documentary method teaches the maker of the film to search for the meaning he sees in his world, and it encourages the viewer to continue that search by comparing *his* values with the values expressed by the filmmaker in the film. The Bio-Documentary method suggests that at times it is fruitful to get away from an examination of man as object and try to learn more about him as subject. The Bio-Documentary, it seems to me, expresses the culture of the maker without much of the self-consciousness of art, without the demands of great amounts of physical skill required in the other arts, and without resort to the traditional ways of seeing inherent in the other visual arts. And most important, Bio-Documentary is, by definition (because the filmmaker must see it to show it), tied to the visible world of the moment.

This allows the anthropologist to compare the view of the world that the filmmaker has shown with the view of that same world as seen by himself and others. It allows not only the anthropologist on the scene to make comparisons, but permits others who are not there to make independent evaluation of the same observations.

Upon these early formulations, we based the research that we are reporting now.

Besides determining if and how members of another culture would use film, we proposed to find out if it was possible to systematize the process of teaching, to observe it on the three levels mentioned earlier (the maker, the film itself, and the viewer) and to collect data about it in such a way as to assist other on-going research exploring the structure and process of meaning inference from film "language" communication.

In recent years there has developed a small but significant body of researchers exploring what has been called the semiotics of film and what Worth has called vidistics, who are interested in developing the rules, codes, patterns, and possibly "language" of film communication.

We would like to emphasize, then, that the purpose of our work was not only to find out about the Navajo. We chose the Navajo precisely because much is known about them. Adair and many others had been conducting research among the Navajo for many years, and we could check our inferences from visual communication against other data. We were interested in studying the general nature of the cognitive processes involved in film use within specific cultural contexts. The Navajo were a people with a contrasting language and culture to that of the investigators.

Before knowing that Navajos could make films and before knowing what or how many rules we would have to teach, we had no clear way to state many of these problems. Before knowing the alternative ways in which Navajos could structure visual events, we had no way of comparing our way with theirs.

A working hypothesis, then, for our study was that motion picture film, conceived, photographed, and sequentially arranged by a people such as the Navajo, would reveal aspects of coding, cognition, and values that may be inhibited, not observable, or not analyzable when the investigation is totally dependent on verbal exchange—especially when such research must be done in the language of the investigator.

We were interested not only in studying the general nature of the cognitive processes involved in this visual mode of communication itself, but we were searching for specific pattern, code, and rules for visual communication within a cultural context. It was the interdependence between a mode of communication and its context as expressed in patterned, interrelated behavior that was sought.

Further, we felt that our research in the methods of photographing filmed image events and then sequencing them through the editing process might create new perspectives on the Whorfian hypothesis, work on which has for the most part been limited to linguistic investigation of cognitive phenomena. Through cross-cultural comparative studies using film as a mode of visual communication, relationships between linguistic, cognitive, cultural and visual phenomena might eventually be clarified. Processes involved in cognition might be better understood if the way in which people produced a structure of visual sequences were compared to the way the same people structured their verbal language; that is, we hoped to be able to compare two communicative structures, one verbal and one visual. By making comparisons across these two modes, we might be able to make statements about language and culture similar to those made by comparing two verbal linguistic structures in a Whorfian manner. The use of both modes—visual and verbal—compared across cultures, could provide an analytic structure which would make it possible to analyze these deeply interrelated verbal, visual, cognitive, and cultural phenomena within one conceptual framework.

We also reasoned that the images, subjects and themes selected and the organizing methods used by the Navajo filmmakers would reveal much about their mythic and value systems. We felt that a person's values and closely held beliefs about the nature of the world would be reflected in the way he edited his previously photographed materials. We were able to elicit data relevant to these areas by asking the students why certain portions of film were totally discarded, or why certain pieces were emphasized by position in the film or by control of length and rhythmic relation to other pieces coming before and after it.

As mentioned earlier, an additional interest of ours was in the process of innovation itself—what happens when that process is guided by the investigators. A process which might be called *guided* innovation, in contrast to the more conventional and otherwise unattainable retrospective and historical studies of innovation and diffusion that have taken place entirely independently of the investigator. Guided innovation allows the investigator to study the introduction of something new to a community in the very act of introducing it.

This process, in which the investigator is intimately involved as the central agent in the diffusion and introduction of a new technology, a new ideology, a new form of social structure, or, as in the present instance, a new mode of communication, is central to studies of participant intervention. Holmberg (1960), for example, after a period of participant observation during which he conducted basic studies of the existing economy, technology, and social organization of a hacienda at Vicos, Peru, intervened in the political process and altered his role to incorporate direct action. The anthropologist in that case deliberately stimulated the community and other levels in the national government to accept innovation. Another example of this approach was Cornell University Medical College's work in introducing new medical practices at Many Farms on the Navajo reservation. Essential to this method of study is the communication to the community of why the investigator is there, what his objective is, and an explanation of his interest in them. Just as we, as members of another society, sought a context for understanding the way

Navajos organized their world, they too needed a context for understanding our behavior as researchers.

Other anthropologists such as Holmberg (1960), Barnett (1953), Spicer (1952, 1961), Adair (1944), Adair and Vogt (1949) and Goodenough (1965) had observed and analyzed the process of technological innovation. It was somewhat easier, however, to explain why one was teaching and observing a process of agriculture or of politics. Little is known, however, about how a new mode of *communication* would be patterned by the culture to which it is introduced, and we had no precedent for explaining what we were going to do or why we were going to do it.

One of the cardinal interests in this research was to see what other peoples had to say about themselves through film, and how one could teach them to say it. Many of our formal theoretical notions may or may not be borne out. What emerges from the film data we have collected, however, is a new form of expression from a group of people in another culture who have never expressed themselves in this way before. Their statements, and the method by which they were made, are now available for study and replication.

It is now time to deal with the specific methods by which we were able to teach filmmaking to the Navajos and our methods of collecting data about what they did and did not do. Before discussing these methods, however, it is essential to understand something of Navajo culture—their history, the particular community in which we worked, and something of the value system common to them and contrasting with ours.

Chapter

3

The Navajo

The Navajo reservation is located across northwestern New Mexico and northeastern Arizona, with a small section extending up into southern Utah. It is high country—part of what geographers call the Colorado Plateau. The altitude varies from 3,500 feet to mountain peaks over 11,000 feet. On the higher ranges are large stands of piñon and juniper which above 6,500 feet merge into ponderosa pine.

The whole of the terrain has very little rainfall, ranging from twelve inches a year in the mountains to as little as five inches in the lower desert regions. During years of drought there is even less, which makes agriculture and sheep raising very precarious, especially for those at the lower altitudes. Most of the precipitation comes in July and August, when there are great cloudbursts which wash the top soil down the *arroyos*. Winter is marked by some snow—a good bit in the mountains—and severely cold nights of sub-zero temperature.

Until recently the Navajo have lived in hemispherical earth and log houses, called *hogans*, where much of the photography by the Navajos in our study took place. The hogan, a one-room, windowless structure about eighteen feet in diameter with a central fireplace (today occupied by a stove) and smoke hole in the roof, provides adequate protection from the cold and the severe dust storms. Its persistence is also due to religious sanctions, since curing ceremonies known as *sings* must be held in such a dwelling. In the summer the people move into brush structures which shade them from the sun and take advantage of the breeze. The Navajo detest extreme hot weather—an important factor in the periodic return to the reservation of those who have gone to seek wage work in southern Arizona or California.

While it is a severe land, marked with recurrent droughts, dust storms, and blizzards, it is a land of great beauty. Vast panoramas of red rock and deep canyons with beautiful pine-studded parkland attract visitors from all over the United States. Tourists also come to see the Navajo in their picturesque dress—the women in long full sweeping skirts of calico and blouses of velveteen, useful garb for a people who make much of bodily modesty. Many of the men, especially on the northwestern edge of the reservation, still wear their hair long, put up in a double knot at the nape of the neck.

Compared to tribal peoples living in the interior of New Guinea, the upper Amazon River drainage, or the remote highlands of Southeast Asia, the Navajo are in no sense a primitive people. Most of them share, to some extent, twentieth-century technology, live in part in our economy and speak some English. The Navajo, however, do have some characteristics in common with other tribally organized peoples. They retain in good measure their own traditional social organization and religion which differ greatly from those of urban-living peoples with a Euro-American orientation such as ourselves, and from subcultures in our society such as Mexicans, Negroes, Puerto Ricans, and others, who share our religion, language, and variations of our social organization. They think of themselves as a coherent group. In their own language, they call themselves *Dine*, which means "the People."

The very facts that the Navajo do share much of our technology, are involved in our wage economy, and speak our language as well as their own, make them representative of a very large segment of the "developing world." Those developing societies share with us features of twentieth-century life, but also share with tribal peoples many of the ideological and social principles of human organization that give them a very different approach to living and a very different system of understanding their total environment.

It should be noted that although the Navajo speak English in ever-increasing numbers (most of the population under thirty is bilingual), only a small percentage of those over sixty are fluent in spoken English and an even smaller number are literate. Navajo remains the language of the home and the community. It is the language in which the child first learns to think, and it remains the language that he reverts to when, as an adult, he meets a crisis.

It is also well to appreciate that the Navajo living on the edge of the reservation have been in contact with the white man, his values, his family, and his community organization for one hundred years.

In 1869 the Navajo were returned to their homeland from Fort Sumner in eastern New Mexico, where they had been interned for the previous five years as part of an all-out attempt on the part of the War Department to put an end to raids on Anglo- and Spanish-American settlements in the Southwest. Upon their return the present reservation was established by treaty.

The next fifty years was a period of forced assimilation. The white politicians, civil servants, and educators of that era thought that if the children of the Navajo (and of all other Indians) were isolated from their own people, placed in boarding schools distant from the reservation, and kept out of touch with their families and communities, they would automatically be "educated," assimilated into white culture, and thus become "civilized."

It is now apparent that this program was a failure; it produced misfits unable to function in either their own or the dominant society. Nor did the attempts to Christianize the Navajo meet with great success. Except for a small number of converts, the Navajo have retained their own religion and its elaborate ceremonial life.

It was not until the reform administration of John Collier, Commissioner of Indian Affairs under the presidency of Franklin D. Roosevelt, that government officials began to entertain a more sympathetic and understanding view of Indian culture. Under Collier the trend in education was reversed, from distant boarding schools to high schools near the reservation and elementary schools in the local communities. Indian arts, religion, mythology, and tribal ways were officially sanctioned by the government officials in the Bureau of Indian Affairs on both the Washington and district levels. But the less educated, run-of-the-mill school teacher, doctor, or land management officer, who was working on the local tribal and community level on the reservation, did not necessarily go along with what they thought to be the impractical idealism of Collier and his staff.

At this time there was another very important development on the Navajo reservation—the beginnings of tribal government. Before 1920 the Navajo had no political unity as a tribe. The people had been organized into local bands, each with its own leaders, but there was no overall tribal identity. In the 1920s a tribal council was established and by the end of the thirties it began to have recognized authority, even though during those years many of the Navajo thought of the council as a rubber stamp for Washington. After the Second World War the council became an effective political and legislative body with a chairman and vice-chairman and seventy-four councilmen elected by secret ballot from as many voting districts spread across the reservation. While at first the tribal government was under the tutelage of some able federal civil servants at Window Rock, Arizona, today it is completely in the hands of Navajo leadership. Additionally the tribe has developed its own committee system responsible to the tribal council, for example, a committee on education, a committee on health and welfare, a committee on grazing. The Navajo have successfully assumed the responsibility for governing their own affairs after a period of over a hundred years of dependence on the federal government. That dependency had crushed Indian groups elsewhere, notably the Indians on the plains whose economy was drastically altered by the disappearance of the buffalo and the encroachment of white settlers.

Political growth has been matched by economic growth on the Navajo reservation. Uranium, natural gas, oil and timber became sources for the building of capital funds under federal guidance. The income from such wealth (held tribally, not individually) has been used to develop a tribal timber industry, to further arts and crafts production, to set up merchandising centers, to encourage small businesses, to improve roads, and to advance community development. Additionally, the tribe has a generous fund used for supporting higher education. Today the Navajo have their own civil service, employing over a thousand men and women; it conducts the administration of their affairs (including their own police force), all of which had been in the hands of federal administrators thirty years ago.

The growth of the Navajo during this period, as a unified people with a nationalized ideology of their own (they have constantly held out against pan-Indian political involvement), may be compared with the growth of national pride in the developing nation states of Africa and elsewhere.

The social organization of the Navajo is based on about sixty matrilineal clans and on an extended family system which traces kin to collateral lines far beyond the nuclear family. The clan's principal function is to regulate marriage; it is an exogamous unit with marriage rules which are still in effect—for example, to have sexual relations with a clanmate is to commit incest. Clan members also have economic obligations to one another—members of the same clan join in putting on the expensive nine-night ceremonies.

Upon marriage, the husband joins the "camp" of his wife, where the couple set up their own hogan (house) adjacent to those of her grandmother, mother, and numerous sisters, all of whom live with their husbands in separate dwellings nearby. This is the classic residence pattern, but it is breaking down today among the members of the tribe who have been off to school; they tend to set up their homes apart from the wife's female relatives.

As mentioned, the economy of the Navajo has changed rapidly in the last thirty-five years. As late as 1934 most of the families and communities were largely self-sufficient, following a subsistence economy based largely on horticulture (corn, beans, squash, potatoes, and other garden crops) and sheep herding. The large herds of sheep were used for food and the wool and lamb crop were used for barter with the traders. The wool also was used for rug-weaving, in which Navajo women excel. Within a radius of fifty miles of Gallup, New Mexico, there grew up a concentration of silversmiths who made jewelry from silver and turquoise obtained from the white traders. In the late thirties and early forties the sheep economy was greatly altered, when the large flocks of sheep and horses had to be greatly reduced. For centuries the arid region had been overgrazed and enforcement of the soil erosion regulations set back Navajo–Federal relations, creating much misunderstanding, bitterness and recrimination. It was not until well after the Second World War that the wounds healed, when the Navajo undertook the enforcement of their own grazing regulations.

During the Second World War thousands of Navajo went to work in defense industries and on the tracks of the western railroads. Within ten years, the tribe became highly dependent on our cash economy. In 1937 there were only a few automobiles in and around Pine Springs. Today almost every family has either a passenger car or a pickup truck.

Many men and women on the reservation are dependent on

federally or tribally sponsored programs. In the last few years the various federal and state poverty programs have had a great effect on communities all over the reservation. It should be noted that while the tribe jointly has considerable wealth, most families which have five or more children fall under the federal law for direct aid.

Along with this rapid economic change has come a breakdown in the extended family, especially among those educated Navajos who live on the edge of the reservation or in the bordering small towns and cities. In such families the rights and obligations of the mother's brother—who traditionally played an important role in teaching the Navajo's moral code to his sister's children—have all but been forgotten by the generation now growing up. The use of alcohol also has greatly increased; today alcoholism is a major mental health problem for the tribe. Coupled with auto accidents, it is a scourge for the Navajo just as for the rest of the nation.

The religion of the Navajo is still central to their identity despite almost a hundred years of mission activity. Its central focus is curing, which in Navajo ideology is the means whereby the patient is restored to a proper harmony with his total environment—his fellow man, his natural surroundings, and the gods. These curing rites include short, one-night sings as well as complex nine-day ceremonies involving sand paintings and the singing of song cycles with sacred texts. The Night Chant, or *Yeibechai* as it is popularly called, is one such rite. It is performed only during the winter season, after the first frost and before the first thunder of the spring. Hundreds of people come from a great distance to attend the final night, when teams of men from various communities vie with each other in the performance of a masked dance. It is an abstracted cardboard mock up of the mask of one of the Yei (gods), which appears in one of the films to be described later. During the previous days the medicine man has been singing over the patient and directing assistants in making the elaborate sand paintings which depict the gods through complex geometric patterns created by sifting colored earth pigments through the thumb and forefinger onto a base of carefully smoothed desert sand. At the completion of each sand painting, the patient sits in the middle of the pattern, and the medicine man transfers its strength and beauty to various parts of the patient's body.

These ceremonials, attended by many relatives and neighbors all praying for the patient's recovery, have considerable psychotherapeutic value. Thousands of Navajo retain faith in the curing properties of these religious observances. They are an essential complement to the therapy given by medical doctors, which may rid the body of germs but fail to bring about the harmony required for health. Physicians from our culture who have worked as doctors or researchers on the reservation have only recently been learning the effectiveness of the curing ceremonies in the total health of their patients.

With the passing of each decade there are fewer medicine men with control of all the knowledge essential to the enactment of a nine-day chant, a knowledge which entails memorizing the original myth and the texts of long chants and songs, knowing the formulae for medicinal plant infusions, and having sure control of the design of the sand paintings. Such skill takes many years of training, starting in adolescence, as it is believed that the slightest error in any part of the ceremony may cause the death of the patient. This religious system was geared to a subsistence economy, and now that young apprentice medicine men must work off-reservation for wages, the essential time for learning, not only these most elaborate rites but the shorter ones too, has been sharply curtailed. The resulting loss of these and other aspects of traditional Navajo culture might provide some insight into the motivations of our Navajo students; almost all of them quickly chose subjects for their films depicting the "old ways."

But many of the shorter and less elaborate ceremonies, including the very sacred Blessing Way, which is used as a prophylaxis against evil and disease, are still performed in great number in every Navajo community. Kluckhohn and Leighton (1946) estimated that the Navajos spent approximately a quarter of their waking hours in religious participation. While participation is probably much less than that today on the reservation as a whole, traditional religious activity is still a dominant theme in the lives of most Navajo and a focus for community participation.

In recent years, starting in the 1930s, use of the hallucinogenic drug peyote, a sacrament in the Native American Church, diffused to the Navajo by way of the Ute Indians of southern Colorado. This religion, which is widespread among Indians all over the western United States, has provided the Navajo with an alternate religious system which is not so dependent on a long period of training and one which is a fusion of Christian and pagan elements. Today the peyote cult has many thousands of Navajo followers and continues to grow. For many years this religion and the use of peyote was outlawed by the tribe, but recently that law was revoked and the Native American Church now conducts its ritual openly.

There is some evidence of a revival of Navajo custom, not only of traditional religious practice and mythology, but of the older code of ethics, including kinship behavior. Today such a revival is to be found at the Rough Rock Demonstration School in the very heart of the reservation. There, eighty miles north of Pine Springs, this elementary school under the direction of Navajo educators has a level of community interest and support no longer enjoyed by the Government and mission schools. It includes in its curriculum the teaching of the Navajo language (both spoken and written) as well as English. Additionally, Navajo history, mythology, and tradition known to the grandparental and earlier generations is being taught to young children. Many Navajos who are now in their middle years, most of whom have lived off-reservation for a considerable period, have faced what psychologists in our culture call an "identity crisis." In several of the films (see Appendix) this search for identity becomes a central theme. Other films show a deep concern for the general concept of the search for origins, whether of self or of their traditions. In the section on analysis of the films this concern for origins should particularly be noted.

In seeking an answer to the question of identity, the Navajo educators at Rough Rock have turned to their own cultural roots in the belief that if the Navajo is more secure as an Indian, he will be more secure living among white men. This is a far cry from the educational policy of fifty years ago, but it is one increasingly respected among those concerned with the education of Negroes, Mexicans, and other minority populations in the United States.

Pine Springs is about forty miles west of Gallup, New Mexico, and ten miles north of U.S. Interstate Highway 40, the main route between Chicago and Los Angeles that follows the Santa Fe railroad tracks from Albuquerque across northern Arizona to California.

Pine Springs is a small community of approximately six hundred people, bounded on the north by the road from Ganado to Window Rock. Ponderosa pine shades into piñon and juniper as one goes south.

Community activity centers in the trading post and the boarding school, which is limited to first and second grades. Both are located on a sort of central square, as is a Roman Catholic mission, which completes the roster of three institutions of the white man usually found in Navajo communities. Half-a-mile away is a large one-room chapter house built by the community for local meetings. There we met with the elders of the community at the outset of the film teaching project.

Political development of Pine Springs has been held back by

its division into two constituencies. The part east of the road from the highway is District 18 which votes at Oak Springs; residents on the west vote at Klagetoh.[1]

Community leadership is in the hands of the local chapter, the smallest unit of tribal government. Such chapters were established in the early years of the century and were essentially based on the old band organization. Juan Tsosie was the chairman of the local chapter and Johnny Nelson was vice-chairman when we came to Pine Springs.

Pine Springs differs from most Navajo communities in only one respect—the high preponderance of craftsmen, both silversmiths and weavers, resident in the area. As early as the mid-thirties Pine Springs began to build a reputation for the quality of its vegetable dye rugs and silver jewelry. The latter was especially noted for its cast work without turquoise. Today many of these silversmiths work in Gallup but keep their homes at Pine Springs. The weavers all still live in the community, where they work in their hogans, assisted in carding and spinning by their daughters and by the older women with failing eyesight. The finely woven rugs bring premium prices and are widely sought by collectors. While these crafts provide considerable income to the community, the Navajos here as elsewhere are largely dependent on cash wages which they earn away from home or on government aid.

---

1. The reservation is divided into nineteen districts set up originally as land management administrative districts, which have since been adapted as the basis for 106 voting precincts for tribal councilmen.

PART TWO

Chapter

4

The Method of Research

As we have said, in order for us to interpret our data it seemed
necessary to understand something of Navajo culture. It is quite
clear that the only way we could show that the movies the Navajo
made, and the way they made—or didn't make—them, were
related to other patterns of their way of life, was by comparing
their films and *filming behavior* to other behavior patterns already
known about the Navajo.

Similarly but less obviously, we feel that the reader must know
not only the methods we used in gathering our information about
the films and filming but also some of the larger concepts that lay
behind our choice of particular methods, for it will be impossible
to determine what in the films came from us (in the sense of being
consciously or unconsciously transmitted) and what came from
Navajo ways of thinking and organizing their world without
knowing what we, the investigators, instructed our students to
do and why we decided upon certain instructions. Our questions
and observations must also be understood in this light. What we
asked our students, as well as our behavior among them, were
certainly influences—even if not always noted and understood—

upon what they thought they should do, or thought we wanted them to do.

In many ways the reader of this report faces many of the same problems that we faced. Just as we were attempting to find a structure in the Navajo way of making a film, so the reader must find a structure in observing and analyzing what we did. What we told the Navajo, what we asked them, and what we observed about their behavior and our reasons for doing so, are much like the Navajo explanations about what they filmed or didn't film, what they chose to include or leave out in their final film, and how they organized their view. The reader can analyze our report in much the way we we attempted to analyze the Navajo's reports and to discern their way of structuring reality.

The methodological and theoretical issues involved in the study of a body of visual expression derived from actual users are varied, complex, and not easy to deal with. It is beyond the scope of this report to deal even cursorily with all of them, for they go beyond visual expression, beyond verbal expression and language theory, and would demand explication of the nature of symbolic expression in general. We feel, however, that we must touch on at least those that we actively considered in determining our method.

A major difficulty in studying the way a group develops the use of a communication code is that of deriving a unique pattern of use or performance when that pattern might itself be derived by imitation from someone else. There was always the possibility that we might ascribe the possibly unique patterns of our students' films to their culture in a situation in which what they did could instead be ascribed to their imitation of us, as teachers, or of movies that they may have seen or heard about.

In many ways this problem is similar to the one encountered by some researchers who attempted to study how children learn to speak their native language—how children learned the unique patterns of particular languages to how children learned to verbalize or to think about such abstractions as causality, size, or time.

It was argued by some (Skinner 1957) that the way a child learned to speak could be explained by means of a functional analysis of verbal behavior, the controlling variables of which could be subsumed under such notions as stimulus, reinforcement, and so on, which are part of a larger theory of learning. To oversimplify, this approach argued that a child learned his language by a complex process of imitation and conditioning; that his parents, schoolteachers, and the people around him rewarded or punished his stumbling attempts to imitate the language he heard; and that after some time he "learned" to speak like other adults in his culture. To some extent of course this is true. When to say something, what not to say, what accent to use, and many other aspects of speaking are learned the way all culture is learned—by living in a group and conforming to group norms. To the extent, however, that such researchers felt that infant speech patterns were "mere mistakes" to be corrected by proper rewards and punishments, they denied the possibility that children learned to speak by learning rules of their language and that all languages had underlying patterns or rules.

Some current researchers in language (Chomsky 1965, 1968; McNeill 1966), for example, are returning to a position first proposed by Vico and Descartes: that not only are there rules that can describe what happens when a native speaker learns and speaks his language, but that there are innate, basic, universal rules embedded in the human brain which make it possible for human beings to learn language—and which make certain similarities and patterns between all languages necessary. Since the basic structure and pattern of all languages stems from the neurological structure of man's brain, some common set of basic rules or grammar must be the basis from which the differing patterns and grammars of individual languages are derived.

Although the parallel between film and language is not exact, it may be that the manipulation of images events in filming and their structuring in editing is not a random activity. We assumed that anybody making a film would be influenced in many ways, and we assumed that when the Navajo were taught to use motion picture cameras they would develop patterned ways of filming and filmmaking; that the language and culture already known by the Navajo would influence not only their semantic and thematic choices of image, but also their syntactic choices, the very way they put these images together in a sequence.

There are several problems which can be extracted even from this inexact parallel with language and language development. We haven't provided data on all of them, but all were to some extent involved in our problem and it may be fruitful to list them briefly.

(1) Is there a pattern or code in film at all, and is this code similar or analogous to the grammar of a specified language?

(2) Are there culturally different codes in film just as there are culturally different languages with different grammars? And, relatedly, are there culturally different patterns of filming which might not reach the level of grammar but which might correspond to different patterns and codes of speaking?

(3) Is there a universalistic basis for a film code or grammar that would encompass all ways of filmmaking on some basic level, just as the postulated deep structure of language is basic to many different languages?

(4) How does one learn these codes? Here one would have to look historically at film development as well as at individual instances of how each filmmaker learns to make a film.

If one looks at film without trying to make direct inferences from studies of languages, one finds similar questions. Without any concern for notions of grammar we find (1) that persons understand film messages, therefore they must share a code with the filmmakers; (2) not all persons understand all film messages, therefore all codes are not identical or all persons do not share them; and (3) yet there seems to be some universality involved in film since most people understand something from almost all films.

These were some of the questions behind our instructions to our Navajo students concerning motion picture cameras, and which were to a large extent responsible for our choices about what we observed and how we analyzed the films made by the Navajo, their filming and filmmaking behavior.

In the chapters devoted to our analysis of the results of the study we will show that in certain cases specific patterns emerged *despite* what we said in our instructions to the Navajo. In some cases, although our code of filming and filmmaking was so strong that we at first unconsciously urged it upon the Navajo, they would not accept it and developed their own ways. In other cases they developed ways of filming and filmmaking that we never thought of and couldn't possibly have taught.

We also participated in the process we studied, which added to the complexities of sorting out influences upon the process of filmmaking. Although participant observation, or in our case, participant intervention and observation is not a new technique for anthropologists, it has rarely been used in communications research in general and it is even rarer in film research.

Most of the research undertaken in the past several decades into visual modes of communication (in either still pictures or films), with the exception of a small body of work by Collier (1967), Gardner (1957), Rouch (1955) and others, has been "experimental" and has followed closely the research paradigms of sociology or psychology, that is, either testing responses to specific films or other visual stimuli by psychological and experimental procedures or by questionnaires and surveys designed to measure the responses of various groups to visual stimuli of various kinds. The purpose was to learn something about psychological or sociological process; about learning, coding and encoding behavior, group preferences, persuasion, or social networks.

In recent years there has been some exciting work in content or message analysis of films in the aggregate. Here attempts were made to deal with the analysis of the films of several nations and the researcher inferred "national traits" (Mead and Metraux 1953; Wolfenstein & Leites 1957). Some studies compared such concepts as "heroes," "teachers," and so on across cultures. Recently Gerbner (1970) has proposed a large scale content analysis which will include visual material distributed through the so-called mass media. Interestingly, he has proposed that this kind of study be carried on continuously as part of a process of assessing what he has termed "cultural indicators." Rather than concentrating on an analysis of visual materials in the attempt to see how a people *present themselves*, Gerbner, recognizing that the mass media are produced by a few for the many under a variety of cultural, economic, and institutional constraints, assumes that what the public sees in large quantities plays a large part in determining the values, myths and attitudes of a society. He is therefore interested in analyzing the "culture" presented to what has become a "public" by the very act of seeing the same set of films or TV programs. Where the anthropologist and ethnographer have examined individual life histories and behavior and asked people what they believe, Gerbner is examining what they see around them, analyzing that, and proposing that that kind of input is indeed what people are being taught to believe.

But both the content analytic and experimental work have dealt primarily, if not only, with the films or the visual presentations after they were made or with the responses of audiences to these films across psychological or sociological parameters.

Our purpose was somewhat different. We were starting at an earlier stage in the genesis of a communication. Our study was of both the process of development and of the structure by which a beginner or learner goes about organizing a communication.

So instead of describing a process of participant observation, we shall be describing a process of participant intervention.

In selecting a location for our field work, we looked for a community with a set of boundaries in order to check our experience against previous observations. We had found that black youngsters in the slums didn't like making films on their own

block. Their films, made in different cities under varying conditions, were about familiar activities rather than places and
showed the youngsters doing those things they were most comfortable doing in areas associated with the white film teacher. In
a film called "Not Much To Do" a group of eleven- to fourteen-
year-old black youngsters in Philadelphia photographed themselves, as they said, "sneaking into" a university museum, stealing goldfish from a university pond, "breaking into" an
abandoned firehouse, swimming "illegally" in the art museum
fountain, and so on. In all of these cases the presence of the white
teacher made these activities legitimate for a film. There were no
scenes photographed in their own homes, their own churches, or
their own back yards. In other projects in New York and Philadelphia sponsored by settlement houses of community groups,
the first things photographed were the sanctioned activities of
the settlement house—ping-pong in the recreation hall, basketball and football in the playground, etc.

Would the Navajo want to communicate about things in their
own community? Would they photograph their own families in
their own homes? Would they be concerned with activities rather
than places?

We wanted a community that would have a clear-cut sense of
turf so that we could see whether the Navajo would follow us
outside it, would want to avoid it, or would be constrained—and
in what way—within it.

Choosing the Community and the Students

We made a brief survey of the reservation in March 1966, before
selecting the community where we would work. We visited several highly acculturated areas (Window Rock and Chinle, both
centers of Federal and Tribal government) and several more
traditional communities (Many Farms, Piñon, and Pine Springs).
We felt that work in the former would be difficult because they

were large and amorphous. Although Many Farms and Piñon were much more traditional, transporting film in and out of the community would have been difficult. It was important to hold the delay in feedback to a minimum.

Pine Springs, Arizona, was chosen. It was much less acculturated than either Window Rock or Chinle, was sufficiently small (around 600) to give us a feel for community structure and organization, and had the added advantage of being only an hour by car from the Gallup airport.

Aside from these factors, the matter of rapport had to be considered. We had only two months at our disposal. Adair had worked in Pine Springs twenty-eight years before and had kept in touch with his old friends. Adair had also made a film there previously, and we felt that it might be possible to compare his film to the films the Navajo might make themselves.

Pine Springs was also isolated enough that some people in the community spoke no English, but the village was close enough to Gallup, an English-speaking community, that there also were many bilinguals. We didn't know if nonspeakers of English would deal with movie cameras differently than would English speakers. It seemed possible that the language one spoke would influence the way one made films. For the same reason we wanted a community that would not have been much exposed to television and where people had seen no or very few films. Pine Springs qualified. Many of the older people spoke no English and there were many people who had seen almost no films. In addition Pine Springs had only that year been invaded by television. One set was available in the schoolhouse, and at the time we were there no pattern of watching had developed in the community.

We wanted men and women, boys and girls, as students. We wondered whether there would be a cultural difference in who could be allowed to make films. For example, at Hopi there are specialized vocabularies for women and for men. Would there be a similar difference among the Navajo—not in verbal language but in who could use the film language or in how they used it?

We were also worried that, although Worth had been successful in teaching college students and others in our urban American society to make motion pictures, the Navajo would prove to
be so different that the entire study would be impossible. Sam
Yazzie's question, "Why should the Navajo make movies?" had
added a cautious overtone to much of our planning. What if
everyone felt that way? We realized that despite our original
optimism, we had no idea whether the Navajo would want to,
and if he wanted to, could make movies.

As a safeguard against the possibility that the Navajo living in
Pine Springs would not want to make movies, and also to see if
there were any differences between a Navajo making movies in
his own community and a Navajo who was brought in from the
outside, we hit upon the idea of finding a Navajo artist. This
choice proved effective, since as it happened both the dimension
of "artist" and that of "outsider" were particularly important in
the way the Navajo made films.

We therefore chose a nineteen-year-old Navajo artist, Al Clah,
who was born in a community about fifty miles from Pine
Springs, and who had attended the Institute of American Indian
Art at Santa Fe. This school for Indian students, set up by the
Bureau of Indian Affairs, attempts to combine Western notions
of art and artist with the traditional values and crafts that are part
of the heritage of almost every American Indian tribe.

We also felt that as a painter and sculptor, Al Clah would be
accustomed to manipulating visual forms and would be motivated to explore a new medium. We further anticipated close
rapport between such an artist and Worth, who had been trained
as a painter and sculptor, and who felt confident he could teach
the technology of film to someone with an art background.

We will in the chapter on the analysis of the film compare
Clah's choice of subject matter, style of working, and film structure with those of the other Navajo.

Other researchers using participant observation techniques
had found that one complication in choosing participants and

communities for research was the strong feelings in the village or community about who would be chosen (and often paid) to participate. If the community was not involved in the choosing, it often interfered with the people chosen or with the project in subtle ways. We therefore felt that it would be best for the other participants to be selected by the community itself, or by someone within the community who was well placed in the power structure. We also hoped to observe the methods by which people were selected for a task such as filmmaking, and shall report on some of these methods.

Adair therefore went to a young Navajo friend, Johnny Nelson, who was the number two man on the local political ladder, and asked him to help select others from within the community.

By the end of our exploratory field trip, we had decided to seek four different sorts of students: (1) a girl; (2) a craftsman or woman who would be, as it were, a step down in the artistic (in the Western cultural sense) hierarchy; (3) a person with political ambitions, who might see this new way of communicating as a means to enhance his power in the community; and (4) a Navajo who had no craft, artistic, political, or personal interest or aptitude in filmmaking.

Not only did we want the kinds of students we have outlined, but we had planned to bring only enough cameras, editing equipment, and film for four students. One reason for this limitation was that we wanted to observe them wherever they went while filming and so were constrained by the number of observers available. There were three of us: Adair, Worth, and Dick Chalfen, a student of Worth's at the Annenberg School of Communications, who had also had extensive course work in anthropology. He would be part of the team, helping Worth in the teaching and helping us all with our many observations. We felt that more observers could only inhibit the learning process by being constantly underfoot, and would have strained the facilities available to us for living and teaching.

As we have noted above, it has proved best, when working in

a culture whose response to the intended innovation is unknown, to move slowly and to let the people within the culture determine as much as possible about the specific arrangements. In our case we also wanted to gather data about the values and attributes of those persons whom the Navajo chose to learn filmmaking. Data on how filmmakers started and proceeded to become filmmakers was very rare.

When we first met Johnny Nelson during our preliminary trip in March, he was working as an assistant in the trading post. Johnny cheerfully agreed to scout around, to see who was available for the summer.

When we arrived in June there seemed to have been little result. One girl, a silversmith, who had tentatively agreed to be a student in March, informed us that her husband had taken a summer job off the reservation and that he wanted her with him. Everyone was extremely vague, and Al Clah was our only student.

On June 3, after we had been in the reservation area for two days (staying in a motel in Gallup because we still had not made final arrangements with the Navajo nor received final permission from the Bureau of Indian Affairs), Johnny told Worth that people in the community were somewhat confused. They thought our project was a Bureau of Indian Affairs project which would give them jobs in the school for the summer. He asked Worth to explain again why we were in Pine Springs and what we would be doing. Johnny by this time had assumed the role of public relations man for the film project. His manner of talking and acting implied that he understood, but that he just wanted to check so that he could say the right things to his friends in the community.

Worth again made his standard explanation. "Adair and I are professors in large universities, John on the West Coast and I on the East Coast. I am a professor of communications; that is, I study how people get their ideas across to each other. John is an anthropologist; he studies how people different from ourselves—

Indians, for example—live. I am a teacher of movie communication. I teach people to get their ideas across to each other by making movies. Dick Chalfen is one of my students; he studied how to make movies with me and is helping John and me while we teach the Navajo. You understand, Johnny, that the reason we're here is not only to teach the Navajo—out of the goodness of our hearts—how to make movies but also because we want to learn how to teach better. We want to learn how Navajos learn, and how they make movies. We feel we will learn more about communication in general if we learn how people different from ourselves learn to communicate. Remember I told you that our students could make movies about anything they want, in any way they want to—all we want to do is learn what you do."

Johnny had listened intently to this retelling, and while Worth was talking, had led him away from the front of the trading post until they were both leaning on a log fence at the side out of sight of everyone. Johnny's face had become animated as Worth talked, and he said with great enthusiasm, "That's a great idea, that idea of trying to find out how people get ideas across to other people. How do you do that exactly?" Worth replied, "There are all sorts of ways, but the way we wanted to try was to see how Navajos did it when they learned how to make films."

Worth's field notes of that conversation say at this point, "I must have been a little dense because it now occurred to me that Johnny had something very important on his mind and was actually just trying to get up nerve enough to say it outright." The young man said, "You know, I think I would like to be one of your students." (This conversation is transcribed from Worth's field notes made directly after this conversation.)

Worth replied, "Gee, Johnny, that would be great but you have to work at the Trading Post, and when we were here last time, you know, two months ago, you told us you couldn't work any place else."

"How much are you going to pay the students?" Johnny asked.

"I think about $1.25 an hour. That's the government rate."

"You know, I think I could end up making as much working for you as I would working for Griswold (the trader). Anyway, it isn't the money—I got something in me to say, and I want to say it. Tell me how it would work, what would we be doing?"

"Well, we would start out, and I will probably ask you what you want to make a film about, and then we would talk about that, and I will show you how to use the cameras and the exposure meters and film, and the things that you would need, and then you would go ahead and make a film, and I would watch," Worth explained.

"How many hours a week would I be working for you?"

"I don't know. It could be about forty hours, but it's up to you how long you'll want to work. If you wanted to work a long time on the film that would be okay, or a short time, that's up to you. Making a film is up to you. You do it any way you think is right."

Johnny declared, "That's exactly what I want. That sounds like real work, not this working just in the store wrapping packages and bundles. I'll go talk to Griswold."

At this point, we agreed to meet again after lunch. As soon as Johnny met Worth again, he continued as if the conversation had not been broken off, "I really want to get starting in this learning how to make movies. I can learn a lot about it."

"Why is making movies such a good idea, Johnny?" Worth asked.

"I been thinking a lot since you and John came here, and now when you tell me that you study the way people can get to tell each other things about themselves, and that they can understand one another, I really feel it's time some Navajo became a professor in that—just like you. Yep, I think it's about time there was a Navajo professor of this."

Worth looked at him and asked, "You mean you?"

Nelson smiled and said, "Maybe."

During the lunch period, Johnny had introduced Chalfen and Adair to Mike Anderson. Mike was about eighteen and had returned to the reservation for the summer. He had no particular interest in filmmaking but had agreed to talk to us about becoming a student because Johnny told him it was a paying job, and Mike said he wanted something to do.

At one point as Worth and Nelson talked, Mike Anderson and Chalfen walked over to us, overhearing Nelson say, "I can't wait to get my hands on that camera." Later Chalfen reported that Anderson also seemed very interested in the idea of learning to work a camera.

It has been our experience, and that of others working with teenagers or members of other cultures, that people who are normally suspicious and hostile about being taught—of anything like school—will readily accept being studied and questioned if, as Johnny put it, they "can get their hands on that camera." This unusual motivating factor is worth noting in relation to other possible educational or research attempts with people of other cultures. When Worth worked with the Harlem Youth Opportunities group (HARYOU) in New York City in 1963–64, he found high school dropouts willing to attend classes in filmmaking and answer questions about their attitudes and ideas in obvious contrast to their normal school behavior. The same response was shown by five different groups in Philadelphia, who learned filmmaking in projects run by several of Worth's students.

Even middle-class white college students, both graduates and undergraduates, seem to gravitate to film courses in universities throughout the United States. The white students articulate it clearly: "Film is where it's at. Film is the thing to know." The attitude expressed by Johnny, "I got something in me to say, and I want to say it," might easily have been said by any middle-class high school or college student today.

But Johnny was able to express other attitudes which reflected very basic Navajo values. Over the next several days, he talked more about what this project meant to him. He said, "Could I go on learning more about film, even after the summer?" "Suppose my film was really good, suppose I was a very good learner, could I learn more, is it possible? I know I can't learn all there is to know only this summer," "I know this is a good chance for me to get a lot of knowledge, I want to get as much knowledge as I can."

In the next several days, Johnny introduced us to Mary Jane and Maxine Tsosie, the daughters of Juan Tsosie, the chapter chairman. Johnny felt that they too should be students. He told us, "Money is not the only thing they want. They want to learn. If you have no money to pay them, it'll be all right. They want the knowledge."

Later he said to us, "I don't have enough knowledge, and I want to do this thing to get more. I told the chapter [the community governing body] that I can't supervise a job for them because I need this summer for knowledge. I want to teach the tribe later on . . . What I want knowledge for is for myself to develop—for my family—everything is for my family—for my tribe—to help them."

It is of course possible that Johnny was telling us this because that's what he thought professors would want to hear. But in the translation of his speech at the chapter meeting later that week which introduced us and our project to the entire community, Johnny said much the same thing. We doubt that that speech was aimed at us (in any event, we didn't speak enough Navajo to understand it). It seemed rather to be a clear reflection not only of Navajo values as reflected in the literature, but of the hierarchy of value. In a pinch, according to the old Navajo values, knowledge comes before money. In the chapter analyzing the responses of the community to the films, we will show the same values reasserted.

We now had agreed to take as students Al Clah, an artist and an outsider; Mike Anderson, a member of Johnny's father's clan, who had worked in a potato chip factory and who "just wanted to do something over the summer"; and Johnny Nelson, a politician. Nelson then introduced us to his young neighbor, Susie Benally, an expert weaver whose husband was away from the reservation in military service.

We had what we thought was an interesting sample in our four students—Clah, who was an artist and who we thought would be most likely to be motivated to learn and to use a new symbol form; Benally, an expert craftswoman, skilled in hand manipulation and in the use of symbolic forms; Nelson, who seemed highly motivated, even though he had no craft or art experience; and Anderson, who seemed totally uninterested in the project other than as a way to keep busy and to earn some money until his return to San Francisco to attend barber school in the fall.

Although we thought that the selection was complete, so that we could start teaching, another principle basic to the Navajo value system first had to be satisfied. Just after we had agreed that Mike and Susie could join him as students, Johnny kept suggesting that what we needed were two men and two women, implying that if we allowed him to suggest another woman, we would be finished. This seemed an obvious slighting of Al Clah, who had been largely ignored by everyone in the community. Johnny was acting as if the outsider didn't exist. Indeed, all the Navajo were making it clear to us that the selection process was not finished; or rather that they were not ready to start school. "We should have two girls to make it right," was said by several of the students after Johnny broached the subject, and when asked why, he replied, "You can't have only one woman—a single woman need a friend—it would be very hard for a bashful girl to ask questions in front of men. It would be possible that she never ask any question about something that bother her because there was no women to ask it of—a woman won't ask a question because there was no women by her side."

These objections also seemed consistent with Navajo values. Balance or equilibrium is a deep Navajo value. The universe is balanced—thus healthy. If a Navajo enters an unbalanced situation, he is bound to become sick—to function poorly or not to function at all. It is not so much that all things come in pairs, such as a boy and a girl, or a night and a day, or being good and being bad, but rather that the universe in its balanced form contained the unity boy–girl, night–day, or good–bad. One didn't exist without the other. A "school" or healthy learning situation couldn't exist without the right balance which meant men–women.

We reminded Johnny that we had chosen three men and one woman but suggested that perhaps we could include one more woman if he could help us find her. It was then that he brought up having introduced us to Mary Jane and Maxine, the daughters of the chapter chairman. We realized that Johnny had brilliantly fulfilled several obligations. As well as maintaining balance, he had managed to include the political leader in the project by finding a source of knowledge and income for his daughters. Johnny had also managed to cover himself ritually, since Juan Tsosie was Sam Yazzie's son. Sam was a renowned medicine man and, should photography be in conflict with ritual, Johnny knew that having a medicine man on his side could only help. Johnny realized that having the medicine man's granddaughters and the political leader's daughters involved would obviate any possible objections in two very important areas.

The sisters agreed to work with us, emphasizing that they were very interested in going to "school" and suggesting that we write a letter to their high school teacher giving them credit for summer school. We asked them how they felt about having three women and three men, and they told us that it would be very hard to learn if there weren't an equal number of men and women. They explained (1) that they would not be comfortable listening to instruction unless the "people were even"; (2) that they couldn't learn well unless "things" were equal; and (3) that neither men nor women would ask questions unless things were equal.

The Community Agrees

As soon as we agreed to accept the Tsosie sisters as students, Johnny informed us that Juan Tsosie had invited us to attend the meeting of the local chapter later that afternoon. Juan would introduce us and tell the entire community about our project.

The Pine Springs chapter house had been completed shortly before we arrived and was the only Navajo building there that had electricity. In contrast to the hogans that most members of the community lived in, the log chapter house had a peaked shingled roof and a wooden floor.

When we arrived, about seventy-five adults and twenty-five children had fairly filled the building (photo 1). Some of the children were a few months old; some of the adults were in their eighties. Many of the men still wore their hair secured and braided with double strands of wool in the back. Most of the women wore velveteen long-sleeved blouses and long calico skirts. Everyone wore jewelry—rings, necklaces, and bracelets. As people came in, each one took one of the new metal folding chairs and sat in one of the rows. Juan Tsosie and a woman (the chapter recording secretary) sat in front on a small raised platform.

Although everyone knew they were at an important and formal meeting, there seemed no restriction on noise, movement, or personal conversation while speeches were being made. Adults kept going in and out casually, passing in front of the speaker, and children continued to play with each other and their parents in apparent total disregard for the formality of the occasion. We found the same attitude later on when we showed the films to the community. It was difficult at times to remember that we were at an official permission-granting council.

The meeting, we learned, was to be in the Navajo language, but there would be interpreters for our benefit.

Juan opened the meeting by announcing the agenda, which included electing certain representatives to the council, arranging for the construction of several shallow wells in the area, and introducing a new group of whites who had come, Juan said, to "help us." In introducing Adair, Juan emphasized, "Here is a man who is not a stranger to the Navajo—he is a good man—a man who knows Navajo religion and respects the Navajo." Adair then explained what we were to do, adding that everyone knew that anthropologists came to the Navajo and often took pictures, but that we were going to teach the Navajo to take moving pictures, and that they could make movies of anything they wanted. Both Worth and Chalfen made short speeches, and then Adair asked the community if Worth could take still pictures of the meeting. Permission was given with much bantering back and forth, and then Juan told us that we were welcome to the community. He said he appreciated that some white men came to help the Navajo and thanked us for respecting Navajo people and ways. He repeated the statement that he wished more white men would respect the Navajo. Worth thanked Juan for inviting us to work there and told him how much he appreciated Juan's understanding and respect for our work. The participants in our project were also there, and Al Clah was introduced to the community for the first time.

On his way out from the meeting, Adair asked an elder, an old friend of his, if he thought the project was a good idea. Would the Navajo be able to learn to make film? The answer was: "I don't know. It's too early to tell. Ask me later." In typical Navajo fashion, the elder would accept, observe carefully, then make a statement based on the outcome.

We then left the meeting knowing that we could move our equipment to Pine Springs and start working with our students —three men and three women—the next day. All spoke both Navajo and English with varying degrees of fluency in both languages. All had seen films before: Al, about a hundred (by his estimate), some of them "documentaries," and Susie about ten (by her estimate), none of them "documentaries."

Al Clah's acquaintance with film was the most extensive of our group. From discussions with Al and his teacher at the Santa Fe school, we learned that he had indeed seen about a hundred documentary films in the last several years. They ranged from Canadian Film Board documentaries to such art films as those made by the San Francisco avant-garde film group. When we asked Al what films he remembered or what films he liked, however, he had great difficulty remembering the names of the films or their directors, which he had been told, or even their story lines. He remembered a film "about a Canadian Indian artist," "a film about nature," and "a film about animals." He said he liked films about rocks and trees and "things like that." Of another film he liked, he recalled, "It's about water and trees and ripples in the water."

When we asked Clah's art teacher in Santa Fe what kind of film he thought Al would make, he replied, "Al will make a film about something obscure—something having to do with old myths or something having to do with the mythical and mystical concepts of his childhood as a Navajo." (See Appendix and Part 3 for a description of Clah's film.) According to the teacher, Al had seen such films as *Beauty and the Beast* by Cocteau, *White Mane*, and a film called *The Sorceress*. He also mentioned that in his years of showing film to Indians, he found that they seemed to like Japanese films best—a particularly interesting comment in the light of the following anecdote.

Worth is a member of the Board of Directors and a trustee of the Flaherty Film Seminars, a group of documentary filmmakers, teachers, and students who meet once a year to view and discuss documentary films produced around the world. In August 1966, he showed Al Clah's film at the seminar, explaining a little about the project and about Clah. Susumi Hani, a guest at the festival and a leading Japanese feature and documentary filmmaker, said to Worth after the screening, "I just want to tell you that that Navajo film was the most beautiful film I've ever seen in America. It is too bad that you Americans cannot understand it—but the Navajo must be like the Japanese since I can understand it."

Worth was astonished by this, not having remembered the comment by Al's teacher which he had recorded in his notes at the time. He asked Hani to tell him what the film was about. Hani's response remains the closest in agreement to Al's own words of any comment about the film. (See Chapter 14 for fuller description.)

5

The Lives of Some of the Navajo Students

Before we continue our account of the research activities, it may be useful to review the backgrounds of some of our students.

Maxine and Mary Jane Tsosie

Like so many Navajo girls of their generation, seventeen-year-old Maxine Tsosie and her twenty-one-year-old sister, Mary Jane, daughters of Juan Tsosie, live in two contrasting worlds. When they are away from home in boarding school or working off the reservation, they live essentially in the white man's world. With that small percentage of Navajo girls who reach high school, they live with their classmates in a kind of adolescent culture typical of the American rural West, or more accurately, the rural West of America some decades ago. Their high school, however, is less a place for college preparation than a place for vocational training.

A school like the public high school at Fort Defiance, run by the state of Arizona, superficially appears to apply to its students the same molding process as those elsewhere in the country. But there is one important point of contrast. The white student in a high school in Albuquerque or Phoenix has some sense of continuity between life at school and home. The language, the religion, the behavior of their teachers, the goals and values taken for granted are not unlike those of their parents. For Maxine and Mary Jane there is very little shared by the two environments. The life style of their parents, and to a much greater degree their grandparents, is in sharp contrast to what they are taught at school. The use of the Navajo language at school has been discouraged if not forbidden. Traditional Navajo religion is practiced at home; starting in elementary school, time is set aside for learning one of the varieties of the Christian faith. The degree to which a Navajo of the Tsosie sisters' generation uses the native language and takes part in Navajo religious practice and belief is largely dependent on the continuity of family and community life. For the Tsosie sisters and many others of their generation, this continuity has been badly fractured by long stretches of time spent away from home.

Maxine

Maxine was born at the government hospital at Fort Defiance, a few hours' drive by auto from where her family was living. When she was only two years of age, her mother died and her father moved to Barstow, California. Maxine attended school there until she was about ten years old. Her father then brought her back to the reservation to live with her maternal grandmother, following the Navajo matrilineal custom. In the old days upon the death of a mother, it was her sisters, her mother, or another woman of her lineage who would assume the responsibility for raising the child, who would not have been taken away by the father as was Maxine.

The grandmother lived at Oak Springs, a community about ten

miles to the northwest of Pine Springs, which became Maxine's primary home. While there, she saw her father only when he returned to the reservation from his job in California.

For three years Maxine attended a government boarding school at Fort Wingate, sixty-five miles to the east, then a public school in Gallup for two years while her father, back from California, worked as a silversmith for one of the local craft merchandisers. She then entered public high school at Fort Defiance and was to start her last year in the fall after we met her during summer vacation.

Maxine did well in school, especially in English. She placed first in a high school speech contest. She told us that since she was a young girl, she had wanted to be an elementary school teacher and she planned to go to Arizona State University for teacher training.

In talking with her during the months of the project and watching her make her film concerned with ritual, we realized that she knew very little of the religious life of her people and had attended very few of the traditional curing ceremonies; she said she had never seen any of the sand paintings. The squaw dance held at Pine Springs that summer was the first she had been to. This is exceptional; most girls of her age have been to many such dances. She had not known her grandfather, Sam Yazzie, the father of Juan Tsosie, a prominent medicine man in the Pine Springs area, until five years before. Although her grandmother at Oak Springs speaks some English and had been married to one of the most acculturated members of the Pine Springs community of that generation, it was she who encouraged Maxine to learn the ways of her people and who scolded her father for not taking her to Navajo ceremonies.

Maxine considers herself a Roman Catholic. She was baptized as a small child when she was living at Barstow. When she is in high school she attends mass every week. Thanks to her grandmother she has learned to speak Navajo, although she was ten years of age before she heard the language spoken by others in the community.

Mary Jane

Mary Jane is five years older than Maxine and the second of the seven sisters (Maxine is next to the youngest). Unlike Maxine, her early years were spent in government schools and her first two years of high school were at a public school in California. While there she did part-time domestic work. She then returned at her father's request to help out at home. Unfortunately appendicitis, followed by a severe infection and intermittent hospitalization, delayed her last two years in high school. Like her sister, her best subject in school was English. She hopes to become a laboratory technician after taking a two-year college course.

Mary Jane also considers herself a Roman Catholic and has been to very few Navajo ceremonies. However, when she was eighteen, she was shown the Yeibechai masks at a Night Chant she attended with another sister; this rite was traditionally part of every young Navajo's initiation into the ceremonial life of the people.

Mary Jane, although shy and less outgoing than her sister, is, perhaps because she was older when she lived away from the reservation, more oriented to the non-Navajo world than Maxine. Mary Jane told us, "I didn't like it on the reservation after living in California; people seemed different. They were not friendly and stared at me." She had a more difficult time learning the Navajo language. "My grandmother and uncle scold me because I speak English nearly all the time." Mary Jane looks forward to returning to California for more schooling, and hopes to live there.

Of the two sisters, Maxine was much the more self-confident in her relations with us and with the members of the community. Maxine, more aggressive, is nevertheless much closer to traditional Navajo ways. If Maxine were to marry a Navajo and settle down as a teacher in an Indian school at Oak Springs or Pine Springs, it is quite possible that in ten years she would be well integrated into Navajo family and community life. For Mary Jane, integration would be much more difficult; she is much more drawn to the world of the white man.

Susie Benally

Susie Benally was the most traditional of any of the filmmakers. She spent the whole of her girlhood with her family at Pine Springs and was over fourteen when she first went to boarding school away from home. She was shy in the presence of strangers and soft-spoken. During the first week of the class she hardly spoke above a whisper. Her demeanor contrasted sharply to the almost bold behavior of the Tsosie sisters.

Susie was born at Pine Springs in 1940, the third of eight children—six boys and two girls. For her first five grades, she attended the local elementary school where our classes in filmmaking were held. During those formative years she was in constant touch with her family and was raised in the conventional Navajo manner. Alta, her mother, was a well-known weaver from a matrilineal line of outstanding craftsmen. Mabel Burnsides, her mother's sister, had taught weaving for many years at various government boarding schools, and other aunts and uncles were well known weavers and silversmiths. Susie's early memories are much like those of other women of her age at Pine Springs. She recalls herding sheep with her mother and grandmother when she was about six. At eight she began to help her mother with weaving, starting with the simplest task of carding the wool; later she was taught to spin. She was able to help her mother weave sashes when she was eleven, and by fifteen, she was weaving her own rugs. There had been a close relationship between the girl and her mother in the learning of weaving.

Susie, like most of the girls of her age at Pine Springs, went o the various *sings* with her mother and father, unlike the Tsosie sisters. At her first menses, Susie went through the traditional girls' puberty ceremony and shared the large corn cake with many clanmates and friends in the community.

At fourteen, after several years out of school, Susie was sent to the Bureau of Indian Affairs vocational school at Stewart, Nevada. There she remained for five years in a course for hospital attendants. She did not like this type of work, however; during the five summers she used her earlier training as a craftsman by working in a curio store at Bryce National Park, where she demonstrated weaving and waited on trade.

In 1963 she married Floyd Benally, a Navajo boy from Bluff, Utah, whom she had known at school. After they returned to the reservation, Susie worked briefly as a waitress at a cafe on the highway not far from Pine Springs. Floyd entered military service and Susie continued living at her mother's home at Pine Springs.

Susie's verbal timidity with us did not seem to handicap her in learning film technique. She was an acute observer. Long training as a craftsman and thorough knowledge of her subject gave her confidence in filmmaking. Hands trained to spin and weave, and eyes trained to distinguish subtle variations in tone and texture and to compose harmonious patterns, were easily retrained to see with critical discrimination through the camera's lens. Further, as a weaver, Susie was accustomed to think holistically about pattern; before she was far along in the weaving of a rug, she had the whole pattern in her mind's eye. Such an outlook is of course a tremendous asset to the filmmaker.

But for the Tsosie sisters, on the other hand, the task of filmmaking presented a very different set of problems. Verbal discourse was the easiest part of the job. Both were able to joke and banter with us from the very first day. They were sure of their ability as students in the classroom at Window Rock, and Worth and Chalfen were immediately accepted as new teachers. The subject of the practice footage shot by Mary Jane and Maxine—the school building and the children at play in the school yard—indicated their feeling of ease in that environment. They wrote careful notes and were more dependent on paper and pencil than was Susie. But lack of training as craftsmen made them much less sure of themselves in learning the technical processes. They were also unfamiliar with the subject—Navajo religion—which they chose for their film.

Susie was much closer to the traditional culture of the community and she chose a subject with which she had been intimate from childhood. Likewise Susie, typically Navajo, had a close relationship with her mother who acted in her film; this intimacy extended to a shared interest in a new technical task. Each woman was able to anticipate the other's demands; Susie's knowledge of the sequences of the process of weaving allowed her to anticipate film sequences in a way that greatly facilitated the shooting of her first film.

In contrast, the Tsosie sisters found it very difficult to handle their actor, their grandfather, in any meaningful way. Not only were they unable to anticipate what would come next in the sing he conducts in the film; but the filming presented them and Sam Yazzie with a reversal of roles. Ordinarily he would tell them what to do, and not they him. But in so far as they were the ones who had the white man's technology to record his actions, he looked to them for directions which they were hard put to give, not knowing what they should expect of him in his role as a medicine man.

Mike Anderson

Mike Anderson was born at Pine Springs in 1942 and was twenty-four when we worked with him. He is the third of five siblings, three girls and two boys. One of his sisters and his brother are older. Two sisters now live in Gallup and one in California. The brother, Terry Lee, an ex-marine, is now on the Navajo police force.

Mike's first education was at a Catholic school in Gallup,

where he remained for five years. When he was in fourth grade Mike was baptized in the Roman Catholic Church as his mother had been years before. Mike thinks of himself as a Catholic; as a boy he was not taken to sings held at Pine Springs nor was he shown the Yei masks at the initiation rite to Navajo ritual.

From Gallup Mike was sent to the Phoenix Indian School for four years, and he then finished high school at the public school at Fort Defiance.

After graduation Mike decided to go to a barber's school in San Francisco, but upon arrival he found that the school was full. He got a job as a machine bag operator at a potato chip factory in Burlingame, California, and remained on that job for three years, eventually earning the maximum union wage, $2.25 an hour. When the factory moved to Texas, Mike quit and got a job as a painter and maintenance man at Dominican College in San Rafael, a suburb of San Francisco. It was the job he held before coming back to Pine Springs for the summer.

While in California Mike would have liked to live with a brother, but since none were available, he lived alone to avoid drunken Navajos, who were constantly asking him for money. Even so they found him, and he changed his place of residence numerous times to elude them. Mike attended Sunday mass regularly and sometimes visited an uncle and a cousin who lived nearby, or another cousin who lived across the bay in Oakland. On other weekends, he would go to the Indian Center in the mission district.

Mike says that he still plans to return to San Francisco and enroll in the barber's school he tried to attend earlier. Questioned about where he will set up as a barber after he has finished the course, Mike spoke once of possibly opening a shop near Window Rock and on another occasion of remaining in San Francisco.

Of the three men, Mike seemed to have the weakest ties to traditional Navajo culture, although he did have an interest in the religion of his people. Like Mary Jane Tsosie, he had spent his childhood away from the reservation and his only close ties were to his immediate family. The chances are that he will, as the years go by, become increasingly involved in urban life away from the reservation.

Johnny Nelson

Johnny Nelson was born at Indian Wells, seventy miles west of Pine Springs, on July 7, 1933. His mother was Florence Yazzie, of Tsina-jinnie clan, and his father was Joseph Nelson.

Johnny's mother died when he was twelve years old and he was adopted by his mother's sister Dorothy Pavatea, the wife of a Hopi, Tom Pavatea, Jr. His foster father was the son of the well-known storekeeper, Tom Pavatea, who had had a trading post for many years at Polacca, at the foot of First Mesa, Arizona; Tom, Jr. helped his father wait on trade.

From the age of twelve Johnny was part of a tri-lingual family. Dorothy had taught her Hopi husband a good bit of Navajo in addition to what he already knew as a storekeeper with many Navajo customers. Both parents spoke English. Johnny said his mother made a regular practice of speaking to him in Navajo and expected him to address her in the language of his people. Hopi was the language of his playmates and he learned enough of that tongue to get along with them on the playground and elsewhere.

Johnny's first formal education was at the Keams Canyon Boarding School, only a few miles distant from Polacca, where he finished sixth grade. There, Johnny remembered, the dormitory attendant punished the children when they spoke Navajo instead of English. During summers much of his time was spent herding sheep for his parents. His next schooling was far from home, at Carson City, Nevada, where the Bureau of Indian Affairs had a special program—essentially an accelerated course in English. Johnny completed the course, designed for five years, in two years. Next came one year in the Bureau's high school in Phoenix, where Johnny was enrolled in the academic course rather than in vocational training.

In 1954 Johnny entered the Marines and went to boot camp at Camp Pendleton, California. Unfortunately, a convoy truck in which he was riding turned over and he suffered injury to his shoulders and ribs. He was given a medical discharge after only seven months in the service. Johnny then got a job on the railroad as a track worker. After a short time with a crew laying and mending track, he advanced to assistant foreman on a track-laying machine and later became its head operator.

Johnny had met Ruby Burnsides, the daughter of Mark Burnsides (a former chapter chairman of the Oak Springs–Pine Springs area), at school in Carson City. They were later married and first lived at her home at Pine Springs; subsequently they set up their own home next to Ruby's parents.

Johnny soon became involved in community affairs. About ten years before, Adair had interviewed him and he had then expressed a desire to be an interpreter, to help his community to have a better understanding of the white man's world, and to improve the local educational opportunities for the Pine Springs children. In fact, he had been chapter chairman before 1957, but the exigencies of politics had replaced him with someone else. Juan Tsosie held the job when we were there in 1966, and Johnny was the number two politico in the community.

Johnny Nelson's life is typical of many Navajo men of his and the previous generation: assorted schooling, military service, shifting residence, and a variety of jobs. The one respect in which Johnny's history is different from that of fellows like Mike Anderson was the exposure from an early age to a family with obvious awareness of the importance of multi-lingual upbringing. Navajo, Hopi, and Anglo-American customs and culture all impinged on Johnny from early life, perhaps shaping his knack for ready communication with a variety of peoples in a variety of situations—good training for anyone with political aspirations.

It is obvious from these short sketches that our students were not what one could call "professional Navajo." If their films showed a common pattern and if the pattern could be related to Navajo language and culture, we could feel certain that there was no deliberate attempt to obey Navajo rules; many of them simply didn't know them. Whatever was Navajo about their filmmaking and filming behavior had to be a result of their internalizing their culture and unconsciously acting in accordance with it when they made their films.

6

Teaching Navajos about Cameras and Film

Even though we planned to pay them a modest wage, we were not certain in the beginning that our subjects would have the motivation essential to learn enough about the camera to produce significant results.

The Navajo, however, are outstanding among American Indians in their willingness to accept innovations. Evon Vogt (1961) has characterized the style of culture change illustrated by the Navajo as incorporative: ". . . the Navajos have had over the centuries to make selective adaptations to cultural elements that were presented to them and which they successfully incorporated into their growing and expanding culture." Thus the Navajo learned a set of agricultural technologies from the Pueblo Indians and adapted it to their own hunting and gathering economy. Also from the Pueblos, who had settled in the Southwest hundreds of years before the Athabascan Indians (of whom the Navajo are one group), they learned weaving and pottery making. Many of the elements in Navajo religion—including sandpainting, prayer sticks, and the dance step seen in the *Night Chant*—have been taken over from other peoples and incorporated into their curing rites. In more recent years sheep and cattle were borrowed from Pueblo peoples and the Spanish American settlers, resulting in a considerable economic growth. The automobile, wage work, small industry, the elective system for their tribal council, and a civil service system are all examples of latter-day adaptations from the white man incorporated into their cultural whole.

The willingness of the Navajo to accept innovation comes, however, only after a careful consideration of its probable value to them. In the words of Ethel Albert (1956): "Technical or ritual innovations are acceptable but only when accompanied by a full set of directions for use, their worth proved by experience, and their contents modified to fit traditional pattern." The behavior of the Navajo in learning filmmaking often illustrated Albert's three criteria; they were crucial in their day-to-day decisions.

The First Day: Getting Ready

We had made arrangements with the school teacher in the Pine Springs Boarding School for our research team to use the boys' dormitory wing as a classroom, editing room, and living space. Al Clah, who was a stranger in the community, would live there as well.

The Pine Springs Boarding School was typical of the schools the U.S. Government had built throughout the reservation in the last twenty years to teach Navajo children the white man's language and customs. Where the older schools had been repressive and authoritarian, the newer ones paid some attention to Navajo culture and religion and attempted to find something better for the Navajo than Dick and Jane readers. The airy and comfortable school was the most modern building in Pine Springs. It was built of cinder block and brick with modern plumbing, heating, and school fixtures, to accommodate the first two grades. The school shared with the Trading Post and the chapter house the distinction of having electricity. Its disadvantage for us was the small-scale furniture and equipment designed for use by six- to nine-year-olds. There were two large classrooms, two dormitories, two bathrooms, and a large, comfortable library and recreation room. The kitchen and dining rooms were well equipped. In general the school looked like any reasonably good camp facility in other parts of the country.

The dormitory wing we had chosen was roughly fifty feet long and twenty feet wide. A four-foot aisle down the center separated four eight- by ten-foot compartments on each side. There were eight cubbies in all, each with two double bunk beds. We left the beds in four compartments for sleeping, and used two compartments for editing, one as a classroom, one for storing equipment, and the aisle for projection.

We did most of our teaching either in the dormitory or sitting just outside it under the piñon trees.

We brought with us all the equipment we needed in four portable cases, easily carried by two people. There were four Bell & Howell 16 mm cameras, four film viewers, four sets of rewinds and related equipment, and all the film we needed. We also had four exposure meters and two tripods.

Our first day at Pine Springs was spent moving beds and improvising editing tables. We all had a chance to get to know one another, and the Navajo had a chance to see and to touch everything. That was by plan—the traditional method of Navajo learning was by doing and touching, exploring new materials directly rather than by lecture or lengthy explanation. In that first day Worth named every piece of equipment and had the students suggest places for storage. We consulted them about placing equipment and arranging the teaching spaces. We wanted to see how they would do it; we also felt that they would probably have some good suggestions that we hadn't considered.

We had our first inkling that the whole thing would work during that first day. The students worked well—full of energy, full of interest, immediately immersed in problem solving. "How can we keep the rewind boards from moving?" Worth asked. One of the Navajos immediately suggested attaching the 1 x 12 boards with C clamps to the small tables which were all we had. When we replied that we had no C clamps, several of the students instantly suggested a trip to town for nails, clamps, extension cords, and so on. They would show us the best store and help us carry things. That was in sharp contrast to other groups of beginners we had known, even in the university. Neophytes tend to feel lost in new situations, especially where technology is involved, and hesitate to offer any suggestions so early: they expect the "teacher" to solve most problems.

We found at Pine Springs that we were working with people so used to solving problems on their own that the normal confusion of setting up shop was minimized. Worth had foreseen days of confusion but the Navajo behavior reminded him at once of the way in which he himself, confident in his knowledge of the process as a professional filmmaker, would go about setting up his own work spaces. The lack of fear in relation to new things, the immense drive to get on with the work, and the cheerful way that everyone cooperated suggested a successful completion of the filmmaking experience.

On the first day, before Worth said anything about movies or how to make them, he interviewed each of the six Navajo in a small office set up in back of the Trading Post. He introduced them to the tape recorder, explaining that he would work it in the beginning, but that later he would teach them to use it, and they would work it for our interviews. We had feared that they would object to talking into a tape recorder, and so introduced it as a part of the filmmaking equipment they were to learn.

Perhaps that was why there was no objection; both the boys and girls watched avidly as Worth loaded tape and tested the machine.

The initial interviews were arranged so that the students couldn't talk with the others before Worth spoke with them. He emphasized with each person, "You can make any kind of movie you want to; you can make it about anything you want; I won't tell you what to do." He then asked what each expected to accomplish during the summer.

To our surprise, three of the students immediately started talking about what they wanted to make a film *about*. The others seemed to have some ideas but for some reason—uncertainty, lack of skill with words, shyness—they seemed to have difficulty expressing them. We learned later that the Navajo had been thinking about subjects for films from the moment they heard about the project.

We originally wondered how the Navajo would define film. We thought they might want to film isolated bits of behavior and show them as snapshots. We were surprised to find that so many of our students had a strong and clear desire to make films on subjects, topics, or themes, and that they were able to articulate them so well. In the first taped interview with Johnny Nelson made on June 6, he gave the following response when Worth said, "What I would like is if you would sort of tell me how you understand what we are going to do":

> I've been thinking a lot about the, what I would try to think of —mostly to make a movie of. What the—how the, our people have been living and how, what—like the landscape, and then how they make their hogans. It's just something they do. I'd like at the same time to make another movie about some of—about how the people used to make their living . . . and then there's another thing that I had in mind. It might be very difficult to . . . like a lot of people they come—some of them come to the Trading Post, or just drive around inquiring how they make those wonderful necklaces and concho belts and all those things that the Indian people have as

their tradition . . . I think this would, you know, this would be very interesting to make the movies, 'cause how the woman weaves, and without having to copy from a certain design. Just like uh, just talking the, see there, it's almost identical to, it's like trying to make up your mind what movie you're going to make, I believe this is the same way that the Indian women have, they have to use their knowledge, something up here [pointing to his forehead], they don't follow any pattern, you know, all they do is set up their looms, and they start weaving and just as they go along they have to use their heads to make the designs that they feel would be interesting to people they sell their rugs to. . . . That's one of the things that I thought about since we met . . . about how to use your knowledge and that would be to making a movie.

Al Clah responded:

I could use a lot of my ideas, and I could go out and film some of those art film which I could show in San Francisco. . . . I might show some film there, you know maybe a shadow. Just a shadow moving along—see how it works, it moves, the colors—and how it moves. There are a lot of rock formations with the shadow. The shadow is intrepid, and on the trees, you know, how the wind blows and under the bush, how it moves, and these combine together like that, you know, dance a little bit. . . . Something like that would really work . . . and at the same time from the ground, up into the air, see the trees moving and look back down again on the ground and it moves again. There's a relation to it. . . . There's some place I want to point, like rocks, I mean in different areas that I want to record on my camera in water colors, and I would run it over again to look at it, you know. . . . I'll be doing that for some time, and I get a little homesick maybe, just let the projector run.

Mike Anderson had little to say in that first interview:

Well, I don't think I have any idea right now and just wait around and I can think about it. . . . Well, see I don't have anything in mind right now, and I think I'll think about something and you know, go out some place and take pictures and then I can put it together.

Mary Jane Tsosie replied to Worth:

> Oh that's a good question. Oh, gee, I really don't know, but I
> think this is wonderful and would be some good experience for me
> 'cause I never had it and I'm pretty sure I'm going to learn a lot.
> . . . I haven't really decided [what to do] yet. Something about
> weaving and uh, maybe squaw dances if they have one around
> here, and some of the traditional ways, you know. . . . I really don't
> know much about the—Navajo ways you know, the traditional
> ways like singing and squaw dancing, and I'm very much inter-
> ested to learn myself because my father, one day he got after me
> because I didn't know anything about singing [Navajo religious
> ceremonies].

Maxine also spoke about the traditional ways, but more purpose-
fully.

> Well, something like this [our project] has never happened
> here, and, well, I'm very interested in this, and, uh, doing it,
> and well, we [her sister and she] could do something that's tra-
> ditional to Navajos. And of course, maybe people out where
> you come from don't know any. Maybe some of them don't
> know how Navajos live and how they do. [Worth asks "for in-
> stance?"] Oh boy, like rug weaving, maybe, well, when a small
> girl gets to be a woman, you know they have some kind of
> party for her where they grind corn and all that . . . and they
> make some kind of cake, they dig down in the ground and they
> cook it overnight, and the next morning they have a celebra-
> tion of her turning to a woman—you might say.

Susie was shy. She said she didn't mind the recorder, but her
voice was so low it hardly registered. In answer to Worth's question she said, "Well, I don't know right now—it's hard to talk—
I guess I'm kind of bashful—I was thinking I would like to make
a film about something this summer. Weaving—"

Most of the ideas mentioned in the first interviews were very
close to the final films that the students decided to make.

The Second Day: How the Camera Works

We had planned for Worth, when he began actual instruction, to stick as closely as possible to the technical and to avoid any conceptualizing of what a film is or how one edits. Even asking the students what they were planning to do would place heavy values on certain attitudes about film. It would imply first, that a film had an idea or was about something, and second, that one could think about it or plan it. We tried to avoid imparting such values by carefully wording the first question that Worth asked: "What I would like is if you would tell me how you understand what we are going to do." We did not want to ask, "What is your idea for a film?" or even "What is your film about?" Upon reflection we realize that even by accepting their free answers to the opening question and showing an interest in the plans and the stories they started to tell us about, we were encouraging them to plan and to make films "about." Still, human interaction always results in some sharing of attitudes. Research that requires communication with others cannot and perhaps should not be so controlled and "objective" that one human's response to another is completely vitiated.

On the second day, after getting the working spaces in order and conducting the interviews, Worth started talking about picture-making in general. He mentioned that peoples across time and across cultures all had made pictures. He mentioned Greeks, Egyptians, Europeans, Americans, Indians, and sand painting, drawing, sculpture and weaving. He tried to point out that the motion picture camera was just a new way of making pictures, and that since people always had special and different reasons for making pictures, they could decide what they wanted to show and for what reason.

After about an hour of general introduction to picturemaking,

Worth asked for questions. Most of the students either said, "Very interesting," or were quiet, except for Mike, who alone was worried about participating in such a novel situation and throughout was more concerned with community acceptance than were the others. On this occasion, Mike asked, "Weren't there people who didn't like to have their pictures taken?"

Worth said he thought there were and asked Mike if he knew of any. Mike said he did not, but asked if Worth did. Mike said that he had been worried for some time that action *might* be taken against him if he took pictures of people "who didn't want you to," or who "might not like it afterwards." He did eventually make a film, but he was the only one who questioned whether we should show the finished films to the community.

Worth tried to relieve Mike's apprehension by saying that he had been in a situation such as Mike feared. He once had made a film which included a scene of a Jewish wedding ceremony. When Worth appeared at the wedding to film it, the rabbi told him that his religion forbade the making of pictures in a holy place. Worth immediately left and didn't even try to make any pictures, since doing so would be in conflict with religious observance. He told the students that on his earlier trip to Pine Springs he had been invited to a sing and had walked into the hogan where the sing was taking place wearing a still camera around his neck. Immediately he was told that pictures weren't allowed, and he removed his camera and didn't take any pictures.

Mike seemed satisfied and there were no further questions.

About eleven o'clock Worth took the camera out of the case and passed it from one student to the next, asking them to look it over before he explained how it worked. Al took hold of the camera with confidence (and a bit of bravado), Johnny with a firm grasp, and Susie with a delicate touch; Mike, Mary Jane, and Maxine were less sure of how to handle it, but showed no fear in doing so.

Then Worth started explaining the workings of a movie camera in much the same way that he did with graduate students at the University of Pennsylvania. He briefly outlined the principles and historical development of photography, touching upon how lenses worked, how silver salts on film reacted to light just as household silver (which the Navajo knew and worked with) tarnished when exposed to light, and how an image was fixed by hypo salts so it wouldn't continue reacting to light. He then continued, using drawings on an improvised blackboard, to show how a movie camera functioned. He described a movie as a series of still photographs made in rapid sequence and projected back at the same rate of speed, and discussed the mechanisms by which the film was transported from one spool to another, passing behind the lens, stopping for the correct exposure, and then moving on so that the next still picture could be made. He pointed out the camera gate, shutter, claw for advancing the film, and the film loops necessary for smooth and even passage of film across the lens. He explained briefly about the ways to control exposure, describing the shutter and the f stop markings on the lenses, telling the students that the exposure meter would be described the next day. He continued by explaining the function and effects of different focal length lenses.

This preliminary introduction took about an hour. We noticed then that the students seemed relaxed, attentive, and to be absorbing all that Worth was saying, although some of the words must have been quite strange to them. (On the other hand, Worth was quite tense in this strange situation.) The tapes of this session showed that a great many technical words ("gamma," "diaphragm," "variable," and so on) crept in, despite our intention to avoid them at this stage. It became evident in later sessions that learning to *use* and manipulate the materials was not dependent on knowing the names of specific parts but rather on understanding their function. The diaphragm ring on a lens which set the correct exposure, for example, was commonly called "the thing you turn for exposure" or "the exposure turner," much as we frequently refer to a thing as "the gizmo that—"

This becomes clear when we listen to Susie teaching her

mother, Alta Kahn, who was about 55. Since Alta spoke no English, the following comments are translated (all translations are by William Morgan) from tapes made in Navajo. Here Susie asks her mother what she remembers from a previous explanation.

> SUSIE: I showed you some things on the camera. Which ones do you remember?
>
> ALTA: I just remember the little knob which you turn back and forth [the winding handle on the Bell & Howell].
>
> SUSIE: How about the little black knob? What is the little knob for?
>
> ALTA: They adjust the lightings and the shadows [exposure].
>
> SUSIE: How about the knobs that adjust the distances, like one for close shots, not so far away, and the far away shots?" [Here Susie referred to the turret which could be turned to bring a different focal length lens into shooting position, and also to the focusing ring on each individual lens.]

At that point Susie and her mother were calling everything a "little knob that—" It was her mother's expression and Susie adopted it. Later she taught her mother the correct words, which were sometimes used by the older woman and sometimes not. The Navajo students showed some desire to learn the names of parts, but mostly they wanted to know, "What does this thing do?" or "What is this for?" Rarely did they ask, "What do you call it?" Worth's and others' college students seem to feel much more comfortable using a thing when they know the proper name for it, perhaps because our culture has emphasized the naming function so heavily in its instruction. One has only to think of the anxious white middle-class mother saying to her infant, "This is a book, dear, say *book*," or "Use your *spoon*, dear, *spoon.*"

We would usually break for lunch at noon and eat together in the schoolhouse dining room, always joking about the child-sized tables and chairs. The Navajo, excepting Al, tried to sit by themselves, but a slight encouragement from us was enough to bring a few over to fill our table. The ice had been broken simply and naturally, by mutual involvement in learning and eating.

After lunch Worth continued his demonstration of the workings of the 16mm Bell & Howell triple lens turret camera, pointing out the exposure and focus markings on the lens, how the viewing system worked, and how the camera was loaded.

As soon as Worth finished his first run through on loading, he passed the camera around so that each of the students could examine it. He thought they would require individual teaching before they could load and be ready to use it. His graduate students had required four or five hours of explanation and practice before they were able to do so properly. To his surprise, however, Johnny asked if he could load the camera, and, when Worth gave him a scrap piece of film, he was able to load the camera perfectly after only two tries.

Within an hour all six students had showed they could load the camera, a job that requires a fair amount of finger dexterity in order to get into tiny spaces, an ability to manipulate several small parts in a definite sequence, and the ability to understand the notions of film loop size, claw engagement, and accurate windup.

Despite the Navajo's reputation for being comfortable with innovation, we were still surprised at how rapidly and easily they mastered this and most other mechanical and conceptual tasks of filmmaking.

In a meeting several weeks later with the former treasurer of the Navajo Tribe, Maurice McCabe, we described how quickly the Navajo learned filmmaking. The Treasurer remarked proudly that Navajos had also been trained very quickly to use some IBM equipment just bought by the tribe. He remarked with a smile, "Maybe you didn't tell them it was hard and that they couldn't do it. Maybe they didn't know making movies was supposed to be a tough job."

After the students had practiced loading for about half an hour, we went outside where Worth showed them how to look through the view finder and hold the camera. He explained that he wanted to shoot a hundred feet of film so it could be sent to the laboratory for developing that day. We had noticed the attraction of polaroid photography for the Navajo, and thought that perhaps motivation would be strengthened by quick viewing of the footage which they would shoot. We therefore had arranged for the film to be developed, printed, and returned within two days after it was shot. By driving to Gallup (a one hundred mile round trip), we could put the film on a small freight plane traveling to Denver and back daily. Our film laboratory consented to pick up and deliver rushes at the plane. The laboratory processed the negative and prepared positive work prints, keeping the negative for safe keeping and further coding for identification purposes. Only the work prints were returned. Thus we could view film shot on Monday afternoon by Wednesday, while the negative remained safely in the lab for further work.

The First Shots and the Notion of Editing

Worth began by taking about ten shots of the students just standing around. He said nothing to explain what he was doing. The students merely observed him taking an exposure reading, winding the camera spring, focusing, and changing lenses.

He then asked each student to take some pictures with the camera—"anything you want." Most spent some time exploring the different images available through the various focal length viewfinders and practiced holding the camera to their eyes. The subjects they chose to shoot were interesting, considering the background of each student. Al Clah shot the geometric pattern of the monkey bars on the school playground and the shadows they cast. Mary Jane took shots of the school building. Maxine directed the camera at children on the teeter-totter in the playground (photos 2–3). Johnny Nelson took shots of a boy on a bicycle, of parched desert plants, and then of a summer rain, which he improvised by having Worth hold a garden hose off camera. Mike took pictures of a piñon seedling. Susie chose to photograph parts of the swing.

We finished shooting at about five o'clock, and Chalfen drove off to Gallup to put the film on the plane so that we could get rushes back by Thursday.

After each student had made the first shots, Worth held a private interview in an improvised office in the back room of the Trading Post. Chalfen remained with Adair to observe how the remaining students went about using the camera but gave no help or instructions.

In the second day of the project and the first day of instruction, then, we had been able to teach them enough to load a motion picture camera and to actually shoot their first footage.

As a guide to how and what we would teach, we had begun amongst ourselves with a speculative analogy: Suppose we could find a group of humans much like us but lacking a little machine in their throats that enabled them to make that large number of sounds which would eventually be coded to become verbal communication or language. Suppose we gave them a "box" that could make all the varieties of sounds produced by the human voice. Suppose that we taught them only how the "box" worked and then observed (1) whether they used it at all, (2) whether, if they used the box, they used all the sounds it could make or just some particular set of sounds, and (3) whether they organized these selected sounds as an observable pattern of sound and a pattern of relationships. What system, if any, would they impose on the sounds? Would they use them to communicate—under what conditions, and so on?

Using the box that made moving pictures as a substitute for the imaginary box that made sounds, we tried as far as possible to limit our instruction to that analogous to teaching them what buttons to push in order to make all the possible sounds. We tried to teach our students only the mechanical rationale of the camera and the chemical rationale of film, and then observed how they went about using the box, what images they wanted to produce with it, what they produced, and what system or pattern they imposed upon the images when and if they organized them.

From that approach, our major problem would be the introduction of viewers, rewinds and splicers—editing equipment in general. Ideally, we would have liked to bury a camera, film, and editing equipment under a tree, and *if* the Navajo discovered them, observe how they used them. It might even have been ideal to leave only a camera and film under a tree and see if they discovered or invented projectors, viewers, splicers, and so on. Time, among other considerations, precluded this form of research and so we had somehow to introduce these materials. We had to tell our students how a splicer worked, and we had to do it in a way that would reflect as little as possible of our system of constructing film utterances, consistent with giving them competence in the technology and the use of the materials.

We decided that we would begin with showing how a simple film splicer worked. We did it as if the splicer was part of the buttons of the camera box. Worth described a splicer as, "a little machine for pasting pieces of film together for any reason you want. You can use it to fix film that tore or for putting lengths of film together for any purpose—like when it comes from the lab in 100-foot lengths and you want to see it all on one reel for projection." We hoped that they would discover or develop some principles of organization, some reasons for putting film together "any way you want."

We were aware that the very notion of putting units of anything—including film—together was a basic first step in the development of a structure. We were willing to go that far in introducing the splicer because what was of paramount interest was *how* they would put pieces of film together, and how their way would compare with our way. We were also concerned to study the development of their rules—the succeeding steps of differentiation of image units and the way they handled the more complex units of which a film could possibly be constructed.

During the first week we therefore had them practice splicing

pieces of "torn apart" film together. They learned the technique
of the splicer in about two hours and seemed to accept it as just
another procedure to be learned, like loading the camera, thread-
ing the projector, and so on.

During the first week we also suggested that each student make
a movie using one roll (100 feet) of film. We had explained that
a movie could be any length they wanted, of any subject or object.
We said that they didn't have to use all of the roll, but they were
limited in this first try to only one. We didn't want to permit
their early experience to become a constraint on the final film
organization that they had planned and discussed with us in the
taped interviews. We wanted first, to allow at least two weeks for
each of them to form his ideas about the film he was to make, and
second, to provide a quick opportunity for exploring the medium
and their own intuitive ways of organizing it.

The Developmental Structure of Film

Before describing the first one-minute films made and edited
during the second week, we should review the developmental
structure of film organization. We will then be able to clarify
how and how far each filmmaker progressed in the process of film
communication; and we will be able more easily to analyze the
films that were made.

Let us first distinguish between the shot as it comes out of the
camera, which we will call the *cademe,* and the shot as it is actually
used in the utterance—the editing shot or the *edeme.* The cademe
is that unit obtained by pushing the start button of the camera
and then releasing it, producing one continuous image event.
Limited only by the length of the film in the camera, one cademe
can be a film, precisely as were the first movies made in 1895. A
film also can be composed of thousands of edemes taken from
cademes and sequenced in any of an infinite number of ways.

Historically, the development of film might be described in the following way: First, the filmmaker has at his command one unit of film *just as it comes out of the camera.* He controls the subject by pointing the camera; he controls the length by his decision to start or stop the camera. The result is his film.

At a later stage he realizes that he can join cademes by pressing the button and allowing the camera to start again, putting his next set of images on the same strip of film contiguously. He may do so until his film runs out. He now shows this length (as distinguished from true sequence) of several cademes *as it comes out of the camera,* and that is his film. This stage was achieved by Porter in 1899, when he photographed three cademes contiguously in order to show "The Life of a Fireman." He first made a cademe showing a fire wagon, horses snorting, racing out the door of a firehouse, then photographed a second cademe of the fire wagon racing along a street, followed by a third cademe of the fireman actually putting out a fire. All were shot on different days, and at different fires, but on the same strip of film. Porter kept one film magazine for his fire film; when he had the opportunity to photograph a fire, he put the magazine containing his previous cademes into the camera and continued shooting. Porter himself described it (Porter 1914): "[this film] continued to run for a longer time than any other film previously made. Encouraged by the success of this experiment, we devoted all our resources to the production of stories made this way, instead of disconnected and unrelated scenes."

The first stage might be compared to the holophrastic utterances of children—the one-word sentences that children make—and could be called the stage of the holophrastic cademe. The second stage combines one or more holophrastic cademes within the camera in a simple linear combination. The third stage occurs when the filmmaker realizes that all cademes he shoots need not be shown. Some shots may be thrown away because they are not good or not needed. The filmmaker is still governed by his simple linear succession of holophrastic cademes, merely excluding some complete cademes from the length.

The fourth stage occurs when the cademe itself is seen as divisible. At this point, the edeme idea is developed, and complex sequence becomes possible. The filmmaker realizes that not only is every cademe not necessary in his final film, but that *all* of each cademe may not be necessary. He realizes that he has a larger unit which can be cut apart—part used and part not used. He has still not learned that the original order in which the cademes were shot is not totally determining. The next stages in development might be called the development of a syntactic sense of film sequence. The historical evidence is not clear that the following steps develop in any particular order, but each must have occurred.

First it is seen that the cademes themselves can be arranged in a sequence other than the one in which they were photographed and other than the way the event actually took place. Secondly, given the notion of making an edeme from a cademe, the number of edemes made from a cademe can be expanded and used in a variety of sequences. For example, in the Porter firehouse film we could cut up the three original cademes—(C_1) the wagon leaving the firehouse, (C_2) the wagon dashing down the street, and (C_3) the wagon putting out the fire of the burning house—and get the following sequence: E_1, burning house (part of C_3); E_2, wagon leaving firehouse (part of C_1); E_3, burning house (part of C_3); E_4, wagon dashing down street (part of C_2); E_5, burning house (C_3); E_6, wagon dashing down street (C_2); E_7, burning house and so on, achieving the form of the early Western with its alternating shots of the good guys and the bad guys or the cavalry riding to save the besieged settlers.

We have been using the synchronic (historical) development of film as it actually occurred as a convenient way of describing our stages of development. The next stage that occurred was the development of an object modifier relationship between edemes by the use of varying spatial relationships of the semantic units in the photograph. The early films were photographed in what is now called the long shot. Cademe scenes showed as much of the action as was possible. The object modifier relationship was made possible when the close-up and medium shot were invented. Successive edemes could now show a long shot of a man (shown from head to toe within a scene context) pulling a gun out of his holster, followed by a close-up of only the gun, pointing and shooting directly at the viewers rather than at another person shown on the screen.

The close-up of the gun needed the context of the long shot and was perceived in relation to it, as modifying or clarifying the important action of the preceding edeme.

It is now possible to photograph the following two cademes: C_1, long shot (LS) of a man walking down the street; C_2, close-up (CU) of feet walking on the street, and from them to produce the following simple edeme sequence: (E_1) LS of man walking; (E_2) CU of feet; (E_3) LS of man walking; (E_4) CU of feet and so on. E_2 and E_4 obviously tell us that something about the feet and walking are modifiers of the man. One can also see that with the introduction of a third cademe of a girl walking down the street, or of a car driving wildly along the highway, we can produce a boy-meets-girl sequence, or an ominous man-might-get-run-over-and-killed sequence.

Once the object modifier possibility is learned, a variety of other parameters of syntactic manipulation become possible. An obvious early device would be the length of the edeme which is again illustrated by the alternating good guys and bad guys running across the mesa, where each edeme becomes progressively shorter and shorter until the posse catches up with the bad guys in one long shot.

The next stages revolve around the specific dimensions or parameters along which these cademes and edemes attain overall meaning: their length, their placement in the film, their spatial dimension (long shot, close-up, etc.), their semantic content, and the relation of one set of cues and contexts to the others.

Here, too, semantic usage might provide an analogy with the developmental sequence in which one learns to join cademes into sequences according to some rules of occurrence—casual or associational.

Analyzing precisely what rules the Navajos followed in this scheme, and how far they progressed in the developmental process, was the purpose for which much of our data was gathered. We wished to see at what point they would learn to discard cademes and why. At what point would they break cademes into edemes? What edemes served as modifiers for other edemes? Which cademes were extensively used and which were discarded? How complex a structure, and how predictable a structure, would each Navajo develop individually, and what rules would all of them seem to follow? Did their rules correspond to our rules, or were they different?

The Practice Films

Let us now examine the actual first one-minute films made after the students had seen the rushes of the shots Worth had made and those they themselves had photographed on the second day. They had now learned how to splice and had discussed their first practice photographs as a group before starting to photograph and splice these practice films.

Teaching the use of a splicer was easier than we expected. Worth explained how to scrape the emulsion from one side of the film to be joined, how to cut the film accurately in the splicer, and how to apply solvent to the join. There were no questions about why one joined film. After each student had practiced making about twenty-five splices, everyone declared himself satisfied that he had learned splicing.

The Navajo students seemed pleased when they saw the results of their first shots on the same roll of film that Worth had used when he made some shots to demonstrate the camera. When Worth asked them which shots they liked particularly, Maxine mentioned "the shot of the snake or something in the grass."

Since neither Chalfen, Worth nor Adair had seen anything like that in the screened footage, we asked the students to describe the shot Maxine was talking about. Al and Johnny seemed instantly to know which shot Maxine referred to; Johnny remembered that it was the first shot in the second 100 feet of film and said, "I'm not sure if it's a snake, but it's something moving in the grass."

When we looked at the footage again (photo 5), it became clear that they had assigned meaning to an image that the three of us "knew" was meaningless.

The usual practice in cinematography is to waste the first and last five feet on a roll of film by merely running the required number of feet through the camera. This allows the laboratory some leeway in processing since they must attach one roll of film to the next in their processing machinery. When a cinematographer runs off his film, therefore, he pays no attention to what the camera is doing. In this case, Worth had asked Chalfen to load the camera. Standing outdoors, he inserted the film, closed the camera, and pressed the start button to run off his five feet. As he did, he continued talking and moving his hands in a normal talking movement, even though the camera was being held in one of them. This resulted, inadvertently, in a moving shot of parts of the low grass on which Chalfen was standing. By accident, the lens in the taking position was focused properly. The camera movements were, to our minds, random, meaningless, and chaotic. Nothing was level and parts of the movement were so fast that we couldn't make anything out. When we (the investigators) looked at it several times, we could see that it was earth and grass that we were looking at. But whereas we "knew" that we were not supposed to see anything—that the footage was only leader—the Navajo saw it as the most interesting shot in the roll. They told us that they knew there was something there because of the way "it" moved. "It" was either the grass or the camera —both movements seemed to count, not only individually but in relation to one another. They laughed at our puzzled looks, and when we explained that we hadn't "meant to make anything like that," that it was an accident, they still insisted that they could use the shot to show a thing moving in the grass.

Although we knew that theirs was a motion-oriented language, and we had hoped that when they made movies they would use motion in complex ways, we were hardly prepared for this dramatic example. We were prepared for differences in perception, but we found throughout the project and the subsequent analysis that the *specific* ways in which perception differed were difficult to predict beforehand. The literature on perception, unfortunately, has not yet accumulated much evidence bearing on the kinds of problems we were to encounter.

When Mike started to make his practice film, he said that he wanted to make a movie of a piñon tree. He wanted to show "how it grow. . . ." He then set about finding a piñon seedling and made a shot of it. His next cademe was of a little taller tree, and then one still taller, and so on, until he had photographed a series of seven cademes ending with a full-grown tree. Worth then thought he was finished, but he continued with a cademe of a dead piñon tree that still had some growth on it, followed by one of a tree that had fallen to the ground, followed by some dead branches, then a cademe of a single piñon nut, ending with a shot of the same piñon seedling he started with.

When the film was returned from the laboratory and was shown to the group we detected some puzzled looks. The film consisted of twelve cademes as described above.

Although Mike and the others couldn't, at that moment, make clear the reasons for their surprise at the result of Mike's first shooting experience, Mike later was able to articulate his difficulty. He had photographed a sequence of trees in a particular order, a cademe sequence. Its sequence and semantic content, he felt, should imply the meaning, "How a piñon tree grows." Instead, because all the photographed images had the same spatial relation to the size of the screen—all the trees both small and large were shot as close-ups filling the full frame—he failed to communicate the process of growth which can be shown when something small becomes big. Because all the big things and small things were made to appear the same size in relation to the size of the screen, they lost their representative or iconic qualities of bigness and littleness, which were the relevant semantic dimensions of the cademes. As Mike continued his filming, he was able to master the semantic elements of space to achieve a rather simple syntactic arrangement.

In Johnny's case, we have evidence of the independent discovery of what we have called the modifier-object relationship.

Johnny said that for his first practice film he wanted to make a movie about a horse. He was the only one of the students who used the practice shooting opportunity to make more than a set of shots of an object. While the others made four or five shots of things they saw around them, Johnny had constructed a little story about the dry earth to be found on the reservation. He made a shot of cracked earth, a shot of a man's feet walking over it and raising dust, a shot of a hand crumbling the earth and letting it sift through its fingers, a shot of rain clouds, and finally two staged shots: one of water falling on the earth which he achieved by having Worth hold a hose out of camera range while he photographed the water falling on the ground, and a shot of a tiny desert flower blooming out of the now damp ground. He had picked the flower from another spot and had transplanted it to the area he had wet.

For his next effort, the horse movie, he explained that we (the investigators) as well as many other people knew very little about horses, and that since they were so important to man, it was important to show as much as one could about them. His comments to Worth while shooting made it quite clear that he was shooting his film to explain the importance of the horse personally to Worth. He kept asking, "Do you know about this"— pointing to various parts of the horse's anatomy or gear. The common attitude for all the Navajo, except Clah, was to use the shot to convey information—to communicate subject matter

rather than a personal emotion about it. In general, the difference
between Clah and the others might be said to be one of the
personal film of self-expression as opposed to didactic communication as expressed in a teaching film.

After getting permission from its owner to use a horse tethered
near the Trading Post, Johnny started shooting. First, he examined the horse through the various focal length viewfinders on
the camera. He remained at the same distance from the horse, but
tried to "see" it from the different "distances" that various focal
lengths allow. He finally told Worth that he was going to make
pictures of "pieces of the horse so you [Worth] will get to know
a Navajo horse when you see my film" (photos 6–11).

He shot about ten close-ups of the head, the eyes, the tail, the
legs, and so on. Each shot took him perhaps two minutes of
thought to determine. At one point, the horse began to urinate.
Johnny tried to make exposure readings and distance settings to
be able to photograph it, but he couldn't do it fast enough. He
said to Worth, "I wanted to get that shot. It is important to show
a horse does all sorts of things like people."

He worked quietly, asking few questions, setting exposure and
distance with care. After about twenty minutes, he started looking at Worth frequently, not by turning his head all the way, but
by that quick sideways movement of the eye characteristic of the
Navajo. Then he said, "I got it now—while shooting the picture
of the horse I thought of it. On Sunday there will be lots of horses
at the Squaw Dance. They come riding up with lots of dust. I'm
going to shoot that and use the pictures in the splicing so that
everyone will know about the horses. That horses run and also
how they look."

Worth said that he didn't quite understand what Johnny
meant, and Johnny explained, "Mr. Worth, if I show pieces of
this horse, and then tomorrow take a picture of a complete horse
at the Squaw Dance—or lots of horses—can I paste them together
and will people think that I'm showing pieces of all the horses?"

Worth managed to restrain himself and said merely, "What do

you think?" Johnny thought a bit and said, "I'd have to think about it more, but I think this is so with movies." Worth asked, "What is so?" and Johnny replied, "That when you paste pieces of a horse in between pictures of a whole horse, people will think it's part of the same horse."

We mention these incidents for several reasons. First, it is difficult to know how Johnny learned this rule. Second, no matter how he learned it, Johnny after two days knew that people infer that a close-up (pieces of horse) is a modifier of a long shot (pictures of a whole horse) in certain circumstances. Mike also, as we have seen, intuitively knew that the way his cademes of the piñon tree were sequenced didn't communicate the concept of growth.

In the first taped interview with Johnny before film instruction began, he expressed a notion that seems quite consistent with his later intuitive understanding of film editing. Johnny had been saying that he thought in a movie one didn't have a design ahead of time, that the design developed in the head as one worked, but that after a short time, "the complete design is in your head." Worth asked him to explain, and Johnny replied:

> Designs [for jewelry and other things the Indians made] is just like making a movie. It's the same thing to use your head. They don't just come by, you know—like a certain designs that a silversmiths would sit down and concentrate and make a few designs. He would say, make oh, about half a dozen designs. And then when he's through making about half a dozen designs, he would put them all together and think about each one, and then he would pick out maybe one or two of these half dozen and make that.

What Johnny was explaining was precisely the process he himself used later on. First he would make a number of shots, then look at them and think about them, and choose one or two that he would arrange in the "right way."

Maxine did something very different in her first attempt at making a practice movie. She had made six shots of little boys on a seesaw (photos 2–3). When the film returned from the lab, some of the other students said they wanted to practice splicing and wondered if they might practice on their own film. We agreed to give them several hours at their editing tables, telling them that they could work alone, and that if they had questions, we would be around to answer them. About two hours later, Maxine said she was finished and wanted to see the film on the projector. We quote from Worth's field notes made at the time:

> Maxine had just shown six cuts on action that are phenomenal. You can barely see where she is cutting in this footage of hers of kids on a seesaw. She did it for practice, but said she "didn't want to spoil the film." When I asked her what she meant, she said, "You told us we could make splices, so I decided to make the splices in such a way that it wouldn't spoil what was already there—so you wouldn't see my splices." I asked her, "Did you have to put these splices in special places or did it work out right wherever you put them?" She said, "Oh no, it had to go in special places." At this point, she started making nervous, contorted motions with her hands around her body, which reminded me of Debby (Worth's 12-year-old daughter). "I can't explain it," Maxine said.

What Maxine had done was to separate the several up and down motions of the seesaw as they appeared in a single cademe as well as in all the cademes she shot. Then she changed from one part of a cademe to another and from one cademe to another until she had a strip of film reproducing the original up and down sequence of the seesaw from footage not in the originally shot order. She managed it so skillfully that at a quick viewing, an experienced filmmaker would not know that anything had been changed. Each cut occurred at just the right place in the motion to enable her to pick the motion up again in the next piece of film so that the motion appeared real and continuous. For the most part, she chose minute moments of pause in motion, such as those moments at the beginning or end of a swing in which there were three or four frames of film in which no motion was occurring.

Since at least one frame is lost at every cut, finding those places where the loss of several frames wouldn't be noticed and wouldn't disturb the rhythm of motion was quite an exercise of skill in both conceptualization as well as viewing.

When Maxine was asked what she did she said:

MAXINE: Well [laughs] I just made only one shot.

WORTH: Uh-huh.

MAXINE: And I sort of put them together—and I cut six parts of that one shot, and I switched them around and it came out all right, too.

WORTH: Can you say why you switched it around?

MAXINE: Well, it's real easy. See—this boy was sitting in the same position—and I looked at other parts and I saw another one—it's sitting in the same position so I cut both one out and I first switched it like that. Actually I cut three parts. I cut right here and here and here . . . and I cut this whole part out and I put it in between that one and that's the one I just switched—these two together.

WORTH: And what did that do?

MAXINE: It did come out about—it's just the same, riding the see-saw, remember—it's just the same, you know, going up and down . . . it didn't change it. It didn't change anything. I switched it but it still had the same thing, you know, going up and down like that —that movement the same.

When in the chapters analyzing their films we refer to the Navajo use of motion, we will refer to this example again. It is also important to keep this exercise in mind because we later report that in certain portions of her final film, Maxine edited in complete disregard of these rules. As in this case, she had a very good reason for it.

At this point in their work, a week after instruction started, all the students knew very clearly what they wanted to do, in contrast with Worth's graduate students who frequently are not certain of their subject matter for several (often up to six) months and also in contrast to our work with black youngsters who take a long time to decide "what their films are about." The black youngsters often just shoot, saying that their film is about what they are doing. For example, in the case of the film "Not Much To Do," the 11- to 14-year-old filmmakers shot the things they were doing every day and put the scenes together knowing only at the end that it was about "what they did in the film club."

Susie had decided that she would make a film about her mother weaving a rug. She wanted to "show how hard it is, how good my mother is, and why Navajo rugs must be so expensive." Johnny was going to make a film about a silversmith. It also "should show how good Navajos are with silver," and "how hard it is to make good jewelry." Mike wanted to make a film about a lake. "Just to show all the things there are there." Al kept talking about a film that would have "lots of symbols," that would be about "the world," and that we would understand "later." During one of the class discussions on the fourth day of classes, Al mentioned that his film would be called "Intrepid Shadows." He explained the title of the film to the students as meaning that shadows are fearless, and then he produced a poem which he said he had written and would like to read. The poem as he wrote it is reproduced below.

> Wheels,
> 　wheeling,
> 　　wheeling around, and round, and round
> Rusty shadows pushing outward and bursting into spin
> 　leaving nothing but motion and time.
> The wheel belt traveling into circle
> 　letting its shadows marking it
> 　black highway between its wheels.
> Around, and around the wheel and the belt spins,
> 　the intrepid shadows spinning.
> The winds, nursing the treetops
> 　with little break-up puzzles of black shadows
> 　dancing underneath its root
> 　Dance, and dance of little pebbles

Bath, and not bath
   as the black shadows dance.

I see big rocks
   partially black
   partially white
     making my eyes recall
     the countless painted of grays and ochre whites
     the archaic dance on the surface.

Dancing,
And drumming,
And singing of the ancient lore
   Are heard in the distant forest.

On the ground I hear the intrepid shadows,
   Dancing.

Al later decided to record the poem on tape, thinking that he would then compose and play music on his flute, and use the poem and the music as the sound track for his film.

Al seemed extremely proud of his poem and the other members of the class seemed quite impressed. Johnny immediately started talking about shadows and explaining to us (the investigators, since the Navajos seemed clearly to understand all about the meaning of shadows) why shadows were fearless. He said, "Shadows involves the sun up there," and explained that shadows at different times of day have different lengths, and the fact that shadows could change so quickly was very important in understanding why shadows were fearless. He also pointed out that the "light of the shadow of a person is lighter on the part around the head than in any other place," and that if one looks at his own shadow on a mesa, he will see that the shadow is always lighter around one's head. Worth commented in his notes at this point, "Naturally this is so because the light is more diffused as it gets further away from the object casting the shadow, but why is this important enough to make a film about?"

Johnny continued what was now becoming a group explanation for shadows being fearless, saying "Darkness always approaches from the East." Al interrupted to say, "Of course, that's why I'm going to make a film about this." Johnny then added that one cannot destroy light, and therefore one cannot destroy shadows. As long as the sun exists, he explained, there will always be a shadow. He felt that it was so important for us to understand that he turned to Worth and told him about a movie he had seen about a "war in Arabia" in which people tried to camouflage some tents, cars, and military equipment, but that no matter how hard they tried to camouflage them from aerial view, people could always tell that there was something there because other people could always see the shadows cast by the camouflaged equipment on the ground. Al concluded, "The shadow always reveals the image."

Not only did shadows of objects (rocks, grass, and trees), and the movements of shadows, play a major symbolic role in Al's film, but most of the important action was shown as the movement of an object's shadow rather than of the object itself. One long and beautiful section in the film shows the shadow of Al as filmmaker with his camera held up to his eye searching over the landscape to find a place in the world where his shadow could be as long and as big as possible (photos 53–54). His film will be discussed more fully in Chapters 13 and 14.

Mary Jane and Maxine informed us that they had decided to work together, and that they wanted to make a film about the old ways. It would be "about our grandfather, who is a very important medicine man." Although the girls chose it, it seemed to us that they were uneasy about the subject. Because of their constant, uneasy behavior while making their film, we were always reminded of the remark Mary Jane made in her first interview, "My father, one day he got after me because I didn't know anything about singing."

Once they told us of their decision to make a film about their grandfather and his religious activities, they seemed at a standstill. They didn't know how to make arrangements for photo-

graphing him, nor did they know how to approach him, to ask
him for his schedule of activities.

Fortunately at the time, the third week of the project, that they
were wondering how to find the subject matter for their film on
the "old ways," they found out that the community was planning
a Squaw Dance (part of the Enemy Way Ceremony). The ceremony would involve several days of preparation and several days
of intense religious as well as social activity. It was the same
activity at which Johnny planned to photograph his footage of
horses. The Tsosie sisters decided to photograph their grandfather and their own family making preparations for the Squaw
Dance and to build their film around that activity.

They made some sporadic shots of Yazzie gathering wood and
herbs (photos 35–36), but really didn't know what he was doing
it for. They followed him around whispering to each other and
telling Worth, who was near them, "This is very hard." At one
point, Sam walked into one of the shaded outdoor kitchens and
took a cup of coffee. As Worth walked over to look at the cooking
preparations, the girls decided they would photograph Sam
drinking his coffee (photo 21). They gathered up courage to ask
him to look up and smile. It was the first time they had ever told
their grandfather to do something. He complied readily and happily. This cheered the girls, and they tried directing him for the
first time, telling him, "Move this way." He did, but quickly left
and went into Juan Tsosie's house. The girls didn't know if they
had offended Sam and seemed undecided about what to do next.
Finally Worth asked them why they didn't go into the house, and
Maxine replied, "It's because there are a lot of people there." He
asked, "Did your grandfather say that you shouldn't photograph
in the house?" and Maxine answered with a shake of her head,
"Oh no, it's just that it makes me uncomfortable to photograph
there during a ceremony."

This sense of discomfort about a film concerning a religious
topic seemed general. As soon as they announced their subject,
the class, both boys and girls, burst into a series of giggles and

laughs. Mike was the biggest giggler in the group. Worth recorded in his notes, "I suspect—watch to see if he says anything
—that the idea of a film about a medicine man absolutely terrifies
him [Mike]."

The following day, Worth drove Mike to the lake where Mike
said he wanted to make "some shots about the water." In the
fifteen minute car ride, Mike brought up the conversation of the
preceding day. "What do you think about the film that Maxine
and Mary Jane make—the film about a medicine man?" he asked,
smiling broadly. Worth said he didn't know, and Mike continued, "Maybe he [Sam Yazzie] will change his mind when they
start taking his picture." Worth asked if he would like to make
a film about a medicine man. Mike replied very firmly, "Oh no."
"Why not?" Mike thought for a moment and replied as if he were
finishing a sentence, "and besides I don't know any medicine
men—don't have any in my family since my mother's father died
—don't know any medicine men." Mike not only expressed fear
of photographing medicine men but clearly said that he was more
comfortable not having to photograph people. He hinted
through several conversations that no medicine man would ever
allow himself to be photographed. When it was seen that the girls
were photographing Yazzie and that, further, Yazzie was allowing Worth, Adair, and Chalfen to make stills of him doing a sand
painting, Mike seemed very much relieved and considered adding some shots of people to his film. That week Mike even allowed Al to take some shots of his feet, which Al said he needed
for his film.

Several other interesting behavior patterns regarding visual
imagery became apparent in our observations during these first
days of shooting. The students all showed great confidence in
manipulating what might be called nature or the natural environment, in contrast to their hesitation or reluctance to manipulate
people or the film images themselves.

For example, Mike kept trying to plant grass in bare spots, to
"make it look better when I shoot." He preferred planting grass

to searching for a camera angle that wouldn't show the bare spot or would make the existing grass look good. The first time Mike had a camera in his hands to make his "how a piñon tree grows" film, he first arranged the ground by pulling at stumps and pieces of grass to make the tree look better, where by moving to another angle, he would have been able to keep the stumps out of view. At the lake, he moved rocks, smoothed the earth, changed the contour of the lake edge slightly, and changed the position of several small clumps of grass.

Al started his photography in yet another way. His first several days of what he called "working on my film" consisted of searching and finding various rocks, branches and bleached bones upon which he painted such words as "moving," "flowing," and "spinning" (photo 4). He seemed to need to orient himself first by using his familiar paint and brushes, creating with words and paint the things he hoped to accomplish with the movie camera. His first shots were of the rocks with "moving" and "flowing" painted on them. He never used these cademes in his film, but at the time they were important to him, as if he were making sure that if the movie camera couldn't do it, he would be able to get the idea across anyway. As he progressed he seemed to find that he didn't need the painted motion words.

The most remarkable manipulation of the environment, however, occurred during Al's first week of shooting. Central to his film was an opening scene in which a man would poke a stick into a spider web, which is taboo behavior for a Navajo. Al found several spider webs under some old trees in half a day's search and study, but he informed us that they were no good and that he'd have to make a spider web. Whether that was because the thought of destroying a real spider web was too much for him (he planned to photograph his own hand because he said he knew he couldn't ask anyone else) or because the real spider webs were in fact not right, we don't know. In any event, he bought a spool of very thin string and a package of pins at the Trading Post, found a piece of wood about a yard square, and proceeded to *spin a web* by placing the pins in the wood to form the outside edges of the web (photo 50). We were so taken aback by his unexpected skill that we never did check whether he did it the way a spider would, but Al's web held together and looked exactly like a genuine spider web. He took the finished web outside, placed other pins on the underside of a fallen tree and on the ground below it, and transferred the web from the board to the tree. He made sure that the pins supporting the web would be outside the camera's range by constantly checking through the viewfinder. When the web was photographed in the finished film, we, the investigators and other whites who saw the film, were unable at our first viewing to tell that it was not real.

Al, who was always quite proud of his achievements, seemed not to make too much of this and neither did the other students. They seemed to think it a reasonable thing to do and to be able to do.

We mentioned earlier Johnny Nelson's film in which he made rain, and we will discuss later his manipulation of the environment to create a silver mine.

This general ability and easiness at creatively manipulating a natural environment contrasts sharply with our attitudes or work habits. Only the experienced and very professional filmmaker goes about creating nature. As a matter of fact, this aspect of professional filmmaking is always accompanied in professional cinematography journals and fan magazines by descriptions of the high cost and the experience and ingenuity required. It is also often denigrated as the mark of a Hollywood or commercial film. On the other hand, when a filmmaker like Antonioni spray paints a landscape to change its color (or "to make it look good") we recognize the innovation, since an amateur never monkeys around with the environment, only with people.

During the second week of the project, Worth comments in his notes for June 15,

All this ease at manipulating the environment is in such contrast
to my own feelings—I have to manipulate the world by rearranging images because it seems easier, or I am not confident enough
about my ability to manipulate the real natural world . . . if Mike
could take a bunch of cademes directly out of the ground, I bet
he'd feel much more comfortable and confident about editing
them. . . . If the Navajo think of images as natural events, they will
feel easy about manipulating them in editing. If images are people,
they won't be so happy editing them.

As it turned out, the Navajo showed a remarkable skill and ease
in learning, or inventing, the editing process.

They Start Filming

By the second week when the students started to work on the
"real" film, we stopped any formal instruction. We would answer questions when asked; we drove them wherever they
wanted to go, which gave us a natural excuse to hang around as
observers; and we got the film developed.

For the first few days, there were many questions: "Can I do
this?" or "Is this all right to do?" Mostly, we answered that they
could do whatever they wanted to do. Sometimes we explained
that something wouldn't work, as, for example, if they loaded the
camera incorrectly.

During the first days, the Navajo often asked us if they had to
use the tripod. Worth had explained on the first day that a tripod
was "to rest the camera on" and that an exposure meter was "to
tell you how much light there is."

We answered most questions about whether "Must we use"
something in the same way: "You can if you want to—you can
use whatever you want." All the Navajo students chose to use the
exposure meter and used it all the time. The tripod, however, was
used infrequently—only when they needed to rest the camera in
some position in which they *couldn't* hold it. For example, Susie

used it for her titles, which were the last things she shot (photo 26). She had decided to pin pieces of loosely spun yarn to a blanket into the shape of letters, which required her to walk back and forth from the blanket stretched on the ground to the camera fixed on a tripod. She wanted to see "how it will look as I make it." Al used the tripod to hold the camera so he could photograph his own feet walking along a field. He would rather have used an actor but couldn't find one at the time.

The students remarked at various times that they enjoyed "holding the camera in my own hands," that "a tripod is not necessary."

Our observations during this filming period ranged from notes as to whether, how, and why they did or didn't use particular pieces of equipment such as tripods, lenses, exposure meters, and measuring tapes, to formal life histories of the students, their position in the community, and their relations with various aspects of Navajo political, social and economic life. We were able to observe each other in our roles as teacher, interviewer and observer, and how these roles were accepted or rejected in specific contexts by the Navajo. We kept a running record of the community's reactions to the filmmaking project—how much the various teaching and filming activities attracted interest or complaints. We remained, however, most concerned with how our students conceived, photographed, and edited their films.

Some of the students decided that they wanted to write out some of the things they were going to shoot. Maxine said, "That's how it should be in school—we keep a notebook and write in it." Some wanted to show us their notebooks and some used them as notes during discussions in class. No one, however, took his notebook with him when he used the camera. Susie never used a notebook. Worth casually asked her why, and she replied that she knew "everything in her head" about her film.

The notebooks seemed very much like grade school assignments and very unlike what the actual films were about. In Johnny Nelson's notebook was the following page:

(SILVERSMITH"

"Bang! Bang! came the sounds from a hogan where a Navajo silversmith was busy smelting a government minted coin." The sound was very familiar in the twenties and thirties. As there wasn't any silver to work with. . . ."

This is particularly interesting since Johnny's film had the silversmith mine his own silver. In a later chapter we report on this aspect of his film and his insistence that he made the film the way he did not because it was true, but because "that's how you tell the story in a film."

On another page headed "Birds" Johnny wrote two sentences: "Birds fly on wings. But they must have air and open space to fly in." He never talked about a film about birds and we didn't know he even had contemplated one.

When the film came back from the laboratory in Denver, we viewed all the rushes with our students and asked them how they liked what they had done. "Was it what you thought you were doing?" "Is it right?" and so on. As the editing progressed, we asked, "Why does this shot go with that one?" "Why did you leave that out?" "What's the purpose of that?" "Why did you splice here instead of here?" When the films were finished, we asked each student in an extended interview why he chose each shot and what it meant in the film. Much of the material in the chapters analyzing the films is taken from these interviews.

Another level of observation was our own notes about how the Navajo were photographing and editing. Our daily field notes and those of Dick Chalfen are full of remarks like "They are doing it all wrong," "They don't start at the beginning," "They have no idea of how an event is structured," "They don't know how to spot the important things."

It was Edward Hall, on a weekend visit to Pine Springs to talk with us and to observe our work, who first said to us, "For God's sake, if it is so clear to you that they are doing it all wrong, it must be because they are breaking a set of rules which you have and which they don't. Your job will be to make explicit the different rules you and they are operating under." We will return to that in the chapters analyzing their films.

Susie and Her Family Get Involved in Filming

During the period that Adair was observing Susie at work on her film he noted how smoothly and easily the filming was integrated into the daily life of Susie and her mother and father. Navajo wandering by would stop and ask Susie if they could look through the viewfinder. She was always calm and always allowed them. Susie's mother was quietly curious and asked several times if she could look through the camera. Susie always let her mother examine the camera. At one point, during the first day's shooting at Susie's mother's hogan, while Worth was sitting on the cot observing Susie photographing her mother at the loom, Susie's father, who had been in and out apparently not paying much attention, asked if he could look through the camera. She showed him how to look through it and how to switch lenses so that he could see through the various focal length viewfinders. He looked for about two minutes, turning the turret many times, and then returned the camera to Susie and sat down to watch. After about five minutes, he got up and began opening one of several storage suitcases in the corner of the hogan. Finally, he pulled out a pair of old field glasses and looked through them at Susie and her mother about six feet away, evidently with some difficulty but without trying to adjust the focus. After about five minutes, he smiled broadly—not saying anything because he knew Worth spoke no Navajo—and handed Worth the field glasses, signalling him to look through them. Worth didn't know whether he was being asked to focus the glasses or to share knowledge about things that help one to see better. Worth looked, focused, and, smiling, handed them back saying "Nijuneh" (nice). Her father shook his head as if to say, "No, that wasn't what I meant," and walked over to Susie pointing to the camera and then to the field glasses. He then said something to Susie, who told Worth, "He says that the field glasses and the camera work the same way."

The evident satisfaction and ease shown by Susie and her parents in relation to making a movie provided us with the opportunity to attempt to pass on to a non-English speaker the same technology we had taught the bilingual, and so gather comparative data. It had been Adair's experience in observing the transfer of medical technology that it had been greatly facilitated by a several-step operation of first teaching an English-speaking Navajo and then having him teach the monolingual Navajo. In effect it was a structuring of roles in accordance with theories of diffusion of a new technology from one society to another. The more acculturated individuals served as intermediaries between the outsiders and the more conservative members of their own social group. Thus Adair reasoned that Susie might be more successful in teaching her mother than would Sol Worth.

We asked Susie if she would teach her mother to make movies. Although Susie was extremely shy, she responded to this in a more overtly positive manner than to almost anything else we asked her to do. In agreeing, however, Susie laid down the rules of the game. She must be alone with her mother at first, and only after that might Worth observe her and record on tape what was said. (Worth was not allowed to come between mother and daughter.) Additionally, she said her mother must be able to see the rushes in privacy and no other Navajo was to be around during the editing.

Thinking to record the first teaching of film in the Navajo language, we asked Susie first to tell us in English what she planned to teach her mother. We then asked her, "Tell me what you—in Navajo—will say to your mother when you explain to her about making a movie—tell me—tell the tape recorder in Navajo."

Susie had no difficulty in replying to these questions in either Navajo or English. She seemed so confident that we asked her if we could go ahead and tape her first teaching session with her mother. She asked her mother, who agreed, and so we were able to tape the first two hours of instruction in which she taught her mother to load the camera, to take exposure readings, and to start photographing.

A tape of Susie and her mother talking was made while Worth, Susie, and Alta were sitting outdoors in the shade of a piñon tree near Alta's house. It was the place and the arrangement Susie made for her teaching. Worth was allowed to hold the microphone of his Uher recorder six inches from the lips of the speakers—a closeness necessary because Susie and her mother spoke to each other in the almost whispering conversational style typical of Navajo women. It was unusual—at least to an observer within our culture—for adults other than trained actors to be able to converse naturally and without annoyance in the presence of a microphone placed so close to their lips. Most adults will bend their heads sharply backward or step back when confronted with a microphone at six inches, but neither Alta nor Susie seemed to mind the microphone, nor did they seem to change their behavior or voice level in any way. They went single-mindedly about their tasks of learning and teaching.

Although it was the first time that the Navajo language had been used for the purpose of teaching someone to use a camera and to make a film, there seemed no problem in adapting the language to such a seemingly foreign use.

What follows are selected portions of the teaching dialogue. We have shortened the time involved in each step and present these selections as an indication of how the teaching was done, rather than as a complete report of the process. It is apparent that although Susie said we could tape her first teaching session with her mother, she had already spoken to her about cameras. How much conversation she had with her mother about cameras we do not know.

> SUSIE: One time [yesterday] I showed you how to use a camera, the thing that you take pictures with. How much do you remember? Would you tell me?
>
> ALTA: I remember some, but not too much. . . . I just remember the little knob which you turn back and forth. I also remember the thing you push to get the pictures. But as I said, I am not sure.
>
> SUSIE: What is the little knob [f stop ring on lens] for?
>
> ALTA: It adjusts the lightings and the shadows.
>
> SUSIE: How about the knobs that adjust the distances, like one for close shots, not so far away, and the far away shots? Do you remember how to do those?
>
> ALTA: Yes, there were three adjustments but I don't remember how to work them. You showed me how to work those things only once. Remember? If we went over it again two or three times, I might be able to do it.
>
> SUSIE: That is why we are here again. We want to know what you don't remember so we can show it to you again. This way you can learn more about it. Not only that, but we would like to see you take some pictures this afternoon. That is why we came over. He [Worth] wants to stay around until noon to watch how things go. He will be back later this afternoon to watch you take some pictures. The pictures you take will be sent off. So be thinking about what you're going to take pictures of.

Notice that Susie instantly tells her mother to "be thinking about what you're going to take pictures of" before her mother has learned to use the camera. This is consistent with the way Susie's mother went about the process of weaving. As Susie described it, "When a weaver gathers roots and berries for the dyes she is already thinking of the design. She is thinking of the design in her head when she is preparing the wool—and for everything she does—because the colors and the fineness of the wool are all part of the design—how you make a rug." There were many instances in both the weaving and silversmith film in which the filmmakers indicated that their actors were thinking of the design while preparing to work. See the discussion of face close-ups in Chapter 9.

> SUSIE: What do you think about that? We will show you some of the things about the camera that you don't remember so you will learn how to use it. . . . You hold it [camera] here and hold it up like this. This long thing here takes pictures at close range. The next one takes pictures not so far away, just a short distance.
>
> ALTA: This one?

The description "long," "short," or "medium" refers not to the actual length of the lens but is American cinematographers' argot for telephoto, wide angle, and normal lenses.

> SUSIE: The ones on this side. This is the long one [a 75mm lens], this is the medium size and this is the short one. The medium size one [a 25mm lens] takes pictures about half the distances. This shorter one, the 10 [a 10mm lens], takes pictures which seem to be far away and yet they may be close by. Whatever range you wish to take pictures you can always set it by turning these things. They have numbers on them. They are called long-shot lens, medium and close-up lens. But you can also adjust it to what this other little thing I had while ago. They called it exposure meter. It records the amount of light or picks up the amount of light. They have numbers on them so you adjust your camera accordingly. Now I want you to thread this thing. I will show you how to do it as you go along. But first, hold it up and look into it. No, hold it like this. You notice how I'm holding it? Now look into and look off into the distance. . . . The other way, to the left—Now turn it. Hold it like this. Now turn this one here. Here, get your hand out of the way, from this side. Not these, just this one. You see these red marks? This one says *run*. This side says *lock*. When this red mark is over here and you pull this other one down it won't run. They are not at the right place, that's why. If you put it here where it says *run* in red, it will run and you can take pictures. . . . [Run and Lock were said in English and in a louder voice.] Now let's try loading the camera. The film goes here. . . . Now watch carefully how I do it. You push it together and lift it. Don't touch this [turret], it will get out of place. Then you take this out. This is

made so you can open it like this. When you put the thing [the film]
you run the end into here. Let me get one, I'll show you how to
do it. . . . This is how you put it in. You stick this in here. You
tear this open first. As soon as you open it, take this end and run
it into here. . . . You run this one in here. These have little metal
points to catch these right here along the edge. They turn and pull
the strip along. Sprockets is what they called them. This round
thing has sprockets.

ALTA: Uh-huh.

SUSIE: Here is another one [the camera claw]. I showed it to you
at one time, remember? That also catches the strip down there.
Look at it, it's way inside.

ALTA: Yes.

SUSIE: They go through these little holes. It turns inside and
when it turns one little point of metal comes through one at a
time and pulls the strip to here and through here. When you
press this to take pictures you hear the sprockets working.
Then the film goes around this one. Then you turn here and
make a loop. Like this, and be sure the loops are same sizes.
They say it does not work right if they are not the same. The
loops should be about this size.

ALTA: Both should be the same sizes?

SUSIE: Yes, make them both the same on either side. You see how
these sprockets come through and hold the film. Get them all like
that and close this one here.

ALTA: I see.

SUSIE: Then you put this [the camera body cover] on. Now you do
it. Do it just like I showed you—This is the top and this is the
bottom. The white [emulsion] is on the outside and the green side
[film back] is on the inner side. Now try it. Turn it over.

ALTA: Like this?

SUSIE: Yes, the film goes in coiled up like this, don't you see? Run
it up through here. Not that side. Put it over the round thing like
I showed you. It catches right here. Be sure they are in place. Try
pulling the strip and see if they are secure. Are they in place?
. . . How about the other one that I showed you? You made it too
tight here. Do it like this, you see? Now it's looser and has a little
play in it. Look at it from here. When they are fastened and secure,

they look like that. Now you push this back on it. Take this out from under it. . . . When you push this over it it closes better.

ALTA: Now!

SUSIE: Push this down and let's see if it'll run.

WORTH: [English] Very good! It's perfect!

SUSIE: Press the button again.

WORTH: [English] It's a perfect load, the first time! That's absolutely correct!

ALTA: This is how it goes, does it?

SUSIE: Yes, be sure you put it on correctly. Now, let it run and let it go through all the way. All of it. Now, suppose you do it all by yourself. [In English]: I'll let her do it by herself, without helping her. . . . Exposure meter, the thing that picks up the light.

ALTA: Yes, I see.

SUSIE: There are numbers all over inside of it. I showed you how to use this gadget some time ago. Perhaps you remember some of the things I told you about it. When you take it out into a very bright light this needle moves way over here. You see the numbers on here?

ALTA: Yes.

SUSIE: Yes. When the light is very bright the indicator goes all the way to 16. When the light is not as strong it will not go very far up. When the light is very, very dim it will barely go up, around figure 2 or even less. Now this thing registers around 16. It shows the light is brighter. This thing [the mask that is inserted between the photosphere and the photoelectric cell to cut down the amount of light entering cell] goes in here like this. You see the indicator went all the way back down. This thing that I am talking about goes behind this white round thing which picks up the light. You use it when the light is very bright so the indicator will not go too far up. The indicator now falls between 2 and 8. We are in the shade under a tree. No plate behind it the indicator will go up, perhaps up to 11 or over.

ALTA: I see.

SUSIE: When the light is bright you put this thing between here. When you are using the exposure meter when it's dark, when it's cloudy or indoors you remove this little black thing. This will give you correct readings. We are now working outdoors and the lights are brighter so that is why we have it in there. It says *in* right here and it says *out* over here. When the thing is placed behind the white round thing you read the indicator on the *in* side. When you leave the thing out you work with the *out* indicator. Turn the things accordingly until you get a correct reading. We are now working with the *in* indicator. [Out and In were said in English and in a louder voice.] Now I have it set and the indicator points to 16. You set this one over here [the f stop on the camera lens] with what you can get from figure 16. Now look into it [the camera] and see which lens you want to take pictures with. Pick it up and look through it. You have a choice of either long shot, medium shot, or the close-up. Now pick out the lens you wish to use and adjust it.

ALTA: I want the close-up lens.

SUSIE: It's already in place. How far away is your subject? By that tree over there?

ALTA: Yes, by the tree.

SUSIE: Now back to this thing here. The indicator on figure 16 has changed somewhat. The numbers are all on here. Move it up to this mark, slightly past 16.

ALTA: Figure 16 is right here, right?

SUSIE: How far do you think, or how many feet do you think it is to that tree?

ALTA: About 18 feet.

SUSIE: I believe it's more than that.

ALTA: Perhaps it's 20 feet.

SUSIE: No. Twenty feet is about up to here. I think it's about 45 feet to that tree. How many feet do you think over to that tree? [Addressed to Sol Worth]

WORTH: Which tree? The big one?

SUSIE: The little one.

WORTH: I would say it's about 40 feet. What do you think?

SUSIE: I said 45.

WORTH: I'll tell you what, Susie. Hold these, I'll measure it. I bet it's close to 50 now.

SUSIE: [Talking to her mother] He's zig-zagging!

WORTH: It's 47, you're better than I am. What did your mother say?

SUSIE: She says it's about 20 feet. [Susie and Alta laugh] It's 47 feet to that tree. Now set the reading on 47. You won't find 47.

ALTA: They're not there? What do you do then?

SUSIE: Just set it between, and do the best you can where you think 47 should be. It should be right here. Now go over yonder, take a reading of something else. . . . Look through it and bring your subject in to where you want it. Pick the sagebrush for your subject. How far away is it? If you want it to be closer bring it in in your lens. . . . Look through it and keep turning it until you bring it in to where you want it.

ALTA: There!

SUSIE: Now? You have the subject close by?

ALTA: It's not far away.

SUSIE: Now, turn that one. You passed it. Turn it back. You have to look through it while you're turning it.

ALTA: Now I got it one medium shot.

SUSIE: Yes. Now the distance. How many feet to that sagebrush?

ALTA: I don't know, maybe it's about 20 feet. No, it's that far. I think it's about 16 feet.

SUSIE: [To Worth] She says about 16 feet.

WORTH: That's about right. What do you think?

SUSIE: I think it's about right too. . . . [to Alta] You should practice a lot like that. You can set it at another place and go through the same procedures again. Now you got the camera all set to shoot.

ALTA: Yes.

SUSIE: Let's try another setting. Turn it to another lens. Remember, they're not all the same. Look through the lens.

ALTA: It's getting heavy.

SUSIE: It is kind of heavy, especially if you're not used to handling it. Hold it up close to your eyes. When these things are open, try to keep your fingers away. If you do, it leaves some marks and they will show on the film. Try working it from the side.

ALTA: It's getting awfully heavy, I'll tell you.

SUSIE: Try the other lens you haven't practice on. This, the close-up lens you got here. This is the medium shot. Which one did you use just now?

ALTA: This one?

SUSIE: Yes. Look right through here until you see something. The other way, turn it the other way. Turn it sun-wise [clock-wise]. [The students were never instructed that they should turn lenses sun-wise. Obviously the turret can turn in either direction.] Here, take another reading. Hold it farther away from you, kind of side ways. Now set it accordingly.

ALTA: It's the same.

SUSIE: Read the numbers closely. It's not set right. You have it set on eight instead of twelve.

ALTA: Then it's right here in the middle, right?

SUSIE: Yes.

[Worth checks the reading and finds an error.]

SUSIE: There was a mistake in the setting at another place. Try again.

Afternoon

SUSIE: [To Alta] Explain into that thing [the tape recorder] what you are going to take pictures of. How are you going to make it?

ALTA: Somebody will be walking this way from over there. Come out from over there, walk along the road and enter the hogan over there.

SUSIE: Then what? That's too short. What else would you like to take?

This is one of the few indications we have of Susie's notion of the appropriate length of a shot. In questioning her about why she said, "That's too short," she replied, "Some things take more film to make them the right length. I don't know why." Obviously, however, there was some notion of "right length" for certain events in certain contexts. Other students often remarked that shots they or others took looked "too long," "not long enough," or "too short."

ALTA: Perhaps wood chopping. Yes, I'll take a shot of someone chopping wood.

SUSIE: Which kind are you going to use [meaning which lens]? What would be the distance?

ALTA: The same one which is on here, the medium shot.

SUSIE: Well, turn it and set it.

ALTA: No, it's already set.

SUSIE: No, that is not the right setting.

ALTA: Right here, right?

SUSIE: You passed it.

ALTA: Can I turn it back? [counter sun-wise]

SUSIE: Turn it like this. [sun-wise]

ALTA: Wait, just a moment!

SUSIE: Look into that other thing [exposure meter] again. I think the light changed.

ALTA: The sun came out again. What shall I do now?

SUSIE: What are you going to try now?

ALTA: Nothing, it's set at the same place. [Taking picture of sash weaving] Let's try it from this other side again. I haven't take picture of it yet—I took it only when the weaving just started.

SUSIE: Let me check it again for you.

ALTA: Just right in the area where you are working.

SUSIE: Are you going to take some more or are you finished? Maybe you want to take it in another way.

ALTA: Is this all right again? Now it is in the shadow.

SUSIE: Eight and one-half. Eight and eleven, or some place between the two. It's better in the middle.

ALTA: It's getting a little bit dark in here.

SUSIE: Look through it and keep turning it. Bring it real close.

ALTA: This thing wouldn't go up.

SUSIE: I think you have to push it down a little.

ALTA: I want it to be straight. [or, level]

SUSIE: Push it down first. Loosen this one. Screw this down. Hold it tight, it's liable to come down. Turn it backward to take it off. Now take it off by turning it. . . . This is only about five feet of it left. You are about to run out [of film]. If it's not right you can move it back so you see the whole thing. Put it over there.

ALTA: It's the long shot.

SUSIE: Bring it in closer so you can see it all. Now this is too close.

ALTA: Is this eight right here?

SUSIE: You finished it [or, you got to the end]. Now just turn it down over here and let it run out completely. There is a bit left in it. Wind some more. Press the button again.

ALTA: I guess that finishes it.

SUSIE: I didn't hear anything. Now here take it out. Turn this thing right here. Take it out and put it away in that thing over there [the camera case].

Several important things become clear from this section of actual teaching. First, is the ability of a monolingual Navajo to learn to use a complex mechanical tool so readily, but more importantly it corroborates the method of letting the participants in the transfer of technology structure situations that are compatible with traditional role enactment. The teacher–student relationship structured by the mother–daughter role relation was a familiar one to each of them. While the mother was the customary teacher of the daughter in passing on traditional technology —she taught her to weave in the first place—the daughter had many times taught the mother many of the white man's ways she had learned in school and in her visits to towns and cities off the reservation.

Secondly, we have here a rather unusual illustration of the creative aspects of language use. Susie and her mother were able to adapt the Navajo language to an entirely new purpose, finding ways to describe objects and processes that were entirely new to the language. Susie's mother seemed able to understand the concepts involved in telephoto lenses, wide angle lenses and the like from the use of traditional Navajo words. It may therefore be assumed that at least for Navajos classroom instruction *in Navajo* about "white man's culture" is a reasonable method. Educators and government officials have often feared that concepts and technologies foreign to the Navajo would not be explainable in the Navajo language. Here we have one instance in which Navajo seemed to facilitate transfer in a clear and rapid way.

A Visual Record

In addition to the usual methods of recording in the form of field notes, tape recordings, and still photography, we took some film footage ourselves. As we mentioned in the introduction, we felt from the beginning that we could not, to our own satisfaction, describe verbally a process of communication that was so largely dependent on visual signs and symbols. Not only were our basic data a corpus of image events produced and organized by the Navajo, and therefore essentially not translatable into verbal signs, but they were produced by members of another culture whose semantic interpretation of these signs, and whose particular mode of organization, was the very point of the study. That is, we were attempting to learn how the visual signs they chose to use achieved meaning for them, and how their interpretations might or might not differ from ours. In order to do this, we knew we would have to talk about what *we* saw when we analyzed the films, and that it would have to be possible for those interested in our analysis to look at the same materials. We have therefore made the films and film footage available for study. But we realized that we were also facing a problem common to all ethnographic description—we were reporting on behavior which was not verbal. For example, we say that the Navajo looked very comfortable when using the complex technology, or we describe the community of Pine Springs in words largely inadequate to give a feel of the environment. The use of films made by the anthropologist to describe these things is a commonplace today, and we had to decide whether we would, in addition to presenting their view of their world, present ours.

Apart from the fact that Adair himself had made or was involved in the making of several of the many films about the Navajo, we had another consideration. We felt that if we were, in a sense, to compete with the Navajo students in making a film, we would undermine much of what we were trying to do. If we were seen photographing in the community we would be demonstrating what we thought appropriate to photograph, what we thought interesting or important. Students might at the very least tend to photograph the kinds of things we photographed, thinking that the teacher "knows what is right." The students were sure to want to see our rushes along with theirs when film was returned from the lab. We considered not showing our footage, saying in effect that it was not for them to see, that it was secret. We rejected this plan for several reasons. First, we just felt uncomfortable asking them to open themselves to us while we remained closed. Second, we felt that refusing to show what we had shot would give the impression to the students as well as the community that we were shooting unpleasant or bad things about them—things so bad that we wouldn't show them to Navajos. Obviously, the choice was not whether we should shoot and not show the footage, but rather whether we should shoot at all. If we made a film, we could hardly not show the raw footage, and we would thus impose not only our choice of subject matter, but also our method of organization of the material. Even our unedited footage would teach them a great deal about our rules.

To test our notion that the Navajos saw events somewhat differently from us, we decided to observe Susie photographing a sequence of her weaving film. Worth's wife, who is neither a filmmaker nor photographer but who had studied weaving both

in Finland and the United States, was asked to be another observer. She was instructed to sit quietly near the site of the
weaving and to write down "things Susie's mother was doing
that would explain how a Navajo weaver went about it, " as
Worth's notes put it, avoiding at that stage words like *structure*
and *organize*.

The particular activity that day was the mother's preparation
(even this is our way of stating it) of the loom and the wool before
actually stringing the warp on the loom. She had to remove the
loom from the hogan, carry it outdoors where the stringing of the
warp would be done, arrange all the materials of loom and wool
in their proper order, position and then put on the warp, tying
all the proper knots, and so on.

Removing the loom from the hogan seemed an important task
to Mrs. Worth. She noted how the various parts of the loom were
taken apart, marked so they could be put back together again and
placed on the ground outside. She particularly recorded certain
distances which, she felt, Susie's mother "carefully" measured
between various parts of the loom placed loosely on the ground.
The work took about two hours to complete and was reflected in
Mrs. Worth's notes by over seventy separate "acts" which had
seemed "important" in the process.

Alta's activity also seemed important to Worth, who knew very
little about weaving. The expression on Susie's mother's face, her
intently deliberate actions, the effort of carrying ten-foot-high
wooden supports out of the hogan, the care in placing everything
just right, all conveyed to him that something important in the
weaving process was going on. Although Worth couldn't have
named the steps involved he felt that most of what Mrs. Worth
recorded should be included in a film about weaving.

Susie photographed none of these preparations. She had the
camera in her hand all the time but evidently felt that nothing
important for her film was going on. She started photographing
after the loom was arranged outdoors, after all the measurements

had been taken and only when the actual stringing of the warp began.

The warp is strung by passing the wool over the top and bottom supports of the loom, tying a knot at the top for each pass. Since the warp is composed of several hundred threads, it is a highly repetitive job. Mrs. Worth noted the type of knot used and then simply waited for the next step. Susie, however, made thirty-seven cademes of this process, paying particular attention to the motions of her mother's hands as she passed the ball of wool over the wooden supports in a sort of flipping hand-over-hand motion with the ball of wool passing from one hand to the other. There were many close-ups of the number of knots tied and the exact way they were done. The sequence in the final film showed the entire warp being put on with all the knots shown clearly and often.

Had we been photographing this scene for our records, we would have started at the point where the loom was being dismantled in the hogan. Susie would have noted that we thought certain scenes were important, and further would have noted that certain acts were shot in close-up or long shot. She would have heard the length of time that the camera ran and such an "authoritative" example might well have altered her own design for what to shoot, how long to shoot, and where to shoot it from. It is, however, not certain that we could in fact have influenced her or that everything we did would have become a model for her. In a later chapter we will describe an attempt to instruct some of the students to take the kind of footage that we thought was right. At the time, however, we decided that we ourselves would not try to document extensively the Navajo filmmaking with our own motion pictures. Instead, we used still cameras somewhat more freely, particularly in the beginning. Because some of the objections we mentioned about filming held true for stills also, we used stills only in such places as were obviously not going to be filmed by Navajo, such as the early chapter meeting before the project began. In the later weeks of the project, when our students had begun to develop their own style and were pretty clear about what they wanted to do, we took footage of their interaction with us, at work in the editing rooms, during some of the interview sessions, and during the last weeks of their own shooting. We felt it important to show how the editing rooms looked, and how they were set up, as well as how the students looked working with the equipment. After their films were finished and the project was over, Chalfen took some footage of the community itself.

The teaching process continued for two months with the last several weeks devoted mainly to interviewing the students about their almost completed and completed work. During these two months the Navajo students made seven twenty-minute black and white films and five small one- and two-minute films. They were all silent. Most of the students felt that sound was not needed, that the films explained everything. Al talked about using his poem as a sound track, but didn't get to expressing any specific desire about it.

These films then can be considered the first filmic utterances or expressions prepared by another culture, in which the teaching input, the method of adapting to a new communication mode, and the resultant film structure, were observed and analyzed systematically.

Chapter

7

The Community Attends
the World Premiere

By July 24 all the films, except the one being made by Susie's mother, were finished. Several days before, the Tsosie sisters had approached Chalfen and asked him if it would be possible to show the films to the entire community. "It would be a great idea," we said, "if you think it is a good thing." The students, except for Mike Anderson, were unanimous. Mike had reservations but was persuaded by the group. The students made a poster announcing *World Premiere Navajo Films*. It gave the time and place and concluded, "all invited." The notice was posted on the Trading Post door and the students proceeded to prepare the school dining room for the showing.

Approximately sixty Navajo showed up on July 25, including some children. There was the same informality as at other Navajo gatherings such as sings or chapter meetings: people

---

Much of the research on the response of the community to the films was by Richard Chalfen. This material is more fully developed in his master's thesis.

came and went, mothers nursed their infants, and the older children played in the aisles. Small children ran in front of the projector, putting their faces, tongues or hands in front of the lens. Some children tried to grab the ray of light coming from the projector and showed frustration when they couldn't quite hold onto it. All of this casual behavior surprised Worth, who was accustomed to silent movie and theater audiences. But the activity and conversation did not distract the Navajos from paying close attention to what was happening on the screen. The adults accepted the children's behavior and seemed to take the occasional dimming or disappearance of the screen image as part of the performance. There was laughter during the scene in *Antelope Lake* when the boy washed his clothes (the actor continually had to hike up his beltless pants), more laughter when the weaver's and silversmith's faces were shown at close range (probably out of shock), and loud laughter when Sam Yazzie faced the camera. But on the whole, the audience was quiet and attentive. After the showing, Adair (through an interpreter) interviewed nine of the adults who attended, five women and four men. We were especially interested in what the films "said" to the interviewees, and how they evaluated them.

The films were generally liked because they conveyed information. Some typical responses were: "Yes, that certainly teaches a lot of good things about weaving," "I think they all bring out good points as far as learning is concerned," and "... there is a lot of teaching behind this work." The films concerned with crafts were highly valued because they were related to the economic welfare of the community. One of the respondents said she like the films because they taught

> how to do these things. I think that is what the film is intended for. The same is true of silversmithing. This should also be taught to the children.

Others responded:

> This is the type of work that some of the people are supporting
> their families . . . so it is good and a good thing to know.

> Perhaps the Navajo rugs would bring a little more money from
> now on . . . White people never give much money for anything.
> Maybe this is why they want to show them and how the rugs are
> made.

> It was showing how to make silver crafts which will bring more
> money and will be on demand.

Johnny's film showing how a shallow well is made was liked
because it "teaches how to fix water so you can always have clean
water to use," and the Tsosie sisters' *The Spirit of the Navajo* was
liked because "He [the medicine man] did not make any mistake.
He performed the ceremony like he should."

In the nine interviews there were two instances in which the
Navajos made interesting remarks about their reasons for not
understanding certain films (*Intrepid Shadows* and *Shallow Well*).
Both films were somewhat outside the framework of Navajo
cognition: *Intrepid Shadows* because of its complex form, and *Shallow Well* because of its nontraditional subject matter.

When asked, "Does that film tell you anything?" one respondent, a 44-year-old woman with one year of schooling, who said
in the same interview "I never been to a movie before," replied:

> I cannot understand English. It was telling all about it in English
> which I couldn't understand.

Another response was:

> That picture was also being explained in English. The reason I
> didn't get the meaning is because I can't understand English.

None of the films, of course, had any sound at all. Since these interviews were conducted in Navajo, we didn't see the translated tapes until we left the reservation, and have not been able to question our informants further along these lines. We can only speculate that in a situation such as we are describing, when someone sees a film he doesn't understand, it seems reasonable (not only to the subject in this case but also to the Navajo interpreter) to assume it is in a language different from his. In this case, since we spoke English and our respondent didn't, she may have assumed that when she didn't understand the film that it in effect spoke in English even though it was a silent film.

While the interviews were all too brief and sampled too small a group from the community, they did tend to indicate that the camera in the hands of the Navajo would indeed serve to reveal their value system, since the values of the individual filmmakers were, with the exceptions noted, communicated to the nine viewers. Ethel Albert's statement (1956) about the Navajo value system —[it is] "empirically based, pragmatically phrased, and geared to consequences. . . ."—characterizes the films as well as the values of the viewers who judged them.

PART THREE

Chapter

8

Analysis

Up to this point we have been concerned with describing specific procedures and events in the field. We presented an outline of work already done, and a description of a set of interrelated problems in communications and anthropology which led us to the work described. Now our task is to analyze the data and relate them to the problems under study. The procedure and events in the field are critically important, in our opinion. It is not only the films that will be analyzed, but the films in relation to the filming behavior we observed: patterns of Navajo social and cognitive activities as our students related them to their process of making films. We will consider the films conceived, photographed, and edited by Navajos in the light of our field notes which recorded how we, our students, and the community behaved during the project. We will also refer to transcribed interviews covering the Navajo students' conceptions, difficulties, and achievements during the filmmaking, as well as their explanations of the way they edited and completed their films.

Our analysis draws upon several disciplines: communication, anthropology, linguistics, and cognitive psychology. Hymes

(1967, 1970) has recently dwelt on the theoretical problems of interdisciplinary research, using linguistics as a conceptual paradigm. He correctly points out that the problem is not one of combining a body of theory in anthropology with a body of theory in another discipline and thus being "interdisciplinary." Rather it is a question of certain problems demanding new theories, which (in our case) are not "anthropological" alone or "communicational" alone. What is needed in our case is what Worth has called a theory of "Codes in Context," or what Hymes (1964) has called the "Ethnography of Communication."

While our analysis is not presented as part of a formal theory of codes in context, we did have such a theory in mind as an organizing principle for our analysis.

Our analysis will be concerned with the following kinds of questions: (1) Who, in what culture, with what technology, with what instruction, and in what conditions or context, can communicate by means of motion pictures? (2) Among those who can communicate by means of movies, how do members of some specific culture organize their communication? Is there a discernible pattern or code in the structure of their movies? If so, (3) is it present in such a way that others in their own or other cultures can understand or infer meaning from their patterned film productions? (4) If persons in differing cultures can produce film productions that are patterned and allow communication to take place between filmers and film viewers, what is the relation between the code and the culture in which films are produced and understood?

These are the sort of questions that a theory of codes in context would have to elucidate, and we will deal with them in our analysis. We have obviously not been able to find definitive answers, but our analysis should provide several valuable tools toward such answers. First, there is a need to stimulate more work in this area and this report presents the first exposition of a methodology designed to assist the development of a theory of codes in context. Second, this report documents a large range of findings which make it possible to begin comparative work across cultures using a comparable methodology. Despite the difficulty of generalizing beyond our Navajo experience, enough work has been done by us and by our students to make possible some comparisons between Navajos, black teenagers, white teenagers and other groups. In a concluding chapter we will present data from other comparable research that makes it clear that certain aspects of filming and filmmaking differ from group to group. We can see that persons in different cultures approach the filming situation differently and make films that differ on several important parameters.

It is therefore important to recognize that our analysis is not meant to describe only Navajo films and filming, although we stick very closely in this study to observations of the Navajo. Our work is intended as a paradigm in both a theoretical and a methodological sense of how to observe and compare the way groups go about communicating in the film mode.

It is also important to realize that once a method of teaching people in other cultures to make films is articulated and people of a different culture prove able to make films amenable to analysis, a great variety of complex and controllable possibilities become available for research.

A theory of codes in context such as that underlying what we are doing would suggest testing along homogeneous or heterogeneous linguistic groups or similarly divided cultural groups to see if the coding and patterning of films follow broad cultural, performance or linguistic patterns, and what their relationship is to each other and to film.

Another broad area of research suggested by our findings is that of "universals" in film communication. That is, do the Navajo films as a group show similar patterns and do they show patterns similar to films made in other cultures? Conversely, where do the Navajo films differ from one other, and where do they differ as a group from films made in other cultures?

The Navajo learned to put discrete records of image events

Photographic Section

1. Some Navajo of Pine Springs meet in the chapter house to hear the authors ask permission to carry out their project.

2–3. Two frames of the seesaw sequence filmed by Maxine Tsosie. She cut the sequence apart and reordered it so that the motion of the two boys remained the same as in the unedited film.

4. On the first day of filming, Al Clah painted words on the ground and other objects and photographed them. He said that they represented ideas for his film and he was "just trying them out."

5. One of the frames casually exposed in running up the first five feet of film in the camera during the first instruction. When the first rushes were screened, all the students were struck by this footage, saying that they clearly saw a snake in the grass. Worth, Adair, and Chalfen had difficulty understanding the students' comments because they had disregarded the footage as meaningless.

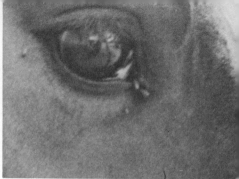

6–11. Frames from John Nelson's short film, *Navajo Horse*. Johnny asked, "What happens when I take bits of a horse and cut them apart and put them in between shots of a whole horse?" **7** and **9** were made on the first day of filming; **6, 8,** and **10** were made at the squaw dance the next day and intercut in editing with the "pieces of a horse." **11** is the shot taken at the end when horses and riders dashed across the field. At this point the drumstick held by the lead horseman broke. Because of this shot, Johnny was asked to pay a fine or return the footage to the family.

12–14. Close-ups of some of the students taken by Worth on the first day before he realized that face close-ups were not something the Navajo did. 12 is Mary Jane Tsosie, 13 is Maxine Tsosie, and 14 is Mike Anderson.

15. The face close-up of John Nelson made by Al Clah as he began his film *Intrepid Shadows*. It follows the action of poking a stick at the spider web. Seeing this shot in the rushes, Johnny refused to act further in any film by Al Clah.

16–21. The only face close-ups made by the Navajo. 16–20 are from "I am thinking about the design" sequences used in two of the films. 16–17 were made by Susie Benally and were on the screen for about two seconds. 18–20 were made by John Nelson: there was about one second of 18, followed by a half-second of 19 before the head turned down in 20. 21 was made of Sam Yazzie by Maxine Tsosie for her film *Spirit of the Navajo*. Most of the audience at the world premiere giggled or whispered at seeing it. In the film, the grandfather's eyes sweep back and forth to avoid looking directly into the camera.

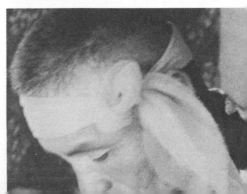

22–25. Frames from three different shots edited into one walking sequence by Mike Anderson for his film *Old Antelope Lake.* (They follow the scenes shown in 56–60.) 22–23 are from one long pan following the boy as he moved behind the tree and emerged on the other side. In editing, Mike jump-cut from 22 to 23 so that the boy vanishes on the left side of the tree and appears on the right. See the full discussion of this cut in chapter 10. In the film, shot 23 continues until the boy reaches the end of the frame, then 24 continues the boy's walk to the end of the frame, then 25 continues until the boy is about three-quarters across the frame. There the walking sequence ends.

26–30. Frames from the film by Susie Benally, *A Navajo Weaver*, about her mother, Alta Kahn. The title (26) was written with yarn on a factory-made (not a hand-woven) blanket. The film opens, as do the others on crafts, with the artist at work (27); then preparations for the project are shown. 28–29 represent the many comings and goings—gathering yucca roots used to make soap to wash the wool, digging roots and gathering berries for dye. 28 is typical of the dozens of walking shots discussed in the text; 29 is a recurrent shot used by Susie to separate sequences, showing her mother always returning to the hogan. 30 shows the warp being put on the loom to begin the actual weaving.

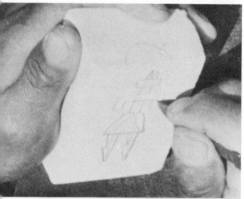

31–34. Frames from the film by John Nelson, *A Navajo Silversmith*. 31 is from the title shot. 32 is similar to the walking sequences in *A Navajo Weaver* (28); here the silversmith looks for sandstone to make his mold. Note that in most of the walking shots, the actor faces away from the camera and walks toward the horizon, usually toward trees or woods. After thinking of his design (see 18–20), the silversmith carves it out of the sandstone block with his knife (33). The figures are cast in the sandstone mold and cooled in a jar of water (34).

35-40. Frames from *The Spirit of the Navajo* by Maxine and Mary Jane Tsosie. **35-37,** made by Maxine Tsosie, represent the jump-cut sequence discussed in Chapter 10 of which she said, "But everyone will know that if he's sitting and then walking, he got up in between." The film cuts from **35,** Sam Yazzie gathering herbs, to **36,** kneeling to gather herbs, to **37,** walking with Mary Jane, to **38,** Sam walking alone.

39 is one of the shots made by Mary Jane when Worth asked her to take close-ups of Sam's face as he worked on his painting. Seeming to comply, she photographed her grandfather from above, not showing his face at all.

40 is one of the close-ups the girls felt permissible, of Sam's hand applying color to the sand painting. (See 21 for the facial close-up the girls did take and use.)

41–43. Frames from *Shallow Well Project* by John Nelson. 41 is the opening shot, showing the kind of well used by the Navajo before they learned the new technology—dirty, fly-infested, and unhealthy, according to Johnny, contrasting with 43, the completed new well. 42 is one of the close-ups of construction meant to show Navajo skill with technological objects.

Johnny asked Worth to pose for 43, saying, "You haven't been in any pictures so far." Worth thought Johnny realized he needed a working shot of the well but felt he could not ask any of the workmen, who were not relatives, to come back to pose for it.

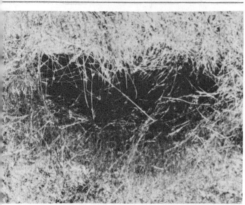

44–47. Frames from the untitled film by Alta Kahn of her daughter, Susie Benally, weaving a belt. In **44,** Susie is spinning; a basin for dying yarn is in front of her. In **45,** Susie weaves on the loom in her mother's house, the same loom and location shown with her mother in *A Navajo Weaver.* Both women presented the process in the same way, but Susie did not think it necessary to sit or dress like her mother: she sat on a metal chair in western-style clothes. **46** is a close-up of Susie weaving. In **47** the finished belt is shown, much as finished blankets were shown in Susie's film. In the background Dick Chalfen makes his own record.

48–55. Frames from the film by Al Clah, *Intrepid Shadows*. In 48, "the intruder" (Johnny Nelson) walks through the field toward the spider web (50, made by Al from cotton thread). In 49, he pokes at it with a stick. 15 followed in the filming, the face close-up that offended Johnny Nelson and led to Al Clah devising ways for himself to appear in his film as "the intruder."

51 shows the wheel rolling through the landscape: in early sequences the shadow is short, and longer and longer shadows were used in later scenes. In

52, the Yeibechai is walking and searching across the landscape. Al made the mask so that the eyes could move back and forth, almost imitating the Navajo way of glancing back and forth to avoid direct eye contact. Note the movie-film-like stripe in the center of the mask, a design unknown in traditional decorations.

53–54 are from the sequence in which Al shows the search for and the finding of his own shadow. The shadow is first short, and at the end it is long and strong.

55 is from the last shot of the film, of the shadow of the wheel spinning, spinning, until it is met by the actual wheel itself, seen entering the frame in the upper left corner. The shot is meant to represent everything coming out all right, being peaceful, the shadow and its object reunited.

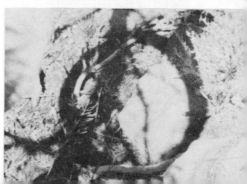

56–60. Frames from the film by Mike Anderson, *Old Antelope Lake*. **56** is the title card. **57** is the first shot made of the lake, showing the source. Mike then filmed sun-wise (clockwise) around the lake. **58–59** represent the sequence discussed in Chapter 10, in which the shot of the footprints of a horse going into the lake (**58**) must be followed by a horse in the water (**59**), and footprints of sheep leaving the lake (not shown, but similar to **58**) must be followed by shots of sheep in the distance (**60**—one of Susie Benally's many shots of sheep, borrowed by the other filmmakers). Worth did not notice the footprints during the filming but thought Mike was photographing mud and trash at the water's edge. For another sequence from this film, see **22–25.**

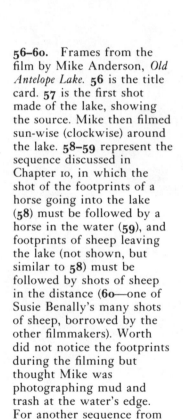

into a sequence which they assumed would be meaningful to someone who saw their film. It is as if they had an innate sense that visual events in sequence have meaning, and more, that other people—certainly people like themselves—would understand the meaning they implied when they chose the events they photographed in the way they photographed them and in the way they organized them into a film. The fact that they strung these image events together in a specific way different from the way we photograph and sequence events seems to us much less important than the fact that they did in fact string them together and assumed that someone else would understand. The important universal of film may be that we "know" that images in sequence have meaning.

Let us state it another way. If we were to start writing in Finnish, most readers of this manuscript would not understand. They would, however, assume we were writing in another language. For our part, we too would assume that many would not understand us. An unspoken agreement in our concept of verbal language is that a *variety* of languages exist and that our ability to speak and to understand all of them is limited.

On the other hand, if we make a film or a Navajo makes a film, we assume that we all can more or less understand it. Whether or not it is true, we somehow do assume that everyone can understand a movie. "A movie is a movie," we seem to imply, and the babble of tongues doesn't change our intuition. That notion is now open to testing, using the materials we have gathered. One can find out, given the statements by the Navajo about what they meant to convey, whether in fact others can infer the same meaning from the film. One can find out how much was conveyed and more importantly who, and from what cultures, with what training, can make inferences from a film similar to those implied by the filmmaker.

Another striking aspect of our research was that, although we found it comparatively easy to teach people of another culture to make a movie, they did not necessarily use it in the same way that we did, show the same sort of interest in it, or seem likely to continue to use it and find a place in their culture for it. The most difficult thing to accept about our Pine Springs experience was our feeling that when we left Pine Springs, so would all ideas about the use of movies by the Navajos. It was not, after all, as if we were teaching graduate students, who were seeking knowledge and techniques to fit into their plans for a career.

We felt that when we pulled out of Pine Springs after two months the innovation would stop. There is good evidence that we were right. The social and economic structure of the Pine Springs community was not geared to support this innovation. Each of the filmmakers was at a dead end, with no opportunity to do anything more with what he had learned. So, while the motivation and ability were there, we too were there—as a stimulant to the innovation process and as an economic resource. In 1970 Adair interviewed Johnny Nelson to learn what had happened in the community after each student had received the print of his film. To the best of his knowledge he is the only one who has shown his films publicly.

Stated in another way, if Johnny Nelson, as a local political leader, wanted to make further use of film for the development of his community, he would have to seek financial as well as psychological support from some outside source. Capital for the use of film at Pine Springs would not be available in that community. If film is to become a functional part of the life of the Navajo themselves, it will have to be funded, at least initially, from some outside source.

Likewise we, as outsiders, would have to gain economic and political support if we were to attempt to test the feasibility and functional use of this innovation to the tribe as a whole. If such an attempt could be made, it is predicted that this mode of communication would be taken up in many parts of the reservation. This estimate is based on (1) the feasibility of teaching Navajos the technology of filmmaking in a community such as Pine Springs; (2) the ongoing interest of the Navajo leadership in modern modes of communication; and (3) the desire of the tribe to communicate to the remote areas on the reservation those methods of development that have proved practical at Window Rock.

We can report that teaching filmmaking to the Navajo and to members of other culture groups in our society was easy. The Navajo seemed to know what films were—even those who said they never saw one—and they learned to make them quickly and easily. They learned to make films much more easily, for example, than we learned to speak Navajo. It is clear, after this experience, that the Navajo learned to express themselves more fluently through film after one month of instruction than members of one linguistic community learn to express themselves in the verbal language of another.

It is this that strikes us as more remarkable than all the differences that we shall report between the way we make films and the way the Navajo make films. Not only the Navajo but all the people—black, Navajo, young, old—with whom we have worked seem able to learn this method of communication readily. Why should people of a culture so different from ours or with such different training learn a new and complex mode of communication so quickly? Could it be that a concept similar to the Chomskian view of an innate deep structure of language operates for the visual mode of communication also? Chomsky's view seeks to explain the almost miraculous ability of children to have mastered at two years of age the complex grammar of speech by suggesting that the human brain has so evolved over the millenia that it is neurologically functional to learn a complex system of rules relating verbal signs to each other and to the outside world to which they refer. The theory suggests that this structure is the same for all verbal language, and that specific languages are variations or transformations from a more basic deep structure. It seems to us not at all unreasonable to assume that just as children have internalized a complete and complex system of rules which can generate original verbal utterances whose meaning is shared within a culture, so have the Navajo—or others who have never made films and whom we can metaphorically consider as film children—internalized some set of rules which may also be innate, which may be based on rules of perception and cognition that are neurologically functional, and which make learning to construct film utterances possible, easy and "natural."

It should be noted here that our use of the word "language" reflects not only an academic difficulty—we have hedged and put quotation marks around it throughout—but reflects a bias in our very use of symbolic forms in communication of all kinds. We simply do not have a good word for the structure inherent in messages in different modes. We do not have the right words to talk about film, dance, facial expression, body positions, and communicative patterns or structures that are not verbal or that accompany verbal communication. "Language" is the word we use when we want to say that communication has occurred in any mode. Thus we find that we talk of the language of dance, the language of gesture, the language of art, the language of film, and even the language of poetry. We are only now beginning to separate speaking from "language" and to make the kinds of distinctions which in many ways the ubiquity of the word "language" has prevented our recognizing. It is only recently that a phrase like "the language of speaking," referring to the pattern, code, or even grammar of speaking, has become meaningful.

We will continue to use the word "language" because euphemisms for it are not really clear enough, but we would like our readers to know that we are concerned with more than the commonly accepted ideas of verbal grammar. We are interested in more than the rules of grammatical utterances or in so-called correctness. In fact, at this point in the development of our understanding of film or in the development of film as a mode of communication, the notion of grammaticality doesn't make much sense. We are concerned with patterns of usage in our film "language," with why a person makes one film cademe rather than another or why he makes one particular cademe at one time and not at another time or in another situation. We are concerned with what things he chooses to say—filmically—and with how he says it, so that we may discover the rules he is unconsciously following.

The Way We Intend to Analyze Our Data

In order to delineate some of the differences we noted, we will need to describe certain elements of the context (the filming behavior) as well as of the code (the film). It is useful, therefore, to think of our work as the report of observations in these two areas, code and context, and to consider (1) the differences we noted as reflecting the different contexts in which we and the Navajo make films and (2) the consequences of those differences on the resultant pattern of film.

The context might be defined as those dimensions which explain some important aspect of the specific situation within which the films were produced. Among them are the following. (1) The learning situation—composed of the students' previous level of learning as well as what we taught them, and including the specific arrangements and methods under which they learned. This would have to include the way the Navajo conceived of learning, its place in their value system in general, how they placed learning *film* within their general notion of learning, and how they structured their own learning situation in relation to our teaching methods. (2) The choice of students—the ways and reasons that we had for choosing certain students, and the ways they devised for controlling our choices. (3) The students' choice of actors for their films—the kinds of activities and talents they felt actors in their films should have, as well as the social relations they felt it necessary for them to have with their actors. (4) The choice of film subjects or themes—the kind of subject matter they thought appropriate to make a film about, and the kind of event they felt appropriate to photograph to express an idea or theme. Under this aspect of context we would include their awareness of the community's feelings about appropriateness of certain themes or events being described or shown in a film. (5) Their method of working, both technical and perceptual —how they handled equipment, what kind they preferred, whether they literally *saw* comfortably or in the same way we did when looking through viewfinders or viewers or at projected images. (6) The interrelation of the filmmaking and the community. Here we would be concerned with analyzing the social controls and freedoms surrounding filming, filmmaking, and learning film within this particular culture.

The second area of analysis includes those elements which relate to the *code*—the film—itself, its description, and the rules or patterns that might be applied to generating or producing what we or they would call a "Navajo film." The areas considered at this stage of code analysis are: (1) The narrative "style" of the films, related to the mythic and symbolic forms of the culture. Here we would be concerned with how a Navajo feels it necessary to tell a film story, and what specific structures he always, or in certain situations, employs. (2) The syntactic organization and sequencing of events and units of "eventing." Here we would be concerned with how an event, an act, or a part of a story or theme is divided into units of cademes and edemes. We would be concerned with the rules of sequencing—they way edemes are joined—which edemes or cademes need "something in between," or "can go together." We would want to know if certain edemes *cannot* go with others, are optional, or must be preceded or followed by some other event. (3) The cultural, perceptual, and cognitive restriction influencing either semantic or syntactic organization and structure. Here we want to show not how they see, in a biological sense, but what they feel they *ought* to see in a cultural sense. Can certain cademes be taken but not used as edemes? Are there cultural restrictions about taking or using close-ups, long shots, or medium shots of specific events, in specific situations? (4) The relation between the structure of their verbal language and the structure of their films. Here we want

to relate specific properties of the Navajo language—its concern
with motion, for example—to specific ways in which Navajo
speakers structure their films.

We have decided to build our analysis around a presentation
of the differences between our films and the Navajo films on the
level of code. Many of the areas delineated above in the first area
of analysis have been discussed in previous chapters and can best
be further discussed in connection with the specific films or parts
of films we will be describing on a coding level. The areas of
context (1 to 6) and code (1 to 4) are in truth necessary intellectual
distinctions which we hope can be kept in mind. The process of
making a film, however, is an ongoing one. A specific person
living in a specific way makes a specific film. He doesn't decide
that certain problems are code problems or context problems any
more than a child speaking makes conscious decisions about syntax or semantics when he wants to tell daddy about seeing a red
fire engine. The process of describing how people make films
seems in some way similar. Things get mixed up in the describing; more than one level of analysis is necessary to describe what
on another level looks like one event.

We will therefore talk about specific films and specific edemes
and cademes, how specific students photographed and edited
them. In the process, we will bring to bear our observations on
the context which influenced them. We will not talk about the
similarities between the way the Navajo make films and the way
people in other cultures make them. We have already mentioned
that the way so many different groups make films understood by
so many others is one of the most significant findings in our
research in this area.

We are concerned in this book primarily with two things: to
present a method of teaching people to make films showing us
how *they* see *their* world, and to present a way of analyzing these
films in their cultural context as a communicative code.

Chapter

9

Narrative Style

First, let us consider that dimension of the code which we are calling narrative style. One element of it might be thought of as those events in daily life which are important enough to show in a film about *any* subject. Or conversely, those events, irrespective of subject, that are always part of a film discourse for the Navajo. For example, when we tell a story in film it is usually about a single person or a pair of people—a hero and heroine—who try to accomplish something against some adversity or odds. We almost always include some aspect of "love," of a girl, a man, a wife, a husband, a mother or father, and often of flag or apple pie. We must show how it comes out at the end, who wins and who loses. We even have institutions in Hollywood supported by national sanctions that act as arbiters so that a bad man doesn't win in the end. Our culture knows what may and may not be shown and what must be shown if the audience is not to be shocked or confused. We know how films begin and end, and how to tell what a film is about from the way the film is made.

How do Navajos construct a film? What elements must it have? What elements doesn't it have? How does it begin? What are the important things to include, no matter what the story is about?

In some ways this kind of analysis calls to mind the analysis of myth and folktales which has long been a part of anthropological and humanistic research. One searches for common themes and common relations or structures between thematic events. Instead, however, of using verbal utterances as our sole datum, we are using what might be called visual utterances.

Although we do not intend at this point to present a complete structural analysis of the films, our aim at this level is to begin

> with a [film] which has not been chosen arbitrarily; rather it has been selected because of an intuitive feeling that it is promising and productive . . . and establish for each sequence the group of its transformations either as they are manifested within the [film] itself or as they are elucidated in isomorphic elements of sequences taken from a number of [films] belonging to the same population. (Lévi-Strauss 1964, with the word *film* in brackets substituted for the word *myth* that appeared in the original.)

Analyzing the films of a culture different from ours on the level of narrative, myth, or tale is a task for which few precedents exist, and our attempt is merely a starting point. Again Lévi-Strauss expresses many of our hopes and fears when he says:

> Mythical analysis is very much like Penelope's task. Each step forward offers a new hope which hangs on the solution of a new difficulty . . . [myth (and also film)] is no more than an imaginary phenomenon implicit in the effort of interpretation. It will be quite enough if we can have the more modest assurance of having left difficult problems in a less bad state than they inhabited when we began working with them. . . . Even a partial grammar or a sketch of a grammar represents a valuable acquisition where an unfamiliar language is concerned. We do not have to wait for a tally of a theoretically limitless series of events in order to see syntactical processes at work, especially since syntax consists of the body of rules which governs the engendering of these events. (Lévi-Strauss 1964)

If we consider the "events" that Lévi-Strauss mentions as the image events we will be discussing, his words reflect our attitude toward the following analysis.

Walking

Almost all the films made by the Navajos portray what to members of our culture seems to be an inordinate amount of walking. As we observed the films being made, excessive cademes of walking seemed to us clear examples of "wrong" filmmaking.

In Johnny Nelson's film on silversmithing, for example, most of the footage he used is composed of edemes of the silversmith walking to get his materials. In his fifteen-minute film almost ten minutes are spent showing the silversmith as he walks to the "old mine," walks to find his silver nuggets, walks back to the hogan, walks again to find sandstone for the mold, walks to his hogan again, and so on (photo 32).

In Susie Benally's film about a Navajo weaver, the same proportion of time is spent in walking. In a twenty-minute film, Susie's mother spends fifteen minutes walking to gather vegetables for dye, walking to collect roots for soap, walking to shear the wool, and walking to and from the hogan between all activities (photo 28–29). Her son walks with the sheep and in one spot rides his horse away from and to the hogan to indicate the passage of time.

In Al Clah's film, the mask of the Yeibechai walks and walks searching for the turning wheel. The intruder is shown walking. There are a number of long sequences of people's feet just walking across the landscape. There is the long shot of Al's shadow walking across the field. Again, in a ten-minute film, close to three-quarters of the footage is concerned with walking (photos 48–55).

The Tsosie sisters also showed their grandfather walking for the gathering of roots, herbs, sandstone, chalk, and other materials he would use for the ceremony they were planning (photos 37–38). Although most of the action in the film occurs indoors and sitting in one place, they also managed to use a great deal of walking footage.

In the interviews, when we asked them what they were going to shoot the next day, or what they had shot "that morning" or "just before," they described the shots in great detail. For example:

> So I decided I take a picture of it—*approaching* the cornfield—the old road that used to *go* to the cornfield. I take a picture of that and just as I *approaching* the cornfield, and then when I *came* to the fence, I took the fence, and then to show this was a field, this was a cornfield, and then after we got into the field then I *went* out there . . . I had my little helper [a young boy Johnny hired to act for him] *walking* here, looking over this field, then he stood there a minute and looked down, picked up some dirt like that [crumbling motion with his hands] to see how dry it was. Kick up the dirt [motion of scuffing with foot] like that. Then I cut that out right there and then I turn my lens on to three [3 inch] which was the closest, the close-up picture. Him kicking up the dirt. I took a picture of that. Then I turn in back to the wider lens.

It was difficult for us to understand that this scene was a scene full of walking. Note the words we have italicized—*approaching, came, walking.* As we listened to Johnny talking, these seemed to be merely connectives of little consequence, joining the actions or images he was talking about. But when Johnny says, "I take a picture of it—approaching the cornfield," the *it* refers to the approach, and the footage Johnny took was of the boy walking toward a field along the road. When he says, "I came to the fence," he doesn't mean that when he reached the fence, he photographed it, but rather that he took another shot of the boy walking toward the fence and then had the boy walk alongside it, moving the camera along the fence.

As the Navajo were working and telling us about their films, we failed to hear or to understand fully the importance of the

words referring to walking. It was only after seeing the footage
that we realized how much walking there was. As we first saw
it, in the screening of the film as it came back from the lab, we
were upset. Worth put in his notes, "When they don't know what
to do they show somebody taking a walk." Although one of our
purposes in doing the research was to discover any differences in
the handling of images and symbols between "us" and "them,"
it took us some time to see how deeply the concept of walking
was embedded in their way of seeing and of showing the world,
and how deliberately they planned and used images of walking.

It was only after studying our interview tapes and field notes
that we noticed the frequent repetitions of phrases like "mother
goes looking for," "then he goes looking for," "then she goes,"
"my brother goes," "he approaches," "he comes to."

We realized afterwards that in listening to their descriptions
of what they were going to do, we had screened out what to our
thought system were mere connectives. We paid attention to
what was important to us. We were looking for "myths" and
"narratives" having to do with old legends, silver mines, etc. Not
until we saw the films, analyzed our interview materials, and
went back to the literature on the Navajo did we understand the
mythic quality of walking as an *act*. For the Navajo, walking was
an important event in and of itself and not just a way of getting
somewhere. We expected the filmmakers to cut out most of the
walking footage—but they didn't. It was the least discarded footage. In questioning them, it became clear that although they
didn't verbalize it, walking was a necessary element to a Navajo
telling a story about Navajos.

Johnny Nelson said to us on the thirteenth of June, "Then the
way the film is going to open—it's going to be John Baloo, he's
going to be walking and wandering around those holes in the
ground—we're going to have the feeling that he's alone, and it's
very hard to find what he's going to find." Further in the same
interview, he tells us that we don't see the face—we'll "see the
silversmith walking."

In reading the Navajo myths and stories later we were struck by how, in most Navajo myths, the narrator spends much of his time describing the walking, the landscape, and the places he passes, telling only briefly what to "us" are plot lines.

> Deer went over there. Then, "It is indeed true!" he said when he came running back. And then Jack Rabbit also started running off to that Coyote. Then, "It is true indeed!" he said as he also came running back and the Deer again started over there. He looked at Coyote again. "It is indeed true!" he said as he too came running back.
>
> Then, "How about you? You run over too!" was said to Prairie-dog. And so he also ran over there. "It is indeed true!" he also said. And then to Chipmunk, "What about you? You run over there too. It is quite true. He has died," was said to him. And so he ran over there too. *(Sapir 1942)*

Or, in the "Night Chant":

> . . . Happily I go forth
> My interior feeling cold, may I walk.
> No longer sore, may I walk.
> Impervious to pain, may I walk.
> With lively feelings may I walk.
> As it used to be long ago, may I walk.
> Happily may I walk.
> Happily with abundant dark clouds, may I walk.
> Happily with abundant showers, may I walk.
> Happily with abundant plants, may I walk.
> Happily on a trail of pollen, may I walk.
> Happily may I walk.
> Being as it used to be long ago, may I walk.
> May it be beautiful before me.
> May it be beautiful behind me.
> May it be beautiful below me.
> May it be beautiful above me.
> May it be beautiful all around me.
> In beauty it is finished.
>
> *(Matthews 1910)*

Or again, from "The Killing of Tracking Bear":

> And then he started to go back [home]. He started to go back to
> the summit of Black Rock. He went back up to the summit of
> Black Rock Encircled with Black. Then he went back up to the
> summit of the Mountain That Lies on Another. He just took a look
> at the place where he had done so. "At noon today something took
> place here," he thought.
>
> And then, yonder across from there, on the summit of Beautiful
> Mountain, the Crystal fool lived. There he was fed. He ate. When
> he had eaten, he went back to his home on the summit of Huerfane
> Mountain way off yonder.
>
> Then he again started off to the east. He went there and back
> in vain. There were no monsters. He also went to the south and
> back. There were again no monsters. He also went to the west and
> back. There were no monsters. He also went to the north and
> back. There were no monsters. He again went back to his home.
> Truly there were no more monsters.
>
> Now here the story stops. Now I have nothing more to tell.
> (Matthews *1910*)

All the films but one (which we shall note later) display this
unusual concentration on images of walking, not only as an in-
trinsic part of the Navajo notion of "eventing," as can be seen in
the quotes above, but as a kind of punctuation to separate activities. The mother and the silversmith, for example, are always
shown walking toward or away from the hogan to indicate a
structural break somewhat akin to phrase, paragraph, or chapter
structure. Compare "Tracking Bear" with Alta and John Baloo
(in the weaving and silversmith films) who go to get roots and
back again, go to get silver and back again, go to light the fire and
back again. Throughout the films the actor goes and comes back,
and as in "Tracking Bear," when the going stops, "Now the story
stops." In Susie's film of her mother, the film ends abruptly (for
us) when her mother holds up the finished rug. We haven't been
shown much of her mother weaving the rug. That portion of the
film showed only the very beginning of weaving and took only

four or five minutes out of twenty. Susie's film is rather a film of coming and going. The actual weaving is only barely started. But the walking parts, of mother and family, are finished. One can almost hear Susie saying, "Now that you've seen how I go and come back in making my rug, I have nothing more to tell. After the going and coming, you see the rug." And in the film—in what to us appears an abrupt cut—we see Susie's mother holding up the finished rug. (In the concluding words of the *Night Chant*, "In beauty it is finished.") The camera pans slowly across it ("before me . . . behind me") in a long shot and then in a close-up, and then repeats the image with a shot of another rug held vertically on which the camera pans up and down (below me . . . above me") also in close-up and long shot.

Several people who have seen these films have commented that it doesn't seem surprising to have first films composed chiefly of walking. "After all," they say, "what do other beginners do? They always show people walking." They also argue that walking is used in avant-garde films like those by Antonioni to show upset, lassitude, or general qualities such as the passage of time. Several facts, however, tend to strengthen our conviction that walking in Navajo films is used uniquely. First, when walking is used in "our" films, it is hardly if ever seen as an event in and of itself. It is used in most cases as a bridge between activities, a structural device to get people from one place to another, similar to the familiar shots of a railroad train speeding along the tracks, or of an airplane taking off, followed by a shot of the main character relaxing in his seat, followed by a shot of the airplane landing. When used as an event, as in an Antonioni film, it is seen as a somewhat unusual event. It is hardly the kind of thing we see in all movies, and certainly we cannot remember films in which the major action is composed of the main character "merely" walking.

It has been suggested that the reason for so much walking is not that the Navajo were following a particular context derived from the structure of their narrative, but rather that they were imitating life. That is, that the Navajo, being "primitive" people, walk a great deal and therefore show walking in their films in imitation of their actual daily activity. The striking thing in this regard is that the Navajo seem to dislike walking and avoid it wherever possible. They will go to great lengths to ride and will at every opportunity use some means other than walking to get someplace. Hardly ever did we observe our filmmakers walking to where they were photographing. They always insisted on driving, and almost all the members of the Pine Springs community owned pickup trucks and used them for journeys as short as a hundred yards. We observed scores of instances where Navajos waited patiently for hours at the side of a road for a ride to another part of the community or to the Trading Post. It may be true that in "the old days" the Navajo walked a great deal; if so they are going back to a traditional form of behavior in order to show how they see the world. Rather than showing behavior as it is, in this instance—walking—they are showing it in a way that they have heard about and that is ritually and culturally "right."

Another striking example to support our claim for difference in the use of walking as event is our analysis of two films on Navajo life made almost twenty-five years ago by Adair on his first visit to Pine Springs. We have compared his films with those made by the Navajo in our research. One of Adair's films is a finished film, photographed by Adair but edited by Mitchell Wilder, then Director of the Taylor Museum in Colorado Springs, and the other is a film that is unedited and contains all the footage shot by Adair in order to make a record of the daily activities surrounding weaving and silvermaking. It was Adair's first attempt at filmmaking and, although made by a young anthropologist, the film can still be said to reflect the young anthropologist's way of structuring events in contrast to the ways of our Navajo students.

What is notable is that Adair does two things different from the Navajo and quite consistent with what "we" do in filmmaking today. Both his films (the cademe version and the edeme version) show almost no walking. People just are in the places they are supposed to be. Nobody "searches for silver that is hard to find" or walks to get roots and plants for dye. Second, his footage is full of face close-ups showing the expressions of the Navajo as they go about their activities.

We mentioned earlier that one film didn't show an inordinate amount of walking. It is an interesting deviation in *support* of our original observation.

Johnny Nelson made two films. The first was about a silver-smith in which walking occurred a great deal. The second was about the building of a shallow well. In that film no walking occurs at all. In style it is similar to Adair's early films of Navajo activity.

Our explanation for this dramatic shift in style is that in the silversmith film, Johnny was telling a traditional story and there-fore he "naturally" told it in the traditional Navajo way. In the shallow well film, on the other hand, he was telling about non-Navajo ways and so told it in "English." This recalls the remark by the Navajo mentioned earlier, that the viewer didn't under-stand the film because it was in English.

It might be thought that a better explanation for the change in style is the fact that no walking occurred in the actual making of a shallow well, while walking naturally occurs in making silver jewelry. The reverse is actually true. Adair was stunned when he noted that Johnny was asking his "actor" to go to "the mine" to look for silver. The fact of the matter is that silver was never mined by the Navajo. This event in the film was derived from necessities imposed on the narrative style by other factors in the context. Remember that in Johnny's notebook he *writes* about the Navajo silversmith, and refers to the fact that the silversmith was using government minted silver coins because there was no silver on the reservation.

On the other hand, in the building of the well, much walking

actually occurred in order to get the materials, and much coming
and going of the trucks carrying the materials was observed by
us. None of this motion and activity is in either the finished film
or the cademe footage.

What we are suggesting here is that people within the context
of their culture have different codes for "saying" different things,
that one's cognitive system might well employ a meta code or
program that would relate the rules for one mode of communication to rules for the other. If someone has one set of rules for
talking and subsets of rules for talking about certain things or
telling certain stories, he might reasonably be expected to apply
those rules to structuring a movie about these subjects. In the
above observations, we seem to have some evidence that the *rules
of Navajo myth and storytelling* are more relevant to showing
events like weaving a rug, making silver jewelry, or building a
shallow well, than are the "real" events that occur when these
activities are actually performed. When Adair questioned Johnny
after the films were made about the fact that Navajos never
mined silver on the reservation, Johnny always answered (without definitely denying Adair's statement), "That's the way you
make a film about it."

Face Close-ups

This leads us to another coding difference, that mentioned in
coding (3): the cultural, perceptual, and cognitive taboos influencing semantic or syntactic organization and structure of an utterance. The Navajo do not use face close-ups, except in very limited
circumstances. Most shots are either cut off at the head or show
the head turned away from the camera. In all the films there are
no more than three face close-ups, and those, as far as we can
determine, are in two specific situations.

The first is most common, showing a full front view of the face
with the eyes looking slightly upward—sort of staring inwardly.

When questioned about what these shots mean, we were told by several of the students, "This shows my mother [or, my cousin] thinking about the design." They occur in those places in the film in which the Navajo is about to embark on the actual work of weaving or making a piece of jewelry (photos 16–20).

The difficulty that the Navajo had in shooting or viewing face close-ups was one of the earliest to reveal itself and one of the most consistent features of their work with the camera. The Pine Springs boarding school had recently installed a television set, and some of the youngsters, ages six to nine, would on occasion come in the evening when we were using the library and ask to watch TV. We noted frequent giggling at what seemed strange points in the dramas they were watching. At points of extremely tense action, for example, when the mother in a story had to leave her sick baby in the middle of the night to find a doctor, the children were giggling, smiling, and sometimes looking away. As we watched this "strange" behavior, it seemed as if the giggles and looking away were correlated with the appearance of a large face close-up on the tube. In the previously described story, when the big face of the mother appeared, looking frightened and, to us, "soap opera concerned," the children watching either looked away or smiled.

After the students had looked for the first time at the film shot by Worth on that first day of instruction, we asked them to describe what they saw in the footage. We have already mentioned the "snake in the grass" sequence, where they saw something in what to us was clearly waste film.

Part of the footage was a series of close-ups and medium shots of the boys and the girls sitting around on rocks near the school. Worth had shot close-ups of heads, feet, and hands, not with any particular plan but as part of his way of showing *any* scene. It seemed perfectly natural—even though we were deeply aware that what we shot could influence how they shot—to photograph ourselves in a simple way. What could be more obvious than to show several long shots of the group and then to make some close-ups of the faces, the hands, and the feet as we sat and stood around. It simply was not possible for us to even imagine at the start of our field work that such things as walking or photographing faces could be relevant areas of difference.

It is important to emphasize this point. When dealing with a communicative mode, one's own way of doing things can be seen *at all* only in contrast to another way. Everything is possibly significant and nothing can be taken for granted as the "way it's done."

Later, while viewing these first films, Worth asked, "Anybody remember anything else they saw—any other kind of shot?" The following exchange took place:

NELSON: Besides the hands and the snake.

WORTH: Yeah.

NELSON: Well, there was that one about the face, the girls sitting up and looking around and about the face there. I think that there was some action there that makes the people feel they do have some attention, have to pay attention, you know—to trying to avoid the camera, all the time.

WORTH: What in the shot made you say that?

NELSON: Well, that shot there, I noticed about two, three of the students there—they gave me the impression that they were trying to, uh, force something to look away from a certain object that was taking their picture.

In expanding his explanation, the other students weren't much clearer, but they all seemed to understand that something was wrong about showing the faces. At the time, we didn't note this concern for faces at all. It was only after studying our tape transcriptions that we were made aware that this concern had surfaced so early in the field work. In examining the photographs being discussed, we discovered that all the eyes were shut or invisible to the camera.

A day or two later, Al was telling us about his film, *Intrepid Shadows*. He was describing how he would show the intruder, who at that point was to be acted by Johnny Nelson. He said, "This person is very, he's very unknown. He's the intruder—but I won't show his face."

It was on the basis of that promise—that his face wouldn't be shown—that Johnny agreed to act in the film. When the footage was shown to the class after processing, we saw several shots of Johnny including a clear close-up of his face (photo 15). Several hours after that screening, Al told us that his film would have to be changed because Johnny refused to be an actor. Neither Al nor Johnny would tell us directly that it was because of the face close-up, but about ten days later, we overheard Al asking Mike to act in his film. Mike asked Al, "Will my face be a part of the picture?" Al answered, "Oh no, I am only going to use your feet, you know, there are no more faces in my film."

While Johnny was telling us about his silversmith film, he explained the permissible face close-up this way:

> He'll [the silversmith] be making some sort of design there on the ground—and then looks around a little bit here, there, maybe up in there [looking upward] . . . then I will make him sit there and think, oh maybe he'll be looking around up there, at the clouds like that . . . that's the way most people think . . . while he's doing that, I will take a picture of the pins that he made, the finished product . . . and insert it right between where he's thinking and then back to where he's drawing. . . .

This is a perfect description, made two weeks before Johnny shot this portion of the film, of the way the sequence looks in the finished film. The silversmith suddenly appears in close-up, his eyes roll slightly upward (in what to us appears almost the beginning of a faint or a trance) and the shot is held for only about half a second. Not only does this shot appear in Johnny's film, but Susie also has a similar scene where her mother is thinking of the design. She used the same kind of close-up with the same slow rolling of the eyes upward, which she said was put there "to show her mother thinking of the design."

The second permissible close-up is in the form of an "in" joke.

The Navajo stares at the camera and makes a funny face. This type of shot is used by the Tsosie sisters when photographing Sam Yazzie. At one point, they catch him almost looking straight at the camera (photo 21). At first he glares in a rather terrifying way but soon smiles and sticks out his tongue. The girls stopped shooting at first and almost left the area, but as soon as he mugged they resumed.

We can speculate that one of the reasons for this "strange" behavior regarding face close-ups is the fact that Navajos generally avoid eye-to-eye contact. Staring at someone or looking him "straight in the eye" is a form of invasion of privacy and a transgression of Navajo interpersonal behavior rules, unless it is done for clearly humorous purposes. A major form of insult is to look someone in the eye without blinking. At one point Al taught Chalfen and Worth to do it and laughed because we couldn't keep looking without blinking. Al said, "I guess you guys can't really insult a Navajo—but we can insult you and you'd never know it." At the time we thought this was a rather subtle way for Al to be able to act out some of his hostility toward his teachers without getting into trouble.

The avoidance of looking at the eyes relates to values of privacy in Navajo culture, where close living and modesty taboos must be reconciled by some form of perceptual avoidance behavior. It seems possible to conclude that this aspect has been carried over into film discourse. Edward Hall has pointed out that proximity in interpersonal communication assumes the level of rule-governed behavior differing markedly across cultures. It might be fruitful to consider research with the above reported method to test whether cultures *seeking* eye-to-eye contact would therefore use a large proportion of face close-ups.

After about a month of observations, we noted that although close-ups were plentiful, face close-ups were hardly ever taken or used. The following incident, told in some detail, will serve to illustrate the extreme difficulty that our students had with the face close-up. Although the major point in this incident is an attempt to influence a deeply held attitude, it also illustrates some of the difficulties inherent in any kind of participant intervention and observation.

During the shooting of a sequence for the Tsosie sisters' film about a medicine man, Al, Mary Jane, and Worth were alone with Sam Yazzie in his ceremonial hogan. Worth was there to observe, Mary Jane was doing the shooting that day, and Al was going to act as the medicine man's assistant. The sequence had taken the two girls over a week to arrange, and not only they, but all the people involved in the project were anxiously awaiting the results of the first Navajo attempt to film a religious ceremony. They had already shot several hundred feet of film depicting their grandfather preparing for this sing and had planned to have the making of the sand painting one of the major sequences in the film. As far as they were concerned, they were on trial. They would be controlling (1) their grandfather—could they do it? (2) a new mode of communication—could they do that? and (3) a Navajo religious ceremony which they really knew very little about.

Worth also was tense in this situation. Although he was an observer, it was difficult for him to divorce himself from the fears and anxieties of his students, and of other members of the community.

Sam had come into the hogan holding two three-foot sticks, whittled and smoothed. He had previously prepared several buckets of sifted and cleaned desert sand. He now sat down crosslegged on the dirt floor, poured the sand into a heap at his feet, and began smoothing the sand first with his hands and then with the smoothing sticks until he had a layer of sand about a half-inch high and about forty inches in diameter.

Up to this point, Mary Jane had done no shooting. She watched avidly, holding the camera at her side. Worth was becoming increasingly upset. In his notes he writes, "I suddenly became aware that it was possible that if left to her own devices nothing would come out of today's shooting. My instinctive desire was to tell her what to shoot."

When Worth noted that the actual sand painting was about to begin and that Mary Jane had done no shooting, he said to Mary Jane, "Don't you think you should have gotten a shot of your grandfather as he walked in and got started?" "Oh yes," she quickly said, and instructed Sam to walk into the hogan and begin smoothing the already smoothed sand. Sam seemed willing to do as Mary Jane told him. She made a quick shot of Sam as he entered the door and immediately dropped the camera to her side and stood watching as before. Worth waited a few minutes, feeling that Mary Jane was going to miss the beginning. Sam sat down again, went through all the smoothing motions and began the sand painting. Worth rationalized that he couldn't allow the girls to fail in their depiction of this scene. It might make Sam and many others in the community angry. Therefore, as Sam started painting, Worth asked Mary Jane if she didn't think she should have a close-up of Sam's hand. She said yes, and took such a cademe.

We spent about an hour in this way—Sam working quietly on his sand painting, Mary Jane watching and occasionally shooting when Worth reminded her that "this was something you should shoot." During this hour and a half, it became clear that Mary Jane couldn't quite get herself to do any uninstructed shooting. Either she was so unfamiliar with the activity that she was unable to divide it into image events and so was completely blocked from shooting or the very notion of structuring and recording a religious event was too much for her.

After the first hour Al Clah, who was avidly watching Sam and making drawings of the sand painting, looked up at Worth and nodded toward Mary Jane as if to show sympathy with a frustration that he shared with Worth. Worth gave Mary Jane an instruction at that point and Al smiled at him, nodding. After several minutes, Al turned to Worth and in a low voice said, "I wish I had a grandfather who did sand painting—I would like to make a film about *that!*" Not only does his remark reveal Al's awareness and essential agreement with Worth about all that Mary Jane was missing by not photographing, but it is another indication of the Navajo's extreme reluctance to photograph anything which doesn't "belong" to them. We will return to this point later.

After two hours, Sam began to tire and asked Al to help him finish. Al agreed with much alacrity and seated himself next to Sam ready to receive instruction. He knew how to drip the sand through his thumb and first finger but wouldn't take the responsibility for the placement of so much as a line, waiting for Sam's instructions.

At this point Worth realized that as far as Mary Jane's shooting was concerned, the day was a fiasco. He determined, not knowing if there would be another opportunity, to get as good a record as possible by both instructing her and taking stills himself. Feeling the need for some close-ups of the faces of both painters, Worth got down on the floor, belly down in rifle-shooting position and positioned his Leica so as to get face close-ups.

Worth stayed that way for about five minutes, making about five exposures, and then as he dusted himself off, he looked right at Mary Jane, who was watching carefully. He hoped that he could get her to make a similar shot without being forced to tell her to do so directly. Sam and Al said things in Navajo and both laughed. Worth asked what was funny, and Al replied, "He said you looked pretty funny down there." Worth waited a few minutes, and when Mary Jane made no effort to move her camera from her side, he asked if she "didn't think she should get a close-up of Sam's face?" Mary Jane nodded and standing upright walked over and pointed the camera straight down on Sam's head. He was sitting crosslegged with his head and body bent over the painting so that his face was about a foot and a half from the sand (photo 39).

Worth asked, "Mary Jane, can you see his face from the way you have the camera pointed?" She said, "No." Worth asked, "Is there anything you can do to get the camera so it will see his face?" She thought for a moment and replied, "I can ask him to look up at me."

WORTH: Will you see his face as it looks when he's working?

MARY JANE: Well no, he can't work if he looks at me.

WORTH: Is there anything else you can do?

MARY JANE: I suppose I can kneel down.

She thought about that for a moment and tried to lower herself to the ground, but seemed unable to make herself. Then:

MARY JANE: Would you do it—lying on your belly the way you did before— I would be ascared to do that.

WORTH: What do you mean, "ascared"?

MARY JANE: I would be afraid to get down on my belly like that.

Worth wanted those face close-ups so badly that he took her camera, lay down on the floor and shot about fifteen feet of close-ups of Sam's face. After that he proceeded to instruct her constantly, telling her to get "cut-away shots" and explaining that these were close-ups of things like the cans of sand, hands, and parts of the sand painting that could be used in the editing process later on to make transitions.

It was the first time that Worth had ever mentioned any conceptual system for either photographing or editing. He was so surprised at his own loss of objectivity that he felt compelled to create something useful for the research out of the experience. While instructing Mary Jane, he realized that it was extremely hard to get her to do it "his way" even when he told her to. He realized that he had failed to get her to take a face close-up, even by direct example, and that it was not a matter of her unawareness of how to lie down so that the camera could see the face.

It then occurred to us that if we could manage in some way to repeat the sand painting and get the two girls to try to photograph it over again with another observer (Adair), we could have a way of testing whether Mary Jane's inability was due to the strangeness of the situation or to the stronger prohibitions of her way of life.

Adair was at first upset at this break in research discipline. He emphasized to Worth that his behavior reflected a common attitude in many representatives of one culture teaching another. He felt that in this case, Worth was fulfilling a preacher's and also a teacher's role, and that although acting as researcher, he was unable to completely divorce himself from his own culture. Worth felt himself as filmmaker to be a representative of the "right" way of doing things, teaching those who were doing it "wrong."

We felt that if we managed to repeat the sand painting sequence in such a way that the girls and Sam wanted to do it over again we would be able to test how far our influence as to what was the "right" way would be accepted by them. If they made face close-ups, or followed any of the instructions Worth had given about what events to shoot and how to shoot them, it would indicate that those were possible choices for them to make. We would learn that they could understand "our" way of structuring and that they could execute it.

Fortunately, the rules of Navajo religious observance were compatible with our research needs. Sam had erased the first sand painting at sundown as no sand painting could be allowed to stand after the sun set—it always had to be destroyed either by a patient's use of it or by the medicine man. Several days later the girls learned that a major part of the ceremony was to have the patient sit on the sand painting. They were so ignorant of ritual that they didn't know this basic fact. They then decided that Sam would have to be asked to make another painting, and since they couldn't or wouldn't use a Navajo for the patient, that they would photograph the ceremony with Dick Chalfen in that role.

The girls left at nine o'clock in the morning with John Adair to pick up Sam and start shooting the duplicate sand painting. Worth drove Susie to her mother's and observed Susie while she was working on her film.

There was no uncertainty there. Susie and her mother worked away, Susie at the camera, her mother at the loom. Susie knew exactly what was to happen next, knew every move in advance and hardly had to say a word to her mother. Occasionally she would turn to Worth, telling him what would happen next and describing what lens she would use and what angle. She seemed to think that he was observing the process of weaving—it hardly occurred to her that what she was doing was very difficult or important.

At about 10:30, Worth drove to Sam's hogan to see what was happening with the Tsosie sisters' film—both Mary Jane and Maxine were to be shooting this time. When Worth arrived he discovered that the camera had jammed and that no shooting at all was taking place. The girls had ruined their first roll of film and the back of the camera was open, exposing the film to the light. It was unusable anyhow.

This accident was very unusual. No one had misloaded a camera up to that point, which was July 7, thirty days after instruction started. The girls had loaded the camera correctly for the twelve rolls of film used before then, doing it perfectly each time. Now Worth found that they had "forgotten" to make a loop of film before inserting the film onto the winding reel. In his instruction, Worth had carefully explained that this was the most important part of loading—no loops, no usable pictures.

When the girls had to photograph the scene for the second time with no chance of help—they knew that Adair would not help them (we had been very careful to avoid mentioning that Adair was a skilled cameraman)—they solved their problem by misloading so that they didn't have to shoot the scene at all. They seemed ready to forget about the whole thing, implying that as long as part of the ceremony was ruined in the camera, they might as well stop. Adair asked Maxine to reload and she did. Worth checked it before she closed the camera, and pointed out to Maxine that again one of the loops was too small. She corrected it instantly and surely. With the camera loaded both girls stood around watching until Maxine started directing her sister, telling her to take certain shots. There were long periods (about fifteen minutes) when no one said or did anything. In the course of three-quarters of an hour, the girls shot about seventy-five feet of film in three or four bursts of activity. Finally Mary Jane walked over to Worth and said:

MARY JANE: Would you do that shot of Sam's face like you did last time?

WORTH: What shot?

MARY JANE: You know the one where you lay down on your belly on the floor and shoot his face.

WORTH: Oh no, not this time. You have to do everything yourself today.

MARY JANE: Oh, I couldn't do that one, I'd be too frightened.

She turned to Maxine and said, "All you have to do is lay down on the floor and shoot Sam's face." Maxine took the camera and lay down on a sheepskin with her feet up against the hogan wall and put the camera to her eye. As soon as she looked through the viewfinder, she turned the camera away and started giggling. When Worth asked her what was the matter, she said, "It's funny, my eyelashes keep getting in the way of the viewfinder so it's hard to see." It was the only time anyone had complained that they couldn't see through the viewfinder, and Maxine certainly had no previous difficulty. Worth replied that she "could so see" and to go ahead. She then looked up at him and said that her arm was "very tired," that it "was shaking," and "that it was very hard to photograph like this." As she received no sympathy from anyone, she started pushing the button without focusing and without setting exposure. She made about a five-second shot that way and immediately arose, took the camera into her left hand

and, looking at us, said, "My God, look at the way my hand is shaking," and held her hand out stiffly in front of her. It was as steady as could be.

Over the course of the afternoon, Maxine repeated at least ten times that her hand was trembling, shaking, or unsteady and said that it was very hard to shoot under "these conditions." Worth asked, "What conditions?" and she pointed around the hogan in reply.

When Mary Jane held the camera, she did no shooting. She circled around, looking at things, at people, but shot practically nothing. She did none of the things that Worth had "taught" her the previous time. Worth's notes of that day sum up his impressions as follows:

> She shot very little while I was there—she didn't do any cover shots—any face shots—or any of the things I showed her. She didn't seem to do any close-ups of anything at all. Not sand painting—not cans of sand—not hands—nothing. She certainly wasn't photographing the sand painting itself so as to show it either take shape or to show it clearly at any point. It is a question of deciding whether she is just an inferior photographer or just terrified to shoot in this situation or whether the entire event is seen by her in a system so different from mine that I can't understand what she's doing.

Although we cannot draw definitive conclusions because of the nature of this "experiment," it seems clear that (1) photographing a religious ceremony was an extremely difficult thing for people like the Tsosie sisters, who had no experience with the ceremony, even if the main character was close kin; (2) face close-ups were a form of syntactic arrangement of an image event that was to be avoided, even though a respected authority requested it. It was not so bad to have the shot (Worth was asked to take it, and in the finished film they used two seconds of it); what was to be avoided was the situation of looking at the face in the camera and taking it; (3) although certain things—mainly technical—could be taught easily, certain ways of conceptualizing were so foreign to these girls and to the other students (although we never tested it in quite this way again) that even direct explanation and directions did not teach it to them.

We had a chance to observe the girls shoot a sand painting for the third time several days later. Sam informed them—at the end of the day of the second painting—that he wouldn't allow anyone to "sit on this painting—it was not correct." (It is possible that Sam was influenced not only by rules of ritual observance but by economic necessity. We were paying him five dollars a day to make the sand painting, and that was Sam's only income at the time other than his government pension.)

On the third try, the girls loaded the camera correctly but photographed the scene in much the same way they had done previously (photos 39–40).

Chapter

10

Sequencing Film Events

In recent years it has become increasingly apparent to people involved in education and in the study of how people take on the customs of a group—that is, learn their culture—that understanding how people manipulate *things* is not enough to explain how people do what they do and become what they become. Increasingly, it has become clear that people manipulate objects that stand for, or refer to, things in a variety of ways: that people manipulate symbols, and furthermore that they manipulate symbols—speech and pictures, for example—in different ways, for different purposes, at different times. There seems sufficient evidence that such manipulations and uses of symbols and symbolic forms or modes are patterned, have regularity and structures, and in some cases have rules of use which are understood or used widely enough within a culture to assume the theoretical level of a theory or a grammar.

We shall now turn to an examination of the Navajo films on the level of symbolic structure; specifically to the way in which the Navajos in our study organized the symbolic events into sequences of symbols meant to communicate some meaning to those viewing the film.

In previous chapters we discussed the ways in which they organized themselves to learn about film, the kinds of things they photographed or did not photograph, and the kinds of actions they thought it important to show. We talked about actions, things (such as faces), events and what they did about them. In this chapter we will discuss how they organized and put together the symbolic representation of these things; how pieces of film representing or symbolizing certain events, ideas, and meanings were organized into a complex symbolic form.

Again we must rely on an inadequate lexicon. We will use words like *semantic* and *syntax*, rather than attempt to find new words which would only add to an already confused jargon. We will be using such words in the sense of syntactic and semantic reasons behind the organization of sequences of cademes and edemes. But we shall try to use syntax and semantics in the semiotic or the ethnosemantic sense rather than in a strictly linguistic sense. Syntax refers to the relations between one sign and another (in our case between one piece of film and another) while semantics refers to the relations between a sign and its referent—between a piece of film and what it is a picture of. In the ethnosemantic sense we are concerned with the way our students divided up their world into little pieces of film and then restructured it by putting the film together.

The distinctions here are subtle and by no means dichotomous. Using such notions is only a convenience. It is almost impossible to talk about putting pieces of unexposed film in sequence, although one can imagine certain art films consisting of a sequence of blank film and black (exposed) film in which neither was an image of anything except possibly blackness and whiteness. One might argue that in such a case the film was about "light" and "no light." As a matter of fact, certain avant-garde filmmakers in the United States are experimenting with just such ideas. Ordinarily, however, one only sequences pieces of film that are about something, and the way one puts these pieces together usually has some relation to what the pieces are about.

We will describe some rules that seem to govern the way the

Navajo filmmakers structured their films, and the way these rules differed from ours. We have already touched upon some of these things in describing our filmmakers' response to the "snake in the grass" sequence, the "how a piñon tree grows" sequence, and the way in which Susie photographed her mother putting the warp on the loom. Certain classes of objects symbolized on film—that is, certain semantic referents—seemed to call for specific syntactical organization. It is these kinds of rules we will be describing. How, and at what point in a cademe, is a piece of film cut apart to make an edeme? What is allowed to follow what? Where does the filmmaker cut two cademes apart because he feels he needs something to go in between?

We found, for example, that the Navajo were joining edemes together in a way quite different from the way "we" do. It became clear to us that our rules were being broken. In fact it wasn't until we noted that the Navajo were doing it "wrong" that we realized the prescriptive strength of some of our rules of syntactic organization.

The following are two (out of many) basic connected rules governing the way we put film together. All American and most Western filmmakers know these rules implicitly; and most explicitly. In later chapters we will offer some evidence that young people exposed to movies and television have learned these rules merely by watching movies.

> RULE 1:   The major purpose of editing and sequencing units is to make it appear that no join exists, so that the viewer sees one continuous piece of "action."

When a filmmaker has two cademes—a long shot of a man walking, for example, and a close-up of a man's feet walking—he will usually try to match action. That is, he will cut the long shot at a point in the walking that can be placed immediately next to a point in the close-up that follows "naturally." If one cuts at the point where the left heel is just about hitting the sidewalk, the next shot will begin with the left heel having hit the sidewalk. The walk will continue *through* the two shots without a break in continuity.

RULE 1A: Things that aren't joined on action are a form of
             magic, or are funny, and are not "the way things hap-
             pen."

When something seems to appear on the screen suddenly and
without "explanation" such as a glass appearing in a person's hand
before his hand reaches the glass standing on the table, we know
we have seen something wrong. For example, imagine two
cademes. One is a continuous long shot of a man sitting in a chair
near a coffee table. He reaches for a glass standing on the table,
picks it up, and takes it to his mouth. Another cademe in close-up
shows a hand reaching for a glass, picking it up, and taking the
glass back toward a mouth. Now imagine that we cut the first
cademe at the point where the hand is some distance from the glass
and insert the second close-up cademe at the point where the hand
holding the glass is returning to the mouth. On the screen we
would have a man reaching out in a long shot and suddenly the
glass would *jump* into his hand as if by magic and would be taken
to his mouth. The technical name for this kind of editing " error"
is the *jump cut*.

It is interesting to note that the French and other avant-garde
filmmakers deliberately break this rule occasionally. They use
the so-called jump cut for some of the same reasons that painters
began using "primitive" art forms; or what is more to the point,
for the same reasons that poets will say "the achieve of the thing,"
knowing that the "wrong" grammar will add power to the
phrase, and further knowing that *we* know the *rule* and know that
the poet is breaking it deliberately.

On the other hand, some of the black teenagers with whom we
worked followed the Hollywood-TV rule, Rule 1. In a film made
by a group of eleven- to fourteen-year-old teenagers working in
a church-related film club set up by one of Worth's students, the
teenagers chose to make a film about their daily activities. The
cademes were photographed in much the same way as the Navajos worked. They seemed to know what to do, did it well, and
worked quickly. When it came to organizing the cademe
material, however, they seemed "innately" to use a different sys-

tem than that used by our Navajo students. They organized their
film according to the standard Western notion of plot, building
to a climax toward the end, employing suspense, and using sequences which in effect provided comic relief. The film ended in
tragedy with one of the boys getting hit by a car and killed on
the street.

Syntactically the film was impressively similar to a standard
television or Hollywood dramatic film. In all cases where one
cademe had to be cut to join another, the cut from cademe to
edeme was made at that point where the action could be made to
flow smoothly. For example, in a fight scene when a long shot of
one boy swinging his fist at another had to be joined to a close-up
(because the cademe was not complete as far as the action was
concerned), the long shot cademe was cut when the fist was in the
center of the screen moving from left to right. The close-up
cademe was cut when the fist was in the same place on the creen.
When the two edemes were shown together, the fist traveled
across the screen smoothly, and the editing join was barely noticeable. The black teenagers seemed to have somehow internalized our system of joining events (although they never verbalized
it). We can think of no other place than watching films and
television where they could have learned our rules for sequencing or "speaking" film.

On the other hand, the Navajo didn't follow the rule of editing
on motion or action at all. The notion of smoothness of action or
making a connective unnoticeable didn't seem to occur to them,
or wasn't important enough to do anything about, except in
specific cases. There are numerous examples of people suddenly
appearing on the screen, "jumping" from one place to another,
"magically" going from a kneeling to a walking or standing position.

It might be thought that these "rule breakings" are evidence
of lack of skill on the part of the Navajo, or lack of a conceptual
ability at that stage in their filmmaking. That is, that when they
"got better" they would "naturally" follow the rule. But remem-

ber the description of Maxine's first editing effort with the see-saw described in Chapter 6. She deliberately and with great skill *chose* to connect her pieces of film so that the motion of the seesaw was uninterrupted. Again, our black teenagers in the Tabernacle Film Club were as much beginners as the Navajo and also were able "technically" to make what professional filmmakers in our culture call smooth transitions. It will become clear that when the Navajo didn't make smooth transitions, or used jump cuts, they weren't breaking our rules at all. They just didn't accept the rule that a jump cut was strange or unnatural. The fact that a symbolic event (walking, or picking up a glass of water) didn't have to *match* the actual event seemed much more reasonable to them than it does to us.

We spent a great deal of time observing the Navaho at their editing tables, trying, at times without questioning at all, to determine their methods of organizing the material. One day toward the end of June, Worth was observing Mike, who was editing his film, *Antelope Lake.* He watched the cademes as Mike ran them through the viewer and watched as Mike cut and joined them. During one period, Mike was working on a sequence in which a boy, who is washing clothes at the lake, walks down the road. This comes at a point between the boy's lighting a fire to warm water and the actual washing sequence. Mike had about four shots of the boy walking (photos 22–25). Each shot was about eight seconds long. He cut pieces from every shot and joined them, but instead of joining them according to the "cut on motion rule" so that the action is continuous, he made each cut a jump cut. That is, the boy walks down the road, then seems to jump magically about twenty feet and continues walking, then jumps again and walks and so on. Worth walked over to the viewer and asked to see what Mike was working on. Mike happily turned the film back, and Worth wound the film through using the rewinds himself. He stopped at the jump cuts, running them back and forth so that the jump was very obvious and asked, "Do these cuts seem okay to you?" Mike looked at them again, knowing that the "teacher" was probably pointing out a mistake. He took the rewinds into his hands and looked twice. Finally, very puzzled, he said, "Yes, they are okay—what's wrong with them?" Worth asked, "Doesn't it seem funny to you that the boy is over here and then in the next frame he's over there?" Mike looked up at Worth and said, "No."

Worth left Mike and walked over to the Tsosie sisters and asked to see what they were doing. They were working on a section in which Sam was gathering yucca roots for his sing. One shot showed Sam on his knees cutting roots. The next shot, which they had already put in place, showed Sam walking down the road holding the roots. Not only was he walking but Maxine had suddenly appeared at his side (photos 35–38). Worth had tried being subtle about his questions previously, but we had realized that we would have to ask very direct questions in order to get answers at all. (Adair had found a similar situation with the Navajos in a previous research project in medical care. He had found that doctors could not get answers to general questions, like "What color is your spit?" in an attempt to diagnose tuberculosis. The Navajo not only had no words for the generic question but had difficulty handling the generality even when bilingual.)

Worth asked the Tsosie girls, "Doesn't it seem funny to you that at this place Sam is kneeling, and at this place right afterward he's walking?" Both said that it did not seem funny. It seemed perfectly all right. Worth said, "Well, it certainly seems funny to me to have him sitting one moment and walking the next. Don't you think an audience will be confused?" Maxine seemed pleased that she had finally understood the point of Worth's questions and replied eagerly, "But everybody will know that if he's walking in this shot that comes last, he must have gotten up between time he was sitting and the time he's walking."

Chalfen later arranged with Mike to go over Mike's finished film, shot by shot. In it there occurred an edited sequence in which the boy in the film walks toward the lake to get his washed clothes (photos 23–25). In the cademe footage, as it came out of the camera, there is one long shot, about ten seconds long, in which the boy walks from the left toward a small clump of trees, passes behind the trees, and just reappears on the right. The next cademe, as it came out of the camera, starts with the boy appearing from behind the trees and walking right, toward the lake. This is followed by a cademe of a still longer (wide angle) view of the boy walking down the road and by another one from another direction. In the first two cademes described, not only is the boy walking toward the tree and passing behind it, but Mike also is panning in the direction of the walk, so that, at the point where the boy is behind the tree, the tree fills most of the frame. As the boy appears on the left side of the screen the tree is on the right in the first cademe. In the second, as the boy appears on the right side of the screen the tree is on the left. In our way of editing, the "natural" place to cut would be while the boy was behind the tree. An editor would cut the first cademe just after the boy moved behind the tree, then cut the next cademe just before he emerged, splicing the two pieces together so the boy walks behind the tree and then emerges again and continues his walk. Thus the boy and the pan would match in action.

Mike edited these cademes as follows. The boy walks toward the tree, but when he is about a second away from the tree, Mike cuts the film. The second shot is cut about a second after the boy emerges from behind the tree. The two edemes are then joined with the resultant jump. The boy appears, as if by magic to jump across the space occupied by the tree. He never goes behind it. Chalfen followed the same procedure that Worth used, asking "Didn't it look funny?" Mike again said "No" in that same puzzled way. Chalfen persisted—pointing out the jump cut twice—and Mike finally seemed to understand what was "wrong," saying, "Well, if I splice the other way, you couldn't see the boy because he was behind the tree. This shot is about the boy goes down to the lake."

Since the two cademes overlap in action, Mike had a great choice of points at which he could cut both pieces of film and join them to get the actor down to the lake.

In a small study done by Worth he asked twenty-five students and faculty at Pennsylvania to indicate on the diagram reproduced below at what point they would cut the film to achieve the effect of having the actor get from the left side of the screen to the right side.

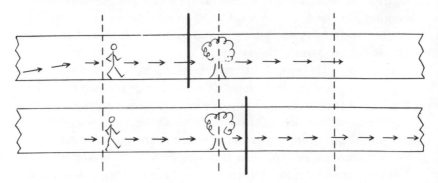

The subjects chosen were faculty members in communication, students at the Annenberg School, and members of the anthropology and psychology departments, randomly chosen, with varying degrees of knowledge about editing. Eighteen of the twenty indicated that they would combine the film in *parallel* fashion; that is, no matter where they would cut the first cademe, they would "match" that point on the second cademe. The dotted lines on the drawing represent some of the places where they indicated they would cut. The subjects more sophisticated in film marked the cut as occurring when the actor was behind the tree. This would make the cut the least noticeable.

Two of Worth's film students, however, marked the diagram for a jump cut, that is, so as not to achieve continuous action. But what is most striking is that both (they did this at different times and had not spoken to each other) immediately looked at Worth after marking the diagram with smiles on their faces. One said, "Fooled you, didn't I?" and the other observed, "That screws up your experiment, doesn't it?"

Both students knew of our work with the Navajo and were clever enough to see the point of the study without being told. They deduced what it was that Worth was attempting to demonstrate. Apparently they knew the rule of continuous action so well that they deliberately broke it—but couldn't resist telling Worth about it. When he pointed out that they were confirming the hypothesis that continuity of action was a rule for "us," they sheepishly agreed.

Mike, on the other hand, cut the sequence as shown by the heavy line in the diagram.

In many ways this result is similar to that of the Brown-Lenneberg study conducted with Navajo and Harvard students, in which the subjects were given color names for color swatches, consisting of the same syllables, *mo, mo; ma, ma*, but spoken with the vowels varying between long and short *o* and *a*. When the subjects were asked to name the colors with the new names, the Navajos correctly repeated the long and short vowel names for the colors while the Harvard students named two different colors with the same syllable, disregarding their vowel length. When Brown subsequently asked the Harvard students, "Didn't you hear the difference?" they replied, "Sure, but we knew it didn't matter." Their rules for language told them that vowel length was not a significant difference, just as Mike knew that continuity of action was not a significant difference.

The Horse Has to Come
After the Footprints of the Horse

Another of the things we tried to learn in interviewing the students at an editing table in our office at the Trading Post was their reasoning in choosing one shot over several others which seemed to us very similar, or why certain shots "went together" at all when we could see no apparent reason for it. In many cases, we were told merely, "Those two shots (cademes out of the camera) are all right together, but these two need something in between." This phrase "it needs something in between" was a frequent explanation. It indicated an acute sensitivity about what could go together and what could not, but the students were never able fully to articulate the rules for this. In our analysis of the complete corpus of film shot, we found large sections of film used as it came out of the camera, and then evidently something was shot which demanded separation. The sections of cademe which they used just as it came out of the camera were sections containing innumerable jumps in action. These were the sections where "we" would need something in between. Western filmmaking finds it intolerable in general to continue actions which are discontinuous. We have a special term for the edeme we insert at that point, a *cutaway.*

It was just this point that Worth had tried to explain to Mary Jane when he told her to shoot close-ups of Sam's hands, face, and cans of sand. So it is not that we do not have the "in between" constraint, but rather that our rules of what specific events need something in between are different from theirs.

One reason, however, for their choice of shots and sequence that seem unreasonable to us might simply be that their knowledge of the world—of nature—is so very different from ours on a simple experiential level. It might have been as difficult for Mike to understand how Worth could edit a subway sequence as it was for Worth and Chalfen to understand how Mike edited the following sequence.

While Mike was photographing his film about a lake, he explained that he planned to walk around the lake, starting at the source and continuing clockwise or sunwise, showing all the things that "happen" at the lake. It was our impression that Mike had made, over the course of several days, a series of cademes of horses, sheep, and what to us looked like several cademe close-ups of mud on the bank of the lake (photo 58). Worth saw the "mud" shot as an interesting one showing some old beer cans lying near the shore spoiling the natural beauty of the landscape. Mike took several "mud" shots during the day, in different places, and when he was editing his film, Worth noticed that he seemed to be looking for something to put "in between" them.

At the time of this interview, Mike had edited these shots into a sequence, and Chalfen was trying to find the logic of his selection of edemes and their organization. The first edeme was a shot of the "mud" followed by a shot of a man on horseback in the water. Chalfen asked why the man on horseback followed. Mike didn't seem to understand the question, and Chalfen then asked about the first shot, "What is that about?" Mike explained, "That shot is a shot of hoofprints of a horse." We realized then that what had been our semantic interpretation of an edeme as "mud" was just wrong. Now Chalfen asked, "Okay, why was this shot of hoofprints followed by this particular man on horseback? You had lots of other shots of men on horseback, and of horses." Mike replied, "You see these hoofprints are leading toward the water and so the horse which these are hoofprints of must be in the water. It's the one going into the water I need to use."

Several edemes later, Mike had placed another close-up of the hoofprints followed by an edeme of a long shot of sheep grazing in the distance. Chalfen asked, "Why isn't there a shot of another horse in the water or of sheep in the water?" Mike looked up very surprised and said, "But these *sheep* hoofprints are going away from the water so the next shot the sheep have to be far away."

This detailed example is one of many instances revealing a similar logic of organization which depends upon the Navajo method of viewing and organizing the world. Earlier in this book we mentioned the Whorf-Sapir hypothesis which in general advances the notion that no individual is free to describe nature with absolute impartiality, but is constrained to certain modes of interpretation even while he thinks himself most free. . . . We are thus introduced to a new principle of relativity which holds that all observers are not led by the same physical evidence to the same picture of the universe. . . . We cut up and organize the spread and flow of events as we do largely because, through our mother tongue, we are parties to an agreement to do so, not because nature itself is segmented in exactly that way for all to see. (Whorf 1952)

Many of the things we have been discussing bear direct relation to the above point of view. It is almost as if Whorf were thinking of filmmaking when he talked about cutting up and organizing the spread and flow of events. It is clear that when we talk about the way Susie shot and organized the sequence in which her mother strung the warp on the loom or the way the Tsosie sisters shot and organized the sand painting or Al Clah his entire film, we are suggesting that "through (their) mother tongue (the Navajo students) were parties to an agreement" to segment nature in a particular way.

Harry Hoijer, a Navajo linguist, might have been explaining in the following analysis of one aspect of the Navajo language why Mike felt it correct or even mandatory to pay attention to the link between a set of hoofprints and their consequent, and not to pay attention to the relationship between one shot of a boy walking and the next.

We are now ready to isolate . . . a possible fashion of speaking peculiar to the Navajo. The Navajo speaks of "actors" and "goals" (the terms are inappropriate to Navajo), not as performers of actions or as ones upon whom actions are performed, as in English, but as entities linked to actions already defined in part as pertaining especially to classes of beings. . . ." (Hoijer 1954)

According to Hoijer there seem to be in this case two types of what we call "action," one seen as entities linked to action already defined and one seen as we do as mere action performed.

The boy in Mike's film walking behind the tree, or Sam Yazzie sitting and then suddenly walking, represent performers of an action for us. They are walking, or kneeling actions, and for us the logic or linkage between edemes must continue the action. For Mike the boy walking was already linked to an action already defined. In Mike's words, "This shot is about the boy goes down to the lake." For walking *in and of itself* there seem to be no mandatory connections when symbolized in film structure. The shot of hoofprints, however, and the horses or sheep which *must* follow them are mandatory connections because they are connected as "entities linked to actions *already* defined in part" by the preceding shot. The horse and the sheep which followed the hoofprints were mandatory because the hoofprints defined, as Mike might have said, that this shot is about a horse goes in the lake, or a sheep goes away from the lake.

Hoijer further writes, "This division of nature into classes of entity in action or movement is the universe that is given; the behavior of human beings or of any being individuated from the mass is customarily reported by assignment. . . ." (Hoijer 1954)

The hoofprints represent a class of "entity in action or movement," and the horses or sheep are a "being individuated from the mass . . . [and] reported by assignment." The horses and sheep are assigned a syntactic position after the edeme representing a class of entity in action.

In Susie's film about weaving we also find instances of mandatory connection of an "entity in action or movement" being reason for the choice of place to start or stop an edeme or an edeme sequence.

In the sequence in which her mother is rolling the spun wool into balls we seem to have too many shots of a seemingly trivial nature. It takes too much screen time to watch her mother rolling yarn into a ball, just as in the warp sequence we spend too much time watching the knots being tied. In both cases we have to continue seeing this action until the end of the wool is in sight —literally. We have to watch until the very end of the hank of wool is on the ball, or has been knotted. The class of entity in action is rolling *all* the wool into a ball, or knotting all the knots. The wool end individuates the action from the mass of wool rolled up or the number of knots.

Examples like these, which can be carried out in many other segments of these films, also point out the value of the Whorf-Sapir hypothesis as one possible method of understanding the way the Navajo present themselves to us in their films. Although much of our analysis stems from a research point of view motivated by what Sapir formulated by writing "Language is a guide to social reality," we do not wish to overstate the point nor to enter the controversy surrounding the Whorf-Sapir hypothesis. For us it is an extremely important heuristic, lending insight to our own development of a methodology by which we can examine the way a people see their world.

Chapter

11

Who Can Be an Actor
in a Navajo Film

The Navajo choice of "actors" for their films and the restrictions of locale were also different from those of people living in our culture. While graduate students at the University of Pennsylvania and at high schools and colleges throughout the country can and most often do make films about anybody, living anywhere—even of Navajos—the Navajo were limited by restricting themselves in their choice of actors and locales.

In fact it seems to us that people in our culture limit themselves in opposite ways. We can make movies of people living somewhere else or being somewhat different much more easily than we can make movies of ourselves. In looking at all the fifty or so documentary films made at the Annenberg School of Communications at the University of Pennsylvania over the last seven years, only one is about the filmmakers' own environment. One is about the school—the easiest subject *technically* that a beginner can make a film about. He doesn't have to travel, he has permission, he knows the people, etc. Rather, they make films about Tibetans living in New Jersey, tugboat captains, autistic children, prizefighters, and so on.

One has only to look at the field of anthropology in general to notice the ease with which observation of far-away people is carried out in comparison with observations of people or cultures close to us. Although this could seem a value criticism of anthropology, it is pointed out here in order to clarify more sharply the differences between those whom we can make films about and those whom the Navajo chose as their actors and subjects.

The Navajo were extremely loath to photograph those distant from themselves, and conversely always sought the closest kin as their subjects and showed the greatest ease and ability with the cameras in those situations. This restriction of closeness did not only manifest itself in people. They also felt extremely uncomfortable photographing anybody else's land, sheep, hogans, or horses. If the situation was such that they had no alternative that fit their plan for their film, they always asked elaborate permission or tried to "borrow" the needed person or object from someone related to them. Apparently the use of a symbolic representation of a person or an object was closely tied to their feelings about the use of the actual person or thing the image referred to. Their attitude toward photographing an animal or a house was similar to the attitude we would have of "borrowing" it. We would feel most comfortable in borrowing houses (for use during a vacation, for example) from our nearest relatives or perhaps from our dearest friends.

The filmmakers, as members of Navajo society, were subject to certain broad underlying moral strictures which tend to regulate their interpersonal behavior. One such stricture concerns property rights. Property for the Navajo is not just the ownership of real estate, silver jewelry, sheep, and other wealth, but extends even to the rights of a medicine man to conduct a curing rite; he may not do so until he has paid his medicine man teacher from whom he learned the ceremony for that knowledge. Human transactions are validated, made legal and binding, by economic exchange in all phases of life.

For this as well as other reasons all of the filmmakers were extremely careful about their choice of people and objects to be photographed in their films. Within the family, and to a degree within the clan, payments may be required or ignored depending on the situation and the relationship between the two kinsmen; but such payment is always demanded between nonkinsmen. The Tsosie sisters felt that it was appropriate for them to pay their paternal grandfather for appearing in the film and did so out of money they earned while making the film. Sam Yazzie also asked that we, the teachers, pay him for appearing in his grand-daughters' film. He explained that his performance was part of our project—part of our teaching—and that since we would be watching him and learning from him, we too should pay. Susie Benally, on the other hand, seemed to feel that it was not appropriate for her to pay her mother. Her relationship to her mother and to weaving were so close that legitimacy was assured without payment.

In the same vein, Al Clah felt that he couldn't make a film about a medicine man or about a curing ceremony because, "I had no father or grandfather who did that." We mentioned earlier that before Johnny felt that he could photograph a horse for his practice film, he had to get the owner's permission.

It was a violation of this code that got Johnny Nelson into trouble when he tried to photograph additional sequences for his horse movie (photos 6–11). We mentioned earlier the moment when he asked whether we thought that inserting pictures of a whole horse between pictures of pieces of a horse would make people think that the pieces were parts of the whole horse. Johnny had said, "I will think about it."

He finally decided to get his photographs of whole horses at a ceremony that was to occur two days afterward. He decided that he would photograph certain parts—sacred parts—of the Squaw Dance. The particular scene that caused difficulty was one when the virgin emerged from the hogan carrying the scalp pole. At this point in the ceremony about twenty to twenty-five horses, gaily decorated with balls of colored wool, race across the mesa chasing the virgin. Johnny felt that this was the best moment to get shots of "whole horses" to use in his film.

The following day, we learned from several of our students and from many members of the community that the entire ceremony had been a failure. We learned that the scalp pole had broken during the charge of the horses, and that now the community faced an unusually heavy economic and ritualistic burden. They would have to repeat the ceremony at great cost in order to insure the health of the patient, who was not a kinsman of Johnny's. We heard rumors the following day that the ceremony was a failure because the white man tried to photograph it. Since all three of us were extremely careful to make no pictures during the ceremony, we were naturally curious about the complaint. We had wondered, at the time that Johnny mentioned photographing the ceremony, whether it would be permissible. We had discussed the photography during the ceremony with him, and he had assured us that it was all right. In an interview with Nelson before the ceremony, Worth asked if people might object if he (Johnny) took pictures of the Squaw Dance. Johnny replied:

> I just don't know. I guess some of these older people, so much rooted in their old way of belief that when you take a picture of some ceremonial that they think is sacred . . . just with a still camera, or maybe with a movie projector . . . they feel that they wouldn't be cured of some evil thoughts that they've had in their —that they wanted to cure. The reason why they have the Squaw Dance—This is something that I've talked to some people and this is what they've said. If you capture any of the secret ceremonies that the Indians do, that they would not be cured because it's been captured by some camera or movie camera. And then when it's being shown somewhere, it'll remain right where he—the same place as where he wouldn't be cured . . .

Some of the older people, like Mr. Sam Yazzie—I talked to him about it, and he said it was a very good idea bout making a movie of the Squaw Dance. Like uh—these kids that go to school, they don't know anything about a Squaw Dance . . . quite a few older people, they are the ones that know how to do it—are getting pretty old and the younger people aren't learning anything about a Squaw Dance. Then he [Yazzie] says that if he can capture it [the Squaw Dance] in a movie, he would, that this would be taught back to the young and make them realize how the Squaw Dance was done and what it meant, what kind of a healing ceremony it was for. So this is what he said to me.

When the scalp pole broke, however, the community finally settled their blame on Johnny. We (the investigators) made it very clear that we had taken no pictures. Johnny, as it turned out, had not arranged permission or payment to any of the sponsors of the ceremony. Had he done so, the sacredness of the subject matter might have been overlooked. From their point of view, Johnny had stolen the ceremony from them, and that, they were certain, was a major cause of the ceremonial failure.

Johnny reported that a delegation of the sponsors of the ceremony visited him objecting to his photographing it and asking to see what he had done. Afterwards they (as Johnny reported it)

wanted to take this out and that out, so I had to take them all out, all them shots out and then . . . there's another point in this thing that uh, which kind of makes me curious . . . then he says if you want to make a film about a Squaw Dance, we would need about four or six head of sheep, plus $20 and oh about six or seven days of groceries—for the Squaw Dance. And thinking about this there, he would run it up to a hundred dollars.

Johnny then told us that he refused to pay that amount of money, and the delegation demanded the film. Johnny gave it to them and he now considered the incident solved. Before he finished, however, he added,

What my curiosity bothered me was if he felt that was real sacred
—that that shouldn't be taken with a camera ... why did they want
payment for it? This is one of my curious bothers—something like
that.

The moral code defining property rights and economic obligations obviously had a restraining effect upon the filmmakers. On
the other hand, the community gave the individuals working
with us a good deal of freedom as long as these obligations were
not violated. Once we had explained to the community what the
purpose of our being there was, and why Navajo people in their
community were making film, there was no attempt on the part
of the community to discourage any of the participants from
working with us.

During an interview that we reported previously, at which
Mike had explained the mud shots, we also asked him why this
particular horse had been chosen when we had seen shots of
several horses in the lake. Mike explained that this particular
horse was his brother's and that the other shots were of horses
that he didn't know, and therefore "had better not use because
the people who owned it [the horse] might not like it."

As you will remember, that film sequence included an edeme
of horse footprints followed by a horse in the water, then an
edeme of sheep footprints followed by an edeme long shot of
sheep in the distance. We assumed that the sheep in the film
belonged either to Mike or to members of his family. After all,
he had just told us that he chose the horse edeme by those criteria.
We therefore never asked him directly about the ownership of
the sheep.

It was not until some months later, during the early stages of
our analysis, that we got to that stage of our work where we were
checking all the footage in the films against the actual negative.
We wanted to put together an accurate chronology of when each
cademe was taken, and to record the context of each cademe in
relation to the other ones on that same roll of film. To our sur-

prise we found the cademe from which Mike's sheep edeme was taken came from a roll of film photographed in its entirety by Susie.

In reconstructing this shooting day from our three individual sets of field notes of that day, we found that Susie had taken that cademe one morning at the start of her work on her film on weaving. On that roll she had photographed several long shots, showing a flock of sheep grazing. Susie was asked, "What are those pictures you are taking about?" She replied, "These go in the film before my mother shears the wool. . . . These are my mother's sheep . . . these are the sheep the wool for the weaving comes from."

From other sections of our notes we discovered that several of the students had asked Susie if they could borrow some film from her. We hadn't known what it was for at the time and simply had overlooked the significance of the interchange. Susie had agreed and had been seen handing over pieces of film to several students.

In thinking about this incident, as we tried to reconstruct it, it became clear that the meaning of "borrow some film" was understood by us in a totally different way from the way in which they used it. We ignored it when we heard it because "borrowing" a "piece of film" to a filmmaker in our culture means to borrow the celluloid, not the image on it. We ask someone if we can borrow some leader or a hunk of film when we are busy working and need a piece of leader, filler, or something for some trivial or technical purpose *not connected* with the fact that it is an image, a cademe, or edeme of anything.

It seems clear that as Mike worked on his film, and started putting his edemes together, he found that the sequence of hoofprints needed the proper edemes to go with them. He found a cademe that he could use of a horse that belonged to his family but couldn't find one of sheep. Since neither Mike nor his family owned sheep, Mike would have had to photograph someone else's sheep without permission, or find someone who had sheep, get permission to photograph them—and perhaps pay them for it—

and then spend all that time and effort going out and photographing, all for just one little edeme. Mike was not the kind of person
who would consider photographing without permission and so
he developed a much better solution. He "borrowed" a piece of
cademe from Susie who had, as we saw on her original roll of
film, plenty of sheep. He got it quickly, for nothing, had to do no
photographing of his own, and had his permission to use it all in
two or three minutes.

These same sheep appeared in Susie's film, of course, and we
discovered pieces of this roll of film in Johnny Nelson's silversmith film also. His actor and silversmith in the film was John
Baloo, a classificatory brother of Johnny's, who had no sheep (or
the sheep were elsewhere at the time of the shooting). So Johnny,
with Susie Benally's permission, used some of the shots she had
taken of her family's sheep and spliced them into his film. No
self-respecting Navajo would want his home environment shown
without sheep, and no apprentice Navajo filmmaker would want
to deprive a relative of such respect.

It must also be pointed out that there were innumerable opportunities for Mike and Johnny to take shots of sheep if they wanted
to do so without permission, if they had felt it was legitimate.
Sheep were everywhere, grazing freely all over the landscape.
There were so many sheep around the schoolhouse that we, half
jokingly and half seriously, put a sign on the dormitory door,
"No sheep allowed in editing room." Despite that, we would
often come in and find the students working at their tables while
one or two sheep from a flock outside were standing near them
watching. Nevertheless, Mike and Johnny chose to borrow from
Susie rather than photograph some sheep themselves. These
sheep shots were the only cademes borrowed by the students.
Apart from those, they used their own footage.

Along these lines it should also be noted that while "we"
photograph almost "anywhere" geographically, these Navajo restricted themselves to the bounds of Pine Springs. In fact, only
one of the Navajo students, Mike Anderson, even suggested mak-

ing his film away from Pine Springs. He at first thought he would make a film at Jeddito (about a hundred miles to the northeast) where his brother was living, but soon decided that he would be more comfortable closer to his own community. He did make one trip to Jeddito, but when he returned he said it had not gone well. "Nobody there knew about film. They don't know what I'm doing here."

In contrast the Negro teenagers with whom Worth worked in a similar manner in Philadelphia showed an opposite tendency. They refused to photograph their own block—their turf—and made their film on other blocks, on university grounds, or on public spaces like museums. Chalfen, on the other hand, who has since the Navajo project worked with five or six other black teenage groups in the Philadelphia area, reports that they tend to feel very comfortable on the "turf" established by the project sponsor. For example, if working with a settlement group, the youngsters will first photograph the settlement house and its activities. If in a neighborhood club, they will gravitate toward the playground or the empty lot in which they usually play ball.

Chapter

12

"They Handle the Equipment Like Pros"

Not only were there differences between our way and the Navajos' in the act of filming and of learning, and the choice of subjects and actors in the films, but there were also differences in their handling of the physical equipment, materials, and processes involved in filmmaking. We found what seemed to be a remarkable difference in the way they actually worked with machines such as splicers, rewinds and viewers. They worked so much faster than we did and with such certainty about what they were doing that we often thought that they were cutting film apart and joining pieces at random. For those who have never worked with film, a short description of a filmmaker's editing routine might help to make clear the distinctions we are discussing.

When the rushes (the film as it comes from the processing laboratory) arrive, the filmmaker normally views them in projection on a large screen at the proper speed at least three or four times. He tries to note which cademes he likes, which cademes are unusable (out of focus, overexposed, or spoiled in some way), and which cademes might have some special quality.

He then looks at the film on a table viewer where he can slow or speed the film through easily. He may make notes of what cademes are on each roll or about how he intends to use each cademe. He may cut out the bad shots that he noted during projection.

After all his cademe footage is assembled—after the entire film is shot—he cuts up the film cademe by cademe and puts together a "rough cut," a string of cademes in rough sequential order. He doesn't worry about exact length of edeme, or about the exact place he will cut. He will often have two or three edemes of the same thing, because he isn't sure which one to use, or which one will go best with other edemes in a final sequence. Like the painter who tries to cover his canvas so as to get a feel for the whole thing at the start, the filmmaker makes his rough cut to see how the film might look if it were all on one reel. He knows that he will make many changes later. He deliberately does not try to decide the exact point of a cut, but leaves extra film on each edeme so it can be cut off later.

When his entire film is assembled in rough cut—at this point it is often twice as long as it will be in a finished version—he begins pruning the almost final edemes. Cademes or pieces of cademe are discarded, and he begins working to find the exact points at which to join two pieces of film. Whether working on a Moviola or a simple viewer, he goes through a long process of running the film back and forth, back and forth, deciding on the exact frame in each cademe that will join with the next to form his final edeme.

An editing room presents a scene of intent decision making as the editor winds the film back and forth, over and over, deciding the precise frame of the cademe to cut on. A class of beginners working on their viewers and rewinds looks almost like a ballet, with arms turning one way and then the other in rhythmic movements. When the splice for the "fine cut" is finally made, the

editor usually will run it through several times to check it and
often redo it because he is dissatisfied with the result. For example, in a sequence showing a man walking, the cut between a long
shot and a close-up of the feet may not look smooth enough—the
movement of the leg may jump or hesitate if the foot in the long
shot is not exactly in the same place as on the close-up.

When the Navajo began editing, their pattern of activity was
quite different. They seemed to spend no time at all looking at
their rushes. One viewing on the projector seemed enough.
While observing Susie at the viewer, we felt as if she wasn't
looking at the image at all. She would wind the film through the
viewer and casually take her hands off the rewinds to take hold
of the film. When one lets go of the rewinds while it is turning,
it continues to turn, moving the film through the viewer. We
carefully stop the rewind—and the film in the viewer—at the
correct frame and mark the film with a grease pencil so that we
can cut at the right place. Susie would allow the film to continue
running slowly and would take hold of the strip as it came
through the viewer, lift it up, take her scissors, and cut the film
at some point apparently without looking—all in one smooth,
continuous, and uninterrupted motion.

We (the investigators) were certain that her behavior meant
that cutting on *approximately* the right frame was all that Susie
was interested in. We could think of no way to ask questions
about it and, at one point, Worth walked over as Susie used the
scissors, grabbed the ends of the film, and asked Susie to describe
the point at which she had cut. Susie calmly described the exact
frame. We did this several times, and each time Susie described
the frame—finally smiling as she did so, knowing that we were
playing a game at which she obviously excelled. At this point in
the project, Worth recorded in his notes that Chalfen seemed
anxious and competitive with the Navajo. He asked Chalfen what
was going on, and Chalfen replied, "How do you expect me to
feel? These guys seem to be editing better than I do."

If the students were not cutting at random, which at that point seemed doubtful, they had what seemed to us a very remarkable ability to perceive and remember individual shots and single frames of image events.

Johnny also showed similar behavior. At one point he asked Mike, who had the editing table on the other side of his cubby, if he could borrow it for an afternoon while Mike was away shooting. Johnny then set up dual editing tables for working on one film. He would take one reel of film on one table and another on the opposite table, jumping from one side of the small space to the other, cutting film, taking pieces from one reel to the other at a speed which again made it seem almost random. Worth tried the same game with Johnny. He grabbed a piece of cut film from one table and then another, asking Johnny to describe the exact frame he had cut. Johhny could do it but secmed annoyed at having to stop his work. Our impression was that he was annoyed because we were slowing down his thinking process.

It is not, in our opinion, that their perception of individual frames was better, but rather that their ability to perceive a single "frame" in a motion sequence and to *remember* it for both short and long periods was better than ours. Although we were not prepared at the time to do more extended research in this area, it is interesting to speculate on what was happening. Was their ability due to a specialized coding procedure for dealing with events in motion, or was it due to a highly developed memory? Asked about it, Johnny Nelson explained, "It's because we always have to have the design in our heads." Both Susie and Johnny, early in our interviews, expressed several times the notion that making a film was "like weaving," or "like the way the Navajo do things."

This concept, "we have the design in our head," was expressed in many ways at various stages of the project. There seemed both a need to conceptualize filmmaking in some way which legitimized such thinking, and an ability to think about, to plan, the sequencing of specific images. We felt that for Johnny at least the need to understand how images were manipulated "in the head" had to come before he could be entirely comfortable about doing it with his hands on pieces of film. In the second interview with Johnny, which took place on the day after instruction started, Worth asked him, "Which [part of the previous day's instruction] is the most fun so far?"

> JOHNNY: The most fun I have, let's see, were handling the camera —and having instruction on picture taking—like making films where you have to use your head to make a picture the way you want it to, or make it the way you feel it should be.

Later in that interview Johnny seemed to be struggling to ask about something.

> About that picture there [a possible movie that Johnny was talking about] where . . . you cut out that little pieces from another film and putting it together and making it more of a—something that's real. You know, something that is real and it's—very hard for me to explain.
>
> WORTH: Just exactly what do you want to know? I'm not sure I understand it. What is your question? What do you want to know?
>
> JOHNNY: Well, the question is, if you put like a picture, if I wanted to like take a picture of a bird flying and it'll be flapping its wings back and forth like that, then I take another picture of some more birds flying and I take a picture of a crow and put it in the midst of a bunch of birds flying, will that make it in the wrong place there—that's what I'm trying to get in.

Worth kept trying to avoid saying anything about any specific editing rules and tried to elicit more reasons from Johnny. Note how specific all the examples were. As we mentioned earlier, Navajos find generic questions on an abstract level almost impossible to use.

> WORTH: If you know in your head why you're photographing these birds, uh, let's say you give me a reason. What would be a reason

for photographing those birds and putting them together the way you said?

JOHNNY: I think he [the bird] would be expressing the uh nature, of how the birds migrate from one country to another in a flight, or something like that—and why the birds have to fly, what makes the birds fly.

WORTH: Would it matter if you put a picture of a crow in a movie like that?

JOHNNY: Well, the crows can fly, yes, but I think that a crow is—it makes them some sort of a—well, I'll say that if I was just to take a picture of the small birds flying, like how they fly and all of a sudden, I jump into a crow, they would now be out of—it's not actually out of a picture—the wrong picture—it's just that the birds—all of a sudden then there'll be this great big crow. People will watch the birds, how they fly and how they sit down on a branch or something, and all of a sudden, here comes a crow. . . .

WORTH: Can you think of a place where it will be good to have birds and a crow together?

JOHNNY: Well, I think there's only—the only good place to have crows and birds is in a corn patch, and—let's see, maybe some melon patches. These two places where crows and birds go together..

In this interview we see how quickly Johnny feels the need to understand, in his head—cognitively—how different images on film can be organized. He wants to know and is able to do it in his head even before he starts photographing or editing film. The editing follows a "natural" process which is worked out before he uses the materials. For many of our university students the ability to juggle concrete images in the head is difficult to learn. The ability to visualize specific images in a sequence usually takes many years of filmmaking experience and many people of our culture find it almost impossible to do on the order of complexity Johnny demonstrates in the above quotes.

As with many of our data, aspects of this portion of the interview illuminate sections of analysis discussed in other chapters.

Johnny is not only showing an unusual grasp of the syntactic as well as the semantic possibilities of film, but he is already showing the same sort of category formation for cademes and edemes that exist in his language. We referred earlier to Mike's reasons for placing the sheep after the hoofprints. Here Johnny is dividing his shots as entities linked to actions and is already expressing a set of rules for determining what images go together. Johnny puts images of crows and images of birds into separate categories of entities. Linking them by action, he finds that "the only good place to have crows and birds is in a corn patch."

So that early in the process—after only two days of instruction —Johnny (who was exceedingly skilled in verbalizing) was able not only to conceive and express the notion of organizing separate images and image events into a specific sequence, but also to begin articulating what must have been existing rules for such organization. He went on to develop his ideas in his film about horses.

The Navajo showed an immediate need and ability to organize symbolic events "in the head." They thought about concrete images, and were able to manipulate these symbols cognitively. They not only needed and were able to do it mentally—they did it physically as well. They handled the physical materials of film in the same organized, systematic and patterned way. We have already mentioned Johnny's ability to use two editing tables at once on the same film, putting together sequences from different parts of the film at the same time, using film units coming from widely spaced rolls of film. Susie demonstrated the same kind of physical organization while working on her film. Although she could never verbalize how she thought about visual symbolic events, the following observations will make clear the same need for pattern and a similar ability to juggle complex symbols in her head.

While observing Susie during the early weeks of July, we noted the development of a quite systematic way of working. First, she would cut up tiny strips of quarter-inch masking tape (which we had provided) into one by one-eighth inch strips, which she put on the edge of her editing board so that most of the tiny strip was hanging free. Then as she viewed the film and cut it with a scissors in the manner we have previously described, she would attach some pieces with the bits of tape to a reel of film lying beside her and hang other pieces on paper clips, which were attached to a string hanging over her table. (Worth had shown this method of hanging film from paper clips as he had shown his own students at the Annenberg School. Few college students used the clips, but Susie found good use for them.) As Worth watched, trying to see some pattern in which pieces of film went on the reel and which pieces went on the rack holding paper clips, he finally asked Susie, "Could you tell me your system of editing?" Normally he wouldn't have phrased a question in this way, using a word such as system, but at that moment he felt as if he were addressing a peer, who clearly was working in a systematic way. Susie explained to Worth that she was at that point in her work just before doing the actual splicing on the splicer. First, she organizes the shots she has taken in the following way. The shots that she is going to use go on the paper clips in the order in which they will appear in the film. Worth noticed at that point that the strips of film were hanging in bunches spaced an inch or more from other bunches. Each bunch was part of a separate sequence in the order in which the shots would appear. The film on the reel was film that she had decided not to use. When all the shots on a bunch were assembled—that is, when all the shots that she had to have for a sequence were on the clips in order—she would splice them.

It seemed to us consistently remarkable for anyone to be able to be so certain about which shots were in and which out with so little examination. Her lack of need for reassurance that she had chosen correctly and her lack of need for viewing more than once were certainly different from our experience with other filmmakers. Peraps when she said, "It's like making a design—it's all in the head before you start," she was talking about a perceptual and cognitive process very different from our own, which aided memory and recall and which allowed for the complex arrangements she had to make in her head. Perhaps as with musicians and mathematicians, there is an image or design sense which is highly developed in the Navajo and which allows them to handle the vast quantities of information involved in memorizing cademes shot and editing them in the head. It may also be the case that in the very act of shooting, the cademes are so organized that they "fall into place" as it were.

In writing this book and in doing the analysis of the filmed materials, we have often thought with envy about Susie's and Johnny's ability to manipulate masses of data, ordering it, and putting each piece into its correct place.

Chapter

13

Motion or Eventing

In applying the Whorfian concept to our research, we thought that the category of motion, which was so important to the Navajo language, would also be a good concept for us to use in analyzing the way the Navajo handled motion pictures. It seemed reasonable to assume that the Navajo would express an interest in film because of its very ability to depict motion.

The Navajo were indeed from the very first interested in the motion aspects of film and learned to manipulate it almost immediately and in a controlled fashion. Remember Maxine and her seesaw film, where the possibilities of rearranging the motion without destroying its flow occurred to her as the first thing she could do with film.

The Navajo also use movements which are quite rare in "our" kind of filmmaking and use motion in what seems to be a meaningful as opposed to a stylistic fashion.

Margot Astrov pointed out in 1950 that:

> The concept of motion in all its possible variations is the perennial current on which Navajo culture is carried along and from which

it receives its unfailing stimulus . . . the very language of the Navajo is one of actions, the idea of motion gives it its distinctive character.

The Navajo will always minutely differentiate whether the person in question was walking, speeding, slowing down. . . . The very structure of the language does not permit the Navajo to be sloppy in presenting some type of motion.

. . . the Navajo should consider 'gait' as tangible a part of a man as his nose. . . .

. . . creation with the Navajo is motion . . . in many curing ceremonies the idea of sanctification and restoration through ritually directed movement is paramount.

On motion life depends . . . in a psychologically significant rite of the Enemy Way, the ability to move is taken from the "enemy" by the patient who holds up against the imaginary foe a bundle consisting of back tendons and leg sinews cut from a previously slain enemy.

Most observers of the Navajo agree that motion pervades the Navajo universe; it permeates his mythology, his habit system, and his language. Harry Hoijer (1951) has written:

It would appear that Navajo verb categories center very largely about the reporting of events or better, "eventings." These eventings are divided into neuters, eventings solidified, as it were, in the states of being by virtue of the withdrawal of motion; and actives, eventings in motion. The latter are further subdivided into imperfectives, eventings in process of completion; perfectives, eventings completed; progressives, eventings moving along; and iteratives, eventings repeated over and over again. The customary reports eventings repeated by force of habit or custom; the optative, a desire that an eventing take place; and the future, the expectation that eventing will occur.

But this is not all. A careful analysis of the meanings of Navajo verb basis, neuter and active, reveals that eventings themselves are conceived, not abstractly for the most part, but concretely in terms of the movements of corporeal bodies. Movement itself is reported in painstaking detail, even to the extent of classifying as semantically different the movements of one, two, or several bodies, and sometimes distinguishing as well between movements of bodies differentiated by their shape and distribution in space.

But this high degree of specificity in reporting of movements is not confined in Navajo to verbs having particular reference to motion of one sort or another. On the contrary, it permeates the Navajo lexicon in the sense that many verbs, not at first sight expressive of movement, proved to be so on more detailed analysis. For example, the theme ha.h "one animate object moves (in an unspecified fashion)" is easily recognized in a large number of words, the meanings of which appear to be far distant from any concept of motion. The following examples are typical: oa. -na- . . . -ha. "be busy, 'preoccupied,' " literally "one moves continuously about with reference to it;" ʔe.h.- . . . -ha. "one dresses," literally "one moves into clothing;" hO- . . . ha.h "the ceremony begins," literally "a happening moves;" na- . . . ha "one lives," literally "one moves about here and there;" ʔani.-na- . . . ha "one is young," literally "one moves about newly;" "yisda- . . . ha.H "one is rescued, saved," literally "one moves to safety."

To summarize: in three broad speech patterns, illustrated by the conjugation of active verbs the reporting of actions and of events and the framing of substance of concepts, Navajo emphasizes movements and specifies the nature, direction, and status of such movement in considerable detail. Even the neuter category is relatable to the common conception of a universe in motion. For just as someone is reported to have described architecture as frozen music so the Navajo defined position as a resultant of the withdrawal of motion.

In the Navajo films themselves and in the way they talked about what they were going to do in their films, we can see many examples of this inordinate need both to portray motion precisely and to use it as a recurrent theme. On the second day of instruction Johnny was asked, "What did you shoot today?" He replied:

The other day [yesterday] I shot one shot only that you let us take. . . . I have the whole people [the group of students] standing there . . . and they were talking, they were laughing, so I just stood there

and I took a straight picture . . . today I had to—I thought I might
take something moving. The first one I took was with them standing still, so I won't be—but today, I just kind of figured if I move
the camera a little bit and see how it will come out.

Note how at this early date, Johnny blurts out "today I had to"
and then changes it to, "I thought I might take something moving." He continues:

So I had my little boy, he was riding a bicycle right there—I got
him, I had him on the bike right there [pointing out the window
behind the Trading Post] then he ride right around that little field
right there—got my camera and went all the way round like that
[holding a camera up to his eye and swiveling completely around
in his chair].

WORTH: Where'd you learn how to do that?

JOHNNY: Well, I just wanted, I wanted to take some pictures of
something moving, but you know I just wanted to get the feel of
moving the camera with something moving at the same time.

It is not only that at this stage of learning Johnny expressed
interest in the complex relationship of moving the camera while
an object is moving, but also that he was able to execute these
movements so clearly and smoothly. This first shot showed none
of the shaking or unevenness of movement which is so difficult
to avoid in a hand-held camera. Not only did Johnny, Susie, and
Al Clah show the same ability; all of them combined in very
intricate patterns the various forms of motion. They played constantly with the speed of the object moving and the speed of the
camera movement, sometimes going in the same direction and
often going in opposite directions.

The jump cut for us is an interruption of movement, of the
causal consequences of an action; but motion for them was in
some way differentiated from action in a causal or semantic sense.
That is, a man sitting and a man walking were not parts of the
same motion, whereas a seesaw or camera movement were.

It is a very difficult thing for "us" to remember the kind and speed of camera movement from one shot to another. One of the most difficult editing tasks is to cut on camera movement. One of the prescriptions for standard Hollywood editing is never to cut two pans together. Let us imagine a sequence in which we were to juxtapose two movements of the camera—let us say a pan across a wall in which the camera moves from left to right across one wall and then a shot moving from left to right across another wall. Further, the shot of wall A would be made several hours or even days later, all to be done with a hand-held camera. Worth reports, "No filmmaker I know would be able to handle that sequence easily. Getting the same flow in each shot—the same kind of motion—so it could match is almost impossible to keep in my head. I suppose I'd make fifteen or twenty shots of each, varying the motion of the camera, and hope I'd be able to pick out the best match of motion in editing. But even in editing it would be very difficult for me to see or feel the same motion."

The films made by the Navajo are full of sequences cut on this type of motion, with the students often commenting on how nice [*nijuneh*] it looked.

In Al Clah's film, the movements of the camera are so complex that Worth comments in his notes, "I wish that guy would stop waving the camera around so much. I get dizzy watching." Yet in the finished film, the motion of the images (one doesn't see it as the camera) have an almost inexorable quality.

When Al was talking about his film with Worth during one of the interviews, he attempted to explain his intense dissatisfaction with his state of progress. He was concerned that he was showing only pieces of image and that an audience wouldn't understand his film. In particular he was concerned about how he could explain or make convincing the motivation for the entire film if he couldn't use Johnny as his actor in the sequence in which Johnny disturbs the spider web. (We mentioned earlier that when Johnny saw the cademe close-up of his face, he refused to continue as actor.)

AL: Well the fact how these things happen [without showing Johnny's face] the film is dead, it just don't make sense. If I see him in
there, then I know what the film is about. If he's doing all these
things you know, walking through these trees, making motion
. . . I was looking all through these, you know, little pieces [of film]
trying to put something in there. I got to have an intruder that
pokes in these things, that points out to the audience—This, *this
is the real motion.* . . . [emphasis in speaking]

In looking at the films and at the students' raw footage, we can
better understand the use of walking in the context of their
extreme awareness of motion. An image of a person or a camera
or a shadow in motion provides a means of depicting a certain
form of "eventing" (Hoijer's term). The searching and finding of
the mine, the silver, the herbs for curing, the plants for dying the
wool, the rock for casting are all examples of eventing that must
be accompanied by motion to give them their proper place in the
scheme of things.

We have compared the footage as originally shot with the films
as completed by the Navajo students. For example, in the films
Navajo Silversmith and *Navajo Weaver* analyzed so far, we find that
their makers have included almost all the scenes depicting their
subjects walking and have used less than half of the many
cademes that they had depicting the actual fabrication of the
jewelry and rug.

During the second week of July, Adair interviewed Johnny
about his life history. During the course of the conversation,
Johnny started talking about why films are so interesting to
Navajos. He said,

You make a movie about it and then it's moving around where you
can actually see what is being done *how it moves* [our italics]. See,
in a letter you can read it over and over, but you can't express
exactly what, how the shallow well was, unless you want to write
a whole book about it. But . . . if you write a whole book about it,
then it's still. You try to give it to somebody, and he reads it
through, and he does not really get the picture in his mind. You
cannot express just exactly how a shallow well was erected.

At another point Johnny said, "What I really want to see is something that can move in front of my eyes, that I took myself."

The Long Journey and the Origin Myth

In previous sections of this book we have noted how important a place sequences of walking have in the films made by the Navajo. In this connection it is important also to note that in Navajo myths, tales, and in the narrative style itself, the "long journey" is often the central theme for the origin myths.

It has frequently been noted that Navajo myths tell of the culture hero who "travels freely among the gods collecting ritual information as he goes." From this series of supernatural contacts the hero's own fund of power is collected and increased. The structure and narrative style of the films, *Navajo Silversmith*, *Antelope Lake*, *Intrepid Shadows*, and *Navajo Weaver* resemble one of the chantway myths. Johnny Nelson, for example, shows the craftsman at work but has his craftsman set out on a journey for an ancient silver mine. The fact that silver was never mined on the reservation is inconsequential; the origin of silver and the travel to the origin, like the origin of the horse (depicted in the origin myth as emerging with man), must be accounted for in the Navajo universe and is depicted in his film.

It is also worth noting that in the sequence of the growth of the piñon tree, shown in stages from seedling to the mature and then dead tree and then turning back to the pine cone, we find the same basic structure as in several of the other films. Each comes back to the images from which it started, but not exactly to the same scene. This going back to the beginning, to where the action started, is basic to Navajo cognition and is manifested in their mythology and their ritual and visual arts.

There is almost a compulsion in the Navajo to get back to the start, to swing full circle to the beginning. There is need for closure, but closure must not be complete. Thus we find many of the sand paintings enclosed on three sides by rainbow but open on the east, just as the hogan has its door always to the east (the direction from which good and beauty come), and the zig-zag circular pattern on the wedding basket is broken through to prevent complete closure. When a woman comes into the hogan during a ceremony, she must walk clear around the fireplace, "sunwise," as the Navajo say, before she sits on the north side of the enclosure. Another example of the films' adhering to this basic form occurs when Mike Anderson started shooting his *Antelope Lake.*

As they approached the lake, Worth asked where to park the car. Mike chose a place on the shore in the center of the lake, but then proceeded to walk slowly toward one end. They finally came to a very unpretty part of the landscape, muddy and over-grown with weeds and trees. Mike started photographing there and moved around the shore line from east to west. Since he made many trips to the lake, Worth began to notice that he always started shooting at that point of the lake where he had finished the day before. When he had completely circled the lake sunwise and returned to the muddy spot he had started with, he announced that he was finished photographing. Worth asked him what "this spot is here" (the point where filming started and stopped), and Mike replied, "This is the part where the lake begins, where the water starts—it is the head." Worth then asked him, "Why did you walk all around the lake photographing instead of shooting the interesting places first?" Mike replied, "[That] is how to show something the best, by going around it —you show anything by going around it."

His answer is very similar to Johnny's response to Adair when asked, "Why did you have a silver mine when the Navajo never mined silver?" Johnny replied, "That's the way to tell the story."

As in the myths, power accruing from motion and especially from travel is not only a feature that may be depicted in a film, but may also explain the behavior of the filmmaker. Perhaps following his actor in his search for the mine or for herbs, for roots, for stone or for the source of the wheel that turned gave him a sense of assurance in an unfamiliar situation—certainly this is characteristic of Navajo psychology: if you are uncertain of yourself in a particular situation, don't remain still—travel.

Most of the films and the students' discussions of the films reflect what might be called a Navajo worldview—in Whorf's words, a distinctive way not only of looking and organizing the world but a distinctive way of *not* organizing the world. That is to say, not only does the Whorf–Sapir hypothesis suggest that a particular culture will find it easy to use a particular form of categorizing and organization, but it suggests also that certain other ways of structuring reality are more difficult and that certain languages and cultures make certain styles of "saying" less likely to occur.

For example, all but one of the films are without what we would call narrative suspense. The purpose of the film is not to show a suspenseful story leading to an ending which will present a solution or satisfy in some way, but rather to show a journey, a motion describing an event.

In the film on weaving we are immediately shown the weaver making her rug. We then go on to the long journey of gathering roots for dye, caring for the sheep, cutting, carding, spinning, boiling, and so on which is the event of weaving. We then come back at the end to the finished rug—not the same edeme, however, but a similar one. The circle is almost closed.

The silversmith film has an identical structure. The very title shows us the silversmith at work on the finished piece of silver. The first shots show the completed end. Then we go on to the same long journey. Finding the mine, mining the silver, walking endlessly to gather materials. At the end we see a similar shot of the silversmith and the finished jewelry.

There is very little feeling of "how it will turn out." We are told that immediately. Suspense of ending is not the point. The process of becoming, of eventing, of moving toward completion, is what we are made to feel is important; not *what* will happen, but how it happens.

Chapter

14

Intrepid Shadows
and the Outsider

The films made by the Navajo are similar except for one. All the others are direct depictions of eventings. They are specific and somewhat didactic in tone. There is little direct generalization or deliberate "symbolism" as in our university student films. All the other films show "the way it looks"; they are about outer rather than inner processes and things. They are objective rather than personal; we would classify them as documentary. The films obviously objectify the Navajo world according to the Navajo way of structuring things, but they are structuring outer rather than inner or personal events. That is in line with the Navajo language and customs, which do not even have words for generic subjects such as color. One must ask in Navajo, "Is it blue?" not "What color is it?" There is no way of saying, "what 'generalization' is something?"

The exception is Al Clah's film, *Intrepid Shadows*. There was a marked difference on almost all levels of observation between Al and the other Navajos. His way of working, his notion of what he wanted to make a film about, and his behavior while working seemed much more comparable to the students at the Annenberg School than to the Navajo. Al was extremely introspective, hostile, and competitive; he could easily, simplistically, and quite uselessly be characterized as "neurotic," a "middle-class art school type of kid." None of these qualities showed up in the other Navajo.

Yet Al's film is also intensely Navajo in content and manner, particularly his use of motion as a form to convey meaning, his intense involvement and ability to portray a feeling of animism, and his identification with his natural environment rather than his personal one.

A description of Al's film as he finally photographed and edited it appears in the appendix to this book. It might be fruitful to follow its development as Al described it in his interviews. We will insert our comments relating his ideas to the relevant aspects of Navajo culture.

First it should be remembered that Al Clah was a stranger to the community. We chose him and brought him to Pine Springs. He lived with us in the dormitory. He had no kinsman there and was never invited by any person in Pine Springs to any of the hogans. He stuck close to us and the other students during the whole two months. When we left for a weekend, Al usually left Pine Springs, too. Indeed he was not only lonely but said so, and was rejected and resented by the community.

At one point, in what seemed to us an effort to make friends with Mike and Johnny, he participated in a hostile incident at the Trading Post. In discussing the incident with the trader and his wife as well as with other Navajos in the community, the blame was invariably focused on Al, although Mike and Johnny were as deeply involved. As the trader described it,

> Al is the instigator of the whole thing—I feel sure. I looked out and saw Clah and Mike outside. I asked Al to come in and as soon

as I had him in the office, I grabbed his shirt. I didn't hit him—
I wanted to hit him so bad—but I didn't. Ever since he opened his
mouth around here that first day—I wanted to hit him. . . . I know
he is a trouble maker.

As Al tells the story, he treated the trader as a friend but
realized that "like the others, he doesn't want me around."

Al's very title and the discussion of the intrepid or fearless
shadow reflects one of Al's earliest needs to express his lack of
fear in his new situation. He then developed the theme of the
intruder, which at first was a vaguely formulated symbolic event
in no way connected with himself, but rather with the shadows
and the rolling wheel which were the first things he shot.

CLAH: The most important thing is the wheel I have over there.
. . . I let it go, it spins like that [circular motions of his hand].
. . . See the picture's triangle and a third of that piece, that metal
things here [top third]. . . and the rest of this be a shadow—
spinning—it was going that fast—you know—it was a very, very,
very great trans-transform-transformation. That was the first shot
I make.

WORTH: And you shot all of the hundred feet on that?

CLAH: Yeah.

Worth then asked what else was in the film, and Al mentioned
"those rocks," and "a spider web," and "somebody got to see that
wheel moving all the time like that." Worth asked how long it
would take to shoot.

CLAH: It all depends, how I find it—'cause I need certain days—the
shadows have to be—and it depends on how bright it gets, and
how long the shadows. That's important how long the shadows
get. . . . I'm going to try to find me a nice area where there's rocks
. . . what I've seen I like is about a shadow. I need a bright sun like
—a shadow can go through it—a silhouette. Person going to be like
that.

This was the first mention of a person in the film and Worth encouraged Al to go on.

CLAH: I'm going to think about the film because what I seen through the lens or reviewer [viewer] has sort of come out the way I want it. Not just everything move, just some things moving. Maybe the person—the part of the person *in the way* [our italics] that is abstract way of moving—but you can see the person, but I don't want to see the. . . . [At this point, Al gestures vaguely toward the upper part of his body.]

On the twentieth of June, Worth asked Al, "I'd like you to tell me about the shadows called intrepid shadows that I heard in the poem. What's the film going to be, what's the beginning?"

CLAH: It's going to open with Johnny's walking and all that carries down to where we see the tree with the web . . . and, uh, Johnny's still investigating [in the film] the whole idea's round this shadows —which comes first. This will be a very solemn first. Then he hears a snap, he stops—then he starts walking. . . . Remember he heard something—he heard something. He plays with the spider web—pokes a stick in it—then bang—we sees the wheel coming in—he looks up.

WORTH: Did you deliberately shoot that shot with the head in it looking up like that?

CLAH: Yeah.

WORTH: You did?

CLAH: I told him. . . . We stop there and we had a little discussion and I taught him how . . . then he's going to be standing there and uh really surprised faces, then he goes like that [Al snaps his head from side to side with quick jerky movements] . . . after he play with that web that's when he starts running. Try to see what it is. He's going to come right through the trees as he runs. He runs behind the tree—afterwards from another shot, I'm going to find a tree which is very close together and all of a sudden there's a tree like that he's going to come like that and I'm going to take some of his shadow, his foot walking . . . then I take the wheel again and the shadow . . .

He continued to describe motions and specific arrangements until Worth said, "I'm beginning to understand it now. This is a man or a boy, a man out in the world, and there are things that catch his eye—after he plays with a spider web—and then he investigates?"

CLAH: Uh-huh—He's a, he's a intruder see, that's why I call them intrepid shadows.

WORTH: Tell me more about that.

CLAH: The intruder is like Johnny.

WORTH: What does an intruder mean—What does it mean in the film?

CLAH: See he's out there in the world right there observing things. There's nobody been there.

WORTH: Nobody been in the world?

CLAH: Right there in the film—nobody been there. This other person is very—the person that push the wheel he's unknown . . . because I won't show his face—and more mysterious things happen and Johnny's going to investigate—I show his face—then the rain comes in. He finds everything happen. The wheel is mysterious to him . . . his face—there's going to be rain on his face getting wet—the wheel gets wet too. . . . Then he sort of wonders. Then he hears something else, a lot of things. It's sort of complicated, but I—that's the way my mind—I can't, I can't push it —push it out. [Al motions toward his mouth.]

WORTH: I'm interested in this intruder. What is he intruding into. Is he intruding—

CLAH: Into these mysterious—mysterious things happen . . . he uh, he intrudes the spider web. Then something happen because he was there.

WORTH: Is that the shot where he poked the stick?

CLAH: Yeah—into the spider web, he was intruding the spider.

WORTH: And then something happens?

CLAH: Yeah.

WORTH: In the film the next shot is the spinning wheel?

CLAH: Uh-huh.

WORTH: And what does that mean?

CLAH: Well, I, sort of, put it one way. See I need the spider first, in there sometime because it's sort of the spider bewitch him.

In Navajo mythology, the Spider Lady is one of the creators of the world, weaving and holding it together. It is very dangrous to interfere with her function as it might destroy the delicate balances holding the world together. As described by Washington Matthews, Father Haile and others, the Navajo conceive of themselves as in a particular relationship with their environment. Navajo man lives in a universe of eternal and unchanging forces which he attempts to maintain in equilibrium (even to the extent of needing three girls as film students if there are already three boys). There is a constant balancing of powers. The mere fact of living is, however, likely to disturb this balance (which Al will mention later) and throw the world out of gear. The shadow mentioned in the title is also symbolic of the Navajo concepts of soul, that "which is lying in," as they say. The soul can be killed only by the sun, and so we find in this film a play between man and nature and a balance between the two. At the beginning, the sun is strong and the shadows short and weak, and man too is fallible when he interferes with nature.

An intruder, Johnny Nelson in the film, happens on a spider web, and while playing with it destroys it. Poking the web again sets the stage for the intruder's "long journey."

Immediately after Johnny pokes a stick into the spider web, a rolling hoop (an old tire rim) is seen moving mysteriously across the landscape. The intruder looks around but finds no explanation. The hoop seen intermittently rolling through the landscape may be best interpreted in the light of the following quotation:

Closed circles made of meal or pollen or perhaps merely described on the ground, hoops and rings are frequently encountered in ritual. They represent a space so narrowed down that it is under control, an area from which evil has been driven and within which power has been concentrated. (Reichard 1950)

It is the mysterious power which so frightens the intruder. He must find it and become united with it so that balance in the universe may be restored.

WORTH: The spider bewitched him?

CLAH: Almost, yeah, something like that. Then he's out of his mind for a while. . . . All of a sudden there's these mysterious rims—metal setting out of nowhere. . . . I like some kind of motion—some kind of mysterious thing happen.

WORTH: The mysterious thing is like being bewitched?

CLAH: Uh-huh.

WORTH: And the intruder—?

CLAH: Should not have touched the spider web. At the end where the rain is on his face after—I want the rain there then he thinks about it—and I shoot this other part where he was touching the web. I can take it [the shot] back to where the rain is [the end of the film]. Then that will tell that he is thinking about that [touching the web]. That's the reason why it [the rest of the film] happen. . . . It's sort of dark, and water running in his face, and he think back "What did I done. Oh yes, spider in the spider web, that probably what happen." I going to make a shot of him touching it, touching it, you know, just touching it—then a shot of his face looking at it and touching it again. . . . Slowly going into the spider web. Maybe you know, see a spider web and all of sudden his mind fill with those wheels spinning, just those wheels spinning. . . . Then he; still faced with that—he's still faced with it.

WORTH: What made you want to make a film about an intruder?

CLAH: . . . The film [without an intruder] is dead—just doesn't make sense. If I see him in there then I know what the film is about. *I like somebody that pokes in these things* [our italics]. They point out to the audiences . . . I got somebody on *there* to tell me, that's it.

Worth couldn't understand what "there" referred to, but Al soon cleared it up.

CLAH: In other words, the little people on there says, you know, to do it.

WORTH: The little people, you're making a motion as if there are little people on your shoulder, is that it?

CLAH: Yeah; "What are you doing?" one of them asked me. Said I'm trying to make them intrepid. . . . Then one of them said I should have somebody in there to point. So you have to choose one of your own men—one your own people! So I chose Johnny.

WORTH: The little men on your shoulder told you—

CLAH: Yeah, yeah. Then he said, "go 'head." Now I'm telling you, he says. That's telling you, your own people, telling you to point out these things . . . 'cause I can't get in the film when I'm taking the pictures. . . . *This I felt was me on the inside and I have to choose somebody to be me in the film* [our italics]. That's why I tell them to act like I did.

WORTH: In other words, he's going to be you.

CLAH: Yeah!

WORTH: The intruder is you?

CLAH: Is me! That's me that's trying to put it up. This little man [on his shoulder] he says "it's personal—you have to show the other people to make them understand."

WORTH: When did you get the idea for the intruder?

CLAH: I had it in mind all the time—people ask me why you make this shots and you have to explain it. . . . I tried to make you understand it or John [Adair], but you really got confused. Then I have to do it in a way so you can understand.

WORTH: You had to do it [the film] this way to make us understand?

CLAH: Yeah, yes. But the whole thing was in here, in my head. Then I have to put it in another element—Johnny Nelson. . . . It was so personal at first . . . then I lay down during the night to think about it. . . . Then I found the solution in Johnny—said, yeah, this is what I'm going to do. I'm going to do it my action.

WORTH: You felt we wouldn't understand just from seeing the shots you made that it was really you and you were making a film about how it feels to be an intruder.

CLAH: Yeah. I was going to make you an intruder.

WORTH: You were going to make *me* an intruder?

CLAH: The audience, and you, to feel this and you—but I thought it was too complicated so I just have to get Johnny. . . . I was going to do it this way; there'll be no actor except you will be the actor yourself. The audience can feel, see if they can feel it—this didn't happen. They going to get the wrong idea. But now with the actor, they can get, they can make themself Johnny. Now they can do it. . . . I have to make people feel Johnny in the film 'cause I seen with my painting they really understand sometime. Sometime they don't. . . . I want people to understand. I like people to understand. . . . I only got, how can I put it, the center of the film, it's not there yet. I got to get it. The center . . . that the guy really intrudes and he gets that reaction from nature because he was there to intrude.

Later Al informed us that one time he was going to be an engineer, that in an aptitude test at school he was told he could be an engineer, and so he thought that was the thing to do. But as he started drawing, he decided he was meant to be an artist.

WORTH: Who do you think, Al, is more of an intruder, an engineer or an artist?

CLAH: An artist.

WORTH: Why?

CLAH: Well, engineer he just repeat things over and over, buildings and mechanics. But artist—his mind's working. He wants to see things, he doesn't have to touch it, he have to do it with spirit, recapture the image on his pad. There he touch the world, like I touch, like I make a portrait of you—there touched a man's face, I can't say it, I can't describe it, I can't touch it. This is the face [pointing to a pad]. If I want to make a drawing of this [pointing to Worth's face] sure I touch it.

WORTH: . . . that's what Johnny does with the spider web.

CLAH: Yeah!

WORTH: He touches it.

CLAH: Examines it closely. . . . This [his film] is a self-portrait, yeah.

> There you can begin to understand the self-portrait of the artist.
> He portrays himself with a new, with a new theme he's learning
> —like I'm learning this film. . . . It's going to be just *one motion*—
> my portrait, my life, my feeling. This is my feeling."

This is perhaps the sharpest and clearest expression of the
notion of motion in Navajo thinking. A self-portrait is "just one
motion" in which to portray a new theme a man is learning. Not
only is the value of learning and education tied to motion, it is
an integral part of it. The film depicts the motion of learning "my
portrait, my life, my feeling." For Al and perhaps for the others
their films are not so much explanations of events as depictions
of a process of learning these events.

When Mike tells us that he has to photograph the lake by
walking around it sunwise, he too is sharing the idea that the
process of filming is part of the film. He doesn't divorce his own
actions from the events on the film just as Al doesn't separate the
motion of movie images from the motion of his life.

> WORTH: You mean in the film, you can make a portrait of your
> feelings.
> CLAH: Uh-huh. Things happen. This is the artist's mind sometime.
> . . . But if I want to try to self-portrait myself all the way through,
> deep, it would take another thousand, thousand, thousand feet of
> film. This is one way I feel sometime. Being an intruder.
> WORTH: Even in art.
> CLAH: Everywhere. . . .

At this point Al begins to talk about the newest element in his
film—after Johnny had refused to continue acting in the film and
a substitute had to be found. Al refused to remove the shots of
Johnny, but now he couldn't have an actor portray himself. As
he developed within himself his knowledge of who the intruder
really was, he decided to substitute a hand-painted mask of a
Yeibechai god, which he cut out of corrugated cardboard. It was

a free version of the standard ritual Yeibechai mask, with an important variation—the eyes were made in three dimensions, controlled by strings and pieces of wood from the back so that they could be manipulated to swing to and fro in the manner he had originally described as Johnny "looking for the wheel." As soon as Johnny looks up, the wheel appears; we see it rolling and then a Yeibechai mask appears looking in all directions for the cause of the disturbance. Johnny has been replaced by the Yeibechai.

During the course of the film, the intruder gains power by contact with the Yeibechai in his wanderings. At the end of the film Al himself is *intrepid*—to match his shadow (which has also joined the search), and the sun is weak.

Al continues talking about the place of the Yeibechai mask.

> I'm not supposed to paint Yeibechai faces. Sometimes I make the mask, people feel very strong about it. My teacher he says, it's very strong, just a little bit that's all. There I intrude the mask. The sacred mask. People can't understand—this mask is sacred, very ritual. They ask me, "How come you do this? You shouldn't do this—you shouldn't even touch these things." So there I thought about why did I do it. I am an intruder. I find myself the intruder everywhere—well, I want to intrude in myself too. I want to find out more about myself, see what happen—see what happen to me.

In Al's cardboard Yeibechai mask, it is interesting to note the two lines running from the nose upward (photo 52). Such lines never appear in ceremonial Yeibechai masks and these look so much like a drawing of a piece of movie film that one is forced to speculate that Al unconsciously merged the magic of the movie with the magic of the Navajo god represented in the mask, the god who replaced Al himself, and who searches the world to see what happens when the intruder pokes a stick into the web. Here again Al expressed his feeling that the film is one motion of his life.

Al recognized that his film was different from those of the

other students. In many ways he was making the film for fellow artists, for those who could understand, but he wanted to achieve communication. It was important that he be understood. At one point he said,

> I still believe in my Indian ways . . . the other students they making films of the daily lives of the people, but I went beyond, a little beyond that . . . they making films about things out there, the Trading Post, things you can see, I'm making films about inside. I like to see scenes that people never expected, the legends, the gods. I definitely believe in ancient lore, those things which never exists before. Sooner or later you get out of it. I was a Catholic faith and all of a sudden, never went to church no more. I found out the gods never existed, that the church, that the church are just church. . . . The gods aren't really exist because if you, if really exist he could have really went and found that wheel. I mean the wheel was there.

He continued to explain, with much going back over things, that the mask was the Navajo's gods but it was also the intruder and also represented the Christian gods. When the intruder un-balanced the world and the wheel started spinning, everyone tried to find out what happened. If the gods really were gods— if the movies were really motion—they could have found the wheel and stopped its spinning, and all would have been well. Instead it was Al himself, with a camera at his eye—or rather his shadow—growing longer and longer—who searched and searched for knowledge and finally merged with the shadow of the wheel. None of the gods, white or Navajo, could become intrepid shadows, only Al could, because he was on a long jour-ney for knowledge about himself and because he could make the wheel stop. He says the film is "a feeling self-portrait of an artist based on a little bit, part of the legends, the ancient gods and of nature."

> —I found out that I have only one way I can express my self-portrait is through nature and the ancient gods. Because I feel that

way that's why I say that I don't believe in gods. I believe in gods to express by self-por— to self— what's another word? Maybe I can put it this way. *That's* [a film] *the only way that the gods can get me out in the open and they imitate me instead* [our italics]. . . . That was me, that's where my mind was, my body and soul. Also I wore, I wear the white shirt and pants in the film, that's my spirit.

WORTH: The film is your spirit?

CLAH: Uh-huh. That's why I hate to show this to my parents—the ancient gods is taboo—to use gods to take the place of yourself.

In a still later interview, when the film was almost completed, Worth asked Al, "What do you want people to feel after they've seen *Intrepid Shadows?*"

CLAH: In the beginning everything is black, black . . . you know, very good contrast.

WORTH: What kind of emotion is that?

CLAH: I want them to feel their muscles tense. That's the word tense, I guess.

WORTH: Can you think of more words you want them to feel?

CLAH: I want them to feel their emotion . . . very grotick and tense.

WORTH: Growtick?

CLAH: Grotesque?

WORTH: Grotesque?

CLAH: Yes, grotesque, tense—undecided—they feel alone—a this and a that . . . and at the end of the film relaxed. . . . The wheel supposed to be sort of in between grotesque and tense and at the end calm. . . . I'm not sure that would express it 'cause the language . . . the Navajo language is very hard.

WORTH: Could you say it in Navajo?

CLAH: No. In grotesque everything is sort of twisted. And tense is just you get sort of free for a while and see what's happened and the wheel is running and I want to feel the calm again between. The eyes moving and calmness, flowing, walking, just walk, and the mask comes in, goes down that way—nice flowing. And all of a sudden, he stops and just something happens. . . .

WORTH: Is the film still about an intruder and fearless shadows?

CLAH: I was stuck on that yesterday. I was looking at it the intruder, shadows, what's a shadow what's that—an intruder? Who's an intruder? It's a different story now—I'd like to change the title but don't know how. . . . I was going to make it into a dream. . . . The dream, my true image . . . still, just a mask don't portray my image. . . . My—the way I experience things.

WORTH: The mask is you, too.

CLAH: Is me, yes . . . the gods have mingled with people, which is a very paranoid expression, but that's the way the story goes.

WORTH: It's a what kind of expression?

CLAH: Paranoid, it's the gods they never, there's no gods that ever existed.

WORTH: Do you mean paranoid or paradoxical?

CLAH: Paranoid.

WORTH: Paranoid means—?

CLAH: Is when I would say I'm Michelangelo. That's paranoid. . . . I would sleep, and I would dream—I went to sleep, and the gods came looking for something because I didn't believe. Then the god told me if you don't believe go out and look. See if you can find these things. Although I don't believe these gods come at night . . . try to catch me.

WORTH: You sound as if you are talking about yourself.

CLAH: Yes.

WORTH: Are you really?

CLAH: Yes, as I said—but I always say that when I'm the mask no. It's this little, little two scales I'm standing on trying to balance —My real feeling for the right thing that the legend says and on myself I don't believe these legends. It's those little two scales I'm trying to balance.

Here Al finally manages to explain the film in almost perfect accord with one of the deepest Navajo values recorded in the literature. He explains his own need for maintaining equilibrium, a balancing of powers between himself and Michelangelo;

between Navajo god and Christian god, between himself and the old god, between himself and nature, between himself and film itself. He knows that the mere fact of living throws things out of balance, and he justifies his being an artist as a way of compromising or balancing the gods who tell him to undertake the long journey where he will "see what happen."

The "tense" section of his film occurred at the point that the intruder poked a stick into the spider web and the hoop started rolling. The "grotesque" section occurs during the constant movement of the camera as the Yeibechai is looking for the cause of the disturbance set up by the rolling hoop that was loosed by the intruder's poking into the spider web, and the "calm" comes when we see the hoop and its shadow merging into one entity.

The last shot of the film is unaccustomedly long and well planned. It is the longest shot in the film, and as Al explained before he shot it, "This part will be hard because the shadow must combine with the wheel and this might take a long time to happen." The shot opens with only the spinning shadow shown on the screen, slowly, almost lazily making its effortless (and for most audiences, calm) circles across the earth. Then almost imperceptibly the actual wheel hub comes into the frame, never interfering with the shadow but gradually becoming part of the same universe. At almost the moment that an audience is able to perceive this the film ends (photo 55).

The question may be asked: Was Al Clah consciously using traditional Navajo symbols or was the symbolism and narrative style in which it was expressed unconscious? Or is the resemblance between the abstract forms and Navajo ritual stylization purely fortuitous?

It must be remembered that Al Clah had spent seven years away attending the Indian Art School at Sante Fe and, although his home was nearby, he was a stranger to the Pine Springs community. The intruder is of course Al Clah. ("I can't be behind the camera and act in the film at the same time . . . so Johnny will be me.") As soon as Johnny, however, saw the rushes of the

footage Al had shot, in which Johnny not only was made to poke
a stick into a spider web but had his face shown in close-up, as
well, a tension developed between them; Johnny refused to act
in the film and became less friendly to Al.

At this point Al started making the Yeibechai mask out of
cardboard and it became the symbol of the long searches. Al had
originally intended to have the intruder (Johnny) search for "the
thing (the rolling hoop) that started when he poked into the
spider web."

Not only did the mask act out the long search, but Al finally
created a method by which he himself could become strong and
fearless, identify with the ancient gods, and be himself in the
film. He learned first to use the camera in such a way that he
could press the start button with the camera on a tripod, and then
appear in front of it. He arranged the camera to photograph his
white shirt and pants to "show his soul," as he put it. Later he
created a long sequence in which he held the camera up to his eye
in such a way that he could see through the viewing lens and that
the camera could be seen in the shadow he cast before him. He
then photographed his search for that portion of his world in
which the shadow he cast was sharpest, longest, and clearest. It
is a beautiful section in the film in which Al clearly achieved that
"flowing motion—first flow of motion" that he talked about in
his early interviews.

By the middle of June, Adair noted that a relationship had
developed between Sol Worth and Al Clah that was quite different from what we had originally anticipated. Al as an experienced artist was not acting as an intermediary between
Worth and the students. Originally we had chosen Al because we
felt that he would be most likely able to learn filmmaking. We
were still uncertain at the time that Al was included in the
project that any of the other Navajo would be willing and able
to make a film depicting their world as they saw it. Not only did

we feel that Al would be easier to teach, but we thought from previous research that a two-step flow from white innovator to more acculturated Navajo and then to less acculturated would be necessary. That method was used effectively with Susie and her mother, but the facility of the five students from Pine Springs in learning the technology of filmmaking made Al's anticipated role superfluous. Al was forced to take his place in the classroom alongside the others as an equal and was taught as if his needs were the same as the other members of the class. But Al's needs were different on many levels. First, he lived with us, and not with the Navajo in a hogan of his own, with his own kin. Second, he was used to learning new media in a place where every effort was made to explain rules and develop abstract ideas. Worth refused to say what was *good* and hardly mentioned the word *art* to the Navajo. Al knew that film was an art form and was very frustrated because he couldn't talk about art in class—no one really understood it—and Worth wouldn't discuss it. Yet Al knew that Worth had been an artist, had spent many years as a painter and sculptor and had made films that had won prizes and were in museum collections.

Al began to rebel, showing off, becoming aggressive, acting superior, and in general behaving in ways that accentuated his alienation from the Navajo and began to affect the research as well.

Adair called this situation to Worth's attention, suggesting that something be done. Worth realized that Al's talents and background demanded special teaching. The other students allowed Worth to maintain his professor–student role with them, Al insisted that they were equals—both fellow artists. Since this was a difficult role for Worth to maintain while attempting to be a neutral teacher as well as a researcher, he originally responded to Al with some hostility.

When Worth realized that his behavior was supporting Al's alienation from the community by keeping him frustrated, he decided to spend extra private time with him. It worked out well.

Worth would sit down or go for a walk with Al, allowing and even encouraging him to talk about art, his film, and any subject Al wanted to talk about.

It was clear after only a few days that Al was a foreigner to this community; that his training as an artist in a school distant from the reservation—even though run for and by American Indians —had divorced him from Navajo community life and had given him an image of himself very different from that of the other Navajo in the class. The somewhat special treatment that Al received was not enough to prevent his feelings of alienation, although it may have somewhat softened his frustration.

When Al said in his interviews, "The other students are making films of the daily lives of the people, but I went beyond, a little bit beyond that, I like to see in my film scenes that people never expected. In my painting nobody expects me to paint fact. I can always change it," he was leading up to his explanation of his role in the Navajo as well as the white world. When Al later said, "An artist has a world of his own," he was not merely mouthing a cliche common to all art students in the West, he was holding on to the only explanation he could find that would allow him to exist in the essentially paranoid schizophrenic situation he really was in.

For all his similarity to a Western neurotic personality type, Al was a Navajo, and his film in our opinion could only have been made by a Navajo. Through it Al managed to express his attempted reconciliation with both of the worlds he lived in—the Navajo world he was born into and the Western white world he was thrust into. He succeeded in recording the first Navajo bio-documentary film. Al could express himself and explain himself only through his culture, which, by the time of our intervention, was an apparent jumble of white art school abstraction and ancient Navajo lore.

In all the films made, we find repeated reference to standard themes in Navajo mythology which show the strong ties (deliberate or not, conscious or unconscious) that exist between the real problems of the filmmaker, the problems of film technology, and the themes and problems as expressed in the filmmakers' mythology.

Katherine Spencer, in an analysis of the plot construction of Navajo myth, has said, "Rejection by his family or ridicule and scorn on the part of associates may set the stage for the hero's reckless behavior" (Spencer 1957). Not only was the hero of Al's film reckless in the manner we have described, but so was Al himself.

Before meeting his sister for a reunion and just after finishing the calm sequence of the film, Al went to a Squaw Dance in a neighboring community. There, by getting drunk and acting the role of the provocative stranger, he got into a fight, was stabbed several times, and ended up in the hospital unable to complete the reunion with his family and return to the "calm" he said he wanted.

Just as motion and travel give power, and the manipulation of the environment to put people and things in motion give power, so does the manipulation of the environment in other ways— through film—give power and positive satisfaction to the Navajo.

Johnny and Mike were able to give their relatives sheep by borrowing "film of sheep" from Susie and inserting them in a sequence depicting their own relatives. Susie, on the other hand, could be generous by giving away "film sheep" and still retain her "real sheep." One who has so much that part can be given to friends is indeed powerful.

All the filmmakers enjoyed manipulating the environment, from the simple ability to rearrange the movements in the seesaw sequence which Maxine discovered in her first film, to Al's massive manipulation by making the entire world join him in his own personal search.

Susie was able to show that her mother was a superior weaver, and her mother could in return show that Susie was a superior weaver. The films gave the family added prestige and thus power.

Mike was able to make a "haunted" hogan beautiful by

manipulating the environment through editing to make it look as if the haunted hogan was indeed still inhabited. He showed first the outside of the hogan which everyone "knew" could not be lived in, and then cut to a shot of someone else's hogan which was clearly lived in.

Johnny was able to control the making of the shallow well through film while not actually taking the job of construction foreman. Through film he acquired the power to have his cake and eat it. Perhaps Johnny expressed it best when he said, "What I really want to see is something that I can move in front of my own eyes, that I took myself—that I made."

The question of the consciousness or deliberateness with which traditional narrative forms are transferred to new modes of expression is one that aestheticians, anthropologists and art historians among others have asked many times. The important thing to note is that the Navajos on first using film, in an endeavor to communicate their view of their world, chose to create forms which were fulfilling and possibly even therapeutic to them—in traditional Navajo style.

Chapter

15

How Groups in Our Society Act When Taught to Use Movie Cameras

So far in this book we have been describing the films and filming behavior of a single group of people—the Navajo—working as individuals who made films under our instruction within the context of a small community on the Navajo reservation.

Shortly after we returned from the reservation, Chalfen—who had worked as our assistant with the Navajo and shared the teaching with Worth—began to explore the possibilities of using this bio-documentary technique to study the filmmaking behavior of several innercity groups of teenagers living in Philadelphia. As we have said, one of the aims of our research was to develop a method for collecting, analyzing, and comparing how various groups and cultures structured their world when making a film about it.

This chapter will report on several projects undertaken in the

---

This chapter is written with Richard Chalfen.

last few years in which similar methods have been used to study groups differing socio-culturally from the Navajo.

Since 1964 there has been a tremendous growth in the number of teenage and adolescent filmmaking groups in the United States and Great Britain. In 1968 the Community Film Workshop Council (established by the American Film Institute) identified seventy film workshops in thirty-five cities which have produced about two hundred films. Most of these workshops are in urban, black ghetto neighborhoods. Since then many other groups have been established in similar situations (Achtenberg 1967, American Film Institute 1969, British Film Institute 1966, Culkin 1966, Department of HEW 1968, Gilber 1967, Laybourne 1968, Lidstone and McIntosh 1970, Peavy 1969, Robbin 1966, Stewart 1965, Stoddard 1967). One should not assume, however, that all of these projects are designed to serve similar research purposes or that the films made are analyzed in similar ways, if they are analyzed at all. There is little in common between the teaching methods we have reported in our work and those of most other groups learning to make films in the Community Film Workshop. Most of these groups are concerned—and rightly, we feel—with community service and action. They have, however, spent very little of their energies analyzing the results of their activities in ways comparable to ours. In many instances, the filmmaking projects are not reported in the literature. However, the writings of Achtenberg (1967), Larson and Meade (1966, 1969), Ferguson (1969), Robbin (1966), Worth (1963, 1965, 1969, 1970), Chalfen (1969), and Chalfen and Haley (in Press) give some indication of the variety of approaches and functions in the production of teenage movies. In general, apart from the extent of the analysis made of the films, the projects differ with respect to the interests and motivations of the sponsors, the functions of the filmmaking activity, and the settings and personnel involved.

In one instance, Rodger Larson, who has done extensive work

at the University Settlement Film Club on New York's Lower East Side, reported that lower socio-economic blacks and Puerto Ricans turned off to films made by middle-class white kids. This prompted him to seek funds to provide poor adolescents with their own filmmaking opportunities. However, Larson never returned to the puzzling implications of his observation that not all groups of teenagers liked the same types of films. If adolescents of different backgrounds are making different kinds of film that provoke positive and negative reactions, can any generalizations be made to account for the likes and dislikes, the similarities and dissimilarities? Are different patterns of film communication involved? What are the different groups relating to, and reacting to, when asked to see and evaluate a film? Are nonoverlapping social contexts, involving class, race, and sex, structuring the production and interpretation of the film communication?

These problems are seldom discussed in the literature on films made by adolescents. Such questions can be explored only when a systematic means of observation and analysis is applied to different groups as they both produce and evaluate films under similar conditions.

Assuming that there are subcultures living and functioning within any urban setting, and that these subcultures perceive and structure their immediate environment in different ways, we can immediately try to apply to them theoretical questions we have discussed earlier in this book and applied to the Navajo.

Using such a framework, Chalfen attempted to develop further methods that could describe and help clarify various aspects of context as they relate to the analysis of films made by groups with different backgrounds and cultures.

Adopting a socio-linguistic framework (Hymes 1964) which stressed the analysis of speech activity as differentiated from the analysis of speech itself (if speech can indeed be said to exist by itself) Chalfen attempted to develop further ways of describing and analyzing filmmaking *activity* as opposed to analyzing films.

As can be seen from the previous chapters, we have been concerned with the socio-cultural context in which films were made but had not fully articulated the distinction between filmmaking and filmmaking activity. This shift in emphasis, from the study of *filmmaking* as a way of structuring reality to the study of filmmaking *activity* as the study of how social context interacts and determines the use of symbolic forms in communication, seems like a minor change in emphasis but has led to the clarification and understanding of aspects of filmmaking that were heretofore rarely discussed or seen as related to the very forms of the films made by all members of a society.

This approach to the study of visual communication, the ethnography of film communication, suggests that genres of film productions may be distinguished along two dimensions: (1) the type and amount of emphasis placed on different forms of activity within the total film production (such as the actual shooting, or the acting, the editing, etc.), and (2) the comparative use of contextual items such as topics in the film, the settings, the participants, the themes, etc. It is hypothesized that nonoverlapping or dissimilar patterns of elements of these two dimensions will be responsible for a mutual lack of appreciation by the various groups making and seeing the films.

At this point it might be worthwhile to explain another shift in terminology and emphasis. Chalfen has used the term socio-documentary rather than bio-documentary because he felt it was important to contrast his method with that of Worth. Worth, both in his work at the Annenberg School and on the Navajo reservation, has consistently dealt with *individuals* making films. The results of such individual efforts has been generalized to the subculture (as white middle-class graduate students) or the culture (the Navajos) at large. On the other hand, all of Chalfen's work has been done with subjects working in groups, and the films have been products of group decisions. Chalfen feels that the term *bio-documentary* may be misleading in that the individual filmmaker is never working in the isolation of the "bio-self." It is often the case that what the individual does is largely—particularly in filmmaking—a product of a "socio-self," that is, the filmmaker's social context. The question at the moment remains unclear, however. Does a film made by an individual "socio-self" allow the researcher to make accurate or different judgments about filmmaking activity, compared to the judgments made from a film made by a group of people? We will attempt in this chapter tó point out the differences in methodology, but will treat the films made by both socio- and bio-documentary methods as comparable.

Both these approaches can also be criticized on the grounds that the sample chosen for study is inadequate for the level of generalization attempted. We are always faced with the chance that the behavior of a small sample will not be characteristic of the groups we are talking about. To this extent we must assume that certain aspects of culture and communication are revealed by all members of the culture. Our method has been to search for the common items that either the individuals or the group suggest or produce; that is, to look for the common pattern of things. In the case of the Navajo films, it was very obvious that five of the students were working in similar manners, and one, the art student, was behaving in quite a different manner. Thus the deviant was clearly illuminated and identified by seeing the pattern of items (behaviors) common to the other members of the group. In the case of having a group make a film together, the deviant nature of one or two subjects appears to be cancelled out naturally by the comparative normalness of the other group members when they realize that all the ideas for the film must be discussed and agreed upon before the film is actually shot.

There are several other differences in the approach taken by Chalfen to that of Worth and Adair. Worth is primarily concerned with developing an analytic framework for the study of communication based on the semiotic characteristics of the film code. While he is concerned with the context of the filmic utterance, his primary objective is to understand better how film is encoded and decoded, and the relationships between the filmmaker's implications and the audience member's inferences.

Explication of the film code is the focal point of Worth's research. Chalfen's primary interest, on the other hand, is in the context of the filmmaking activity; that is, what social conditions allow or disallow the filmmaking activity itself; what is the relationship of the people in the film to the people who are making the film; is there more of a desire to be *in* the film than to do the actual shooting and editing of the film; are there a common set of topics and settings that the filmmaking group judges as most appropriate to be filmed; and, in fact, is filmmaking activity being treated as "communication" by the movie filmmakers? The context of the code's use then becomes central to Chalfen's approach.

A combination of the two approaches yields a more complete study of what Worth has called "codes in context." When a person of one culture wants to study a communicative code which is utilized by a member of another culture, an analysis of the social, cultural and behavioral context surrounding both codes must be developed. It should be realized that elements of a code are relative to the context within which that code functions. Interpretation (again culturally relative) of the message form can be seen as relative to the social activity that produced the message.

Briefly then, while Worth primarily investigates the film code, Chalfen is more concerned with the film mode. He assumes that by separating and differentiating the pattern of events and activities that combine to produce a finished film product, different genres of film communication can clearly be distinguished. For Chalfen it is not the code that categorizes the film genre but rather the pattern of contextual elements. Examples of contextual likenesses and differences will make this clearer.

Previous and Continuing Socio-Documentary Research

Let us now briefly describe the projects that we will be comparing. Between September 1967 and January 1968, Chalfen worked at the Houston Community Center, a settlement house in a low socio-economic neighborhood in South Philadelphia. During the fall and winter of 1967, he organized a film club of eight black teenage boys between the ages of twelve and fifteen. Meeting as a group for twenty sessions, learning to use the camera in the ways described in earlier chapters, they conceived, filmed, edited, and recorded the sound for a fourteen-minute black and white film titled, *What We Do on Saturdays on Our Spare Time.* This film records what they considered typical activities in the settlement house and at a nearby parking lot, including scenes of ping-pong, dancing, an interview session, a lot of football, and a mass fight sequence. The same group of boys made a three-minute film titled *The Robbery.* This silent production, totally made in two hours, depicts three boys breaking into the locked filmmaking room and stealing equipment. One of the boys is caught by the film teacher (Chalfen) to end the film.

At the Philadelphia Child Guidance Clinic, Chalfen and Jay Haley, Director of Family Research, organized a filmmaking project with eight poor black girls between the ages of twelve and sixteen, members of the Dedicated Soul Sisters, an adolescent group meeting regularly at the clinic under the professional guidance of a social worker and a psychologist. (Chalfen and Haley, 1971.) Between the beginning of June 1968 and mid-March 1969, the girls met twenty-three times and produced a scripted nine-minute sound film titled, *Don't Make a Good Girl Go Bad.* Briefly, the film involves the plight of an unwed teenage mother who is evicted from her home by her mother. The young mother takes her baby to live with a group of girlfriends who share an apartment. They are seen enjoying a party, dancing, drinking, taking drugs, and fighting with one another. The cops raid the party, having learned about the use of drugs. Finally, the unwed girl's mother enters the apartment and takes the illegitimate child from the daughter, who lies drunk on the couch.

In June and July 1969, Chalfen and Haley attempted to introduce a group of black teenage boys to the socio-documentary procedures. The Noble Teens, a brother group to the Dedicated Soul Sisters, also were meeting regularly at the clinic with a social worker. During and after the introductory sessions, pieces of filmmaking equipment were reported missing. The project was cancelled and that group never went beyond their four hundred feet of practice footage. Before the project ended, they had decided to make a film about their activities in the community, playing ball, riding bikes, and generally "messin' around."

In March 1970, Chalfen began work with white middle-class adolescents living in West Philadelphia. The first group consisted of four fifteen- and sixteen-year-old boys. They produced a "pretty pollution" film in the course of forty-five meetings between April and October.

Eight groups will be described and compared. The majority of the observations and findings come from the projects that Chalfen personally directed. However, field notes and interviews given by the filmmaking teachers involved in the Tabernacle Film Project (see Achtenberg 1967, Stoddard 1967), the Shipley School Project (personal communication) and the 12th and Oxford Filmmaking Cooperative have produced interesting and valuable comparative evidence on several comparative subjects. Five of the eight to be considered here were taught by Chalfen, and two others also were taught by researcher-filmmakers trained by Worth. We have attempted to control the contextual variables across the five innercity groups. The groups may be compared as follows:

(1) Seven of the eight participating groups may be defined as "natural groups"—that is, all members of the group were close friends living in the same neighborhood. They did not necessarily go to the same school but generally shared social activities, such as athletics, bicycle trips, going downtown, parties, etc.

(2) Six of the eight filmmaking efforts investigated took place within South and West Philadelphia. Of the other projects, one was in North Philadelphia (12th and Oxford) and another in Chestnut Hill, in a school slightly north of Philadelphia's city limits.

(3) Seven of the eight filmmaking projects took place in or proximate to the group's neighborhood. In all of Chalfen's pro-

jects, the subjects understood that they could regularly meet and make the film in or out of their neighborhoods as they wished. Traveling to shooting sites was generally restricted by time involved and budget limitations. A major exception to this occurred when one middle-class group insisted on filming a sunrise over water and a clear horizon. This required an hour and a half drive to the New Jersey coast line.

(4) In all cases, the participants were volunteers from larger groups; they all chose themselves in different ways after an initial contact was made with a representative(s) of the group. A self-selection process was involved in determining the group's final composition.

(5) Each filmmaking group consisted of either all boys or all girls, all blacks or all whites. No groups integrated by sex or race have been investigated so far.

(6) As one might expect when working with natural groups, all participants were roughly the same ages, ranging between twelve and sixteen. Also somewhat expected, brothers and sisters were included in several of the groups.

(7) In each of Chalfen's projects, there was an attempt to limit the size of the filmmaking group to five members. If the group consists of many more than five, decision making and activity in general become very difficult to observe; many less than five loses the "statement of the group" criterion of the research. Interestingly, after initially requesting five participants, the black groups tended to become enlarged, while the white groups contracted usually to four members. Both the Tabernacle and Shipley groups consisted of between five and seven members.

(8) In seven of the eight productions under consideration, each group was generally subjected to procedures suggested by the bio-documentary filmmaking approach. The basic technological information was given to the group members while the supervisors maintained a determined neutrality in matters of aesthetic preference and choice of film content. In six of the eight projects the supervisor was an admitted investigator, and in these cases the project was called research. Audio tape recordings were regu-

larly made at meetings, written and photographic journals were kept, and a careful film log recorded each piece of film that was shot.

(9) Each participating group had access to generally the same pieces of filmmaking equipment. Three-lens 16mm Bolex and Bell and Howell cameras were used with Sekonic light meters (only the Shipley group had a zoom lens); tripods were available; and quarter-inch tape and taper recorders were used for nonsynchronous sound tracks (only the 12th and Oxford group had synchronous sound equipment). Zeiss moviscop viewers, Moviola rewinds and Griswold splicers were used for editing—generally the same equipment available for the Navajo filmmaking students.

Alternative Expectations

Working from these baseline comparisons in the contexts of filmmaking activity in the groups, three basic assumptions may be put forth as possible hypotheses.

(1) Since all groups consist of novice filmmakers learning and working under a relatively similar set of contextual circumstances with basically the same filmmaking equipment, all films made by different groups will be alike. In this case, universal forms of behavior associated with making a movie or learning to communicate through a visual code for the first time are likely to emerge.

(2) Since there are an infinite number of possibilities in what a group may want to film or actually put on film, and since this mode of communication can be so intensely personal and individual, every group using film for the first time under similar circumstances will make an entirely different type of film. Idiosyncratic differences will rule out the possibility of patterned behavior.

(3) The results of such filmmaking research will fall in between alternatives one and two. This would lead investigators to

hypothesize that patterns of filmmaking behavior do exist and deserve systematic investigation.

Worth and Chalfen's work highly favors the third possibility. The assumptions are that filmmaking is a culturally structured activity, and that the framework of this structure will emerge after consideration of likenesses and differences in *both* the films produced and the behavior surrounding the production of the films. It may be true that a person with a camera *can* take a picture of anyone or anything, at any time in any place—but it is clear that he *doesn't*.

Cross Group Comparisons

One of the first contextual variables we have found is that of geographical location and setting. Theoretically a film can be photographed anywhere, limited only by the time and money available. We do not instruct our students in any way regarding the geographical location and setting of their film. They can go anywhere they want to. Where they do go and what they do shoot, however, is extremely significant. After reviewing film productions made by different groups, a pattern of preferred and proscribed settings emerges.

We have observed that all the Navajo filmmakers selected filming locations in Pine Springs, in most cases near their homes or actually in houses of closely related kin. Mike Anderson, for example, thought that he would like to make a film using his brother as subject. His brother was a Navajo policeman working in a community about twenty miles from Pine Springs and Mike went there one day to start photographing for a film "on my brother." When he returned he told us that he did not do any shooting that day, that he thought he would make another film, that he felt it was "too far away—that film." He decided then to make a film about the lake. He frequently referred in the first weeks to wanting to make a film about his brother, but that it was "too hard to make a film so far away." None of the others ventured very far away from their homes.

White middle-class graduate students at the Annenberg School regularly select locations away from the School or the university setting. In their case, the place common and most familiar to students enrolled in the Documentary Film Laboratory is avoided. For this group, film activity is an excuse for going to far places to photograph the exotic, the unusual, the seldom seen. Many students regularly travel from Philadelphia to New York or to outlying areas several hours away from Philadelphia. They find Tibetan villages in New Jersey, tugboat captains, runaways in Greenwich Village, country folk singers, and so on. The camera is a socially accepted device to make them explorers, to get them away from home and familiar surroundings. Not only do they seldom photograph or make films about the school, the university, or the immediate area, but when they have an opportunity to make a film about or in their homes they almost never do so.

The black lower-class teenagers regularly choose shooting locations near their homes for the practice shooting. Examples include the outside basketball court which was theirs (having been labeled many times with their names written with spray paint and indelible markers), or a vacant local parking lot (used as a football field), or the playstreet where several members of the filmmaking group lived. However, when it came time to produce the final film, they preferred to travel to sites around the city, generally outside of their immediate neighborhoods, or to use fictive settings such as a room in the Child Guidance Clinic made to look like one of their living rooms.

While the black teenagers chose subjects which were "theirs" for practice films, the Navajos reversed the procedure. The practice films were made in "our" geographic territory—the swing in our playground, the teeter-totter in our playground, and the parched earth behind the trading post. They considered the school to be a government, white area. None of the Navajo practice films were on their own land or about their own families.

While the Navajo turned to their families, their homes, and their own possessions as subjects for the final projects, the black teenagers traveled away from such things. The geographical location of *Not Much to Do* was "our" turf; the university, the Philadelphia Museum of Art, the Wistar Institute, an old firehouse, and so on. When the Dedicated Soul Sisters needed a living room for their film they made one up at the Clinic, rather than use one of their own homes. At the Houston Center they filmed themselves playing pingpong in the center recreation room.

Maxine Tsosie made a practice film about Adair hanging out the laundry at the schoolhouse, but she and her sister made their "real film" about their grandfather at his hogan.

The white middle-class teenagers, on the hand, seemed to avoid their neighborhoods entirely, whether practice shooting or making their final film. They consistently chose far away "nature" settings—trees, heavy foliage, rivers, streams, parks, etc. They insisted on filming a sunrise near the ocean (several hours' drive away) rather than film it in the city. They traveled quite a distance to find their nature shots, ignoring a perfectly good park two blocks from where they lived. The white middle-class teenagers seemed to behave toward the filmmaking setting exactly as do their older counterparts in graduate school.

It seems clear at this point that there are group feelings about where filmmaking activity is appropriate. The feeling of the right or appropriate setting seems consistent within the groups and different across groups. Variable relations exist between filmmaking settings and the group producing the film.

It seems that white teenagers or graduate students find the filmmaking activity an appropriate means of controlling images of distant and unusual places and events. They feel free to capture distant space and event on film.

Both the Navajo and the black teenagers, on the other hand, consider filmmaking activity an appropriate means of dealing symbolically with places and events closer to home. In some cases "their" home, and in other cases "our" home, but rarely with the far away, the strange, or the exotic.

It hardly seems unreasonable to speculate that in a white society, white middle-class teenagers and graduate students feel freer to venture forth with a camera, to control symbolically— as they do in other ways—those places and events far away from them. For the white groups we have studied, filmmaking activity is not inconsistent with the conquest of new territory, new people, and new ideas. For the Navajo in contrast to both other American groups (black and white), the family, its home, land, possessions, culture and ideas are the appropriate setting for filmmaking activity. They are not making films about whites as we are about them. They are making films about themselves. The black groups we have studied also deal with themselves, not in their own homes, perhaps, but they do not venture very far away. They too are not capturing on film places and things far away from them.

Topics and Activities

If one looks at the topics or themes about which the filmmakers build their films, and at activities which the filmmakers choose to have their actors portray, one also finds a pattern of relationships between groups.

In all the black teenagers' films, some form of fighting or horseplay appears. It may be in the form of pushing, shoving and pulling, or of wrestling, fist fighting, or kidding around pummeling, in groups or between individuals. The fighting varies from a reenactment of a street gang fight or rumble, to actual fighting during sport or horseplay.

The rough house is almost always accompanied by some form of drinking or dancing and related activities. Sometimes such behavior is part of the story, as when a major scene occurs at a dance, or where the theme of the film is drinking, getting drunk,

242) *Through Navajo Eyes*

or acting badly during drinking. At other times the drinking and dancing, and often the fighting, just happen to be there, or are seen in the background while some other activity goes on. It is almost as if these persistent themes form a common appropriate basis and background for social and individual behavior in their films.

Equally common but not appearing in all the films made by black teenagers is the theme of competition and athletics, varying from organized sports—football, baseball, pingpong—to spontaneous and competitive acts of physical skill shown in a competitive way.

In *Not Much to Do*, for example, the boys break into an abandoned firehouse and each one gleefully takes a turn chinning and swinging on an old water pipe. The filmmaker actors comment on the strength, grace, and skill of each as he does his act. Later they decide to swim (illegally) in the Philadelphia Museum of Art fountain, and the film allows each one to show how he dives, swims, and does tricks. In the soundtrack they again comment on how each compares with the others in physical prowess.

Such topics are seldom if ever treated by the white middle-class filmmakers. They tend to shoot things rather than activities. The most common set of things these teenagers filmed involved elements of nature—clouds, trees, leaves, streams, birds, flowers— or architectural elements—lines and edges of buildings, cement and brick patterns. The activities they do show are relatively inactive, such as a person walking slowly or sitting thinking about something, looking lost. It is interesting to note that the graduate students also rarely show fighting, drinking, or athletic competition. In over forty films only one has a fight in it, and that is in a film about a black prizefighter. It is the only film in which physical prowess is the theme or is shown in any significant way. One film on the other hand satirizes exercise and the use of the gym, and several films attack or are quite critical of fighting, as represented by war. Only one of the white graduate student films shows drinking and dancing: a film about a fraternity party, meant to show in an extremely critical way the behavior of the fraternity party type. There is, however, no fighting in the film.

The Navajo films have no scenes of fighting in them. They show no competitive activities and no drinking. The last is important, for it could be said that of course the Navajo do not show such activities since they do not perform them in their culture. But drinking is a common, and commonly understood, problem for the Navajo. Our male students were no more averse to alcohol than other Navajo, and for some it was a real life problem. They fought bitterly and violently when drunk, and accepted such behavior as part of their lives and as part of the social life of the community. Yet their films never showed it. For the black teenagers fighting and drinking were part of their lives and *appropriate* activities to be shown in their films. For the Navajo fighting and drinking were also part of their lives, but *inappropriate* activities to be shown in their films.

Further differences between groups are revealed when we look at the amount of footage devoted to showing human beings, and when we examine how the filmmakers choose to show human beings.

Almost without exception every cademe made by the black filmmakers showed people, either posing, standing still, or moving in some favorite activity. In direct contrast, the white middle-class male teenage filmmakers deliberately avoided photographing people. In only two ten-foot sections of four hundred feet of their first footage did they show any people at all. In these two sections they asked each other to pose in front of the camera.

In the black films made by groups we have worked with, and in some thirty or forty other films made by similar black groups that we have seen, the tendency was to film other members of the filmmaking group exclusively. The actors were almost always the members of the film club, film group, or film workshop.

In the white groups the opposite tendency was equally strong. The filmmakers were hardly ever the actors, and the films were never about them directly. The white middle-class girls did appear in about 40 per cent of the early practice shooting, but the girls did it reluctantly, as a favor to each other, and clearly felt that it was unsophisticated actually to be in their own movies.

Structuring the Image and Structuring Themselves

The most striking difference that seems consistently to appear in an examination of the patterns of black and white filmmaking activity is whether the importance of the filmmaking activity lies in being the actor in front of the camera or being the image manipulator behind the camera.

In the groups we have studied, we have found clearly and consistently that blacks prefer to *be* the image in front and that whites perfer to *manipulate* the image from the back.

Black groups tended to organize themselves around the activity in front of the camera. They talked most about who would be in the film. They usually decided that it would be themselves. They planned to exclude others from that preferred position and competed for the best roles.

On the other hand, white groups tended to organize themselves around the behind the camera activities. They competed for the best jobs as image manipulator—cameraman, editor, director, and so forth. They never competed to appear *in* the film, and never competed for acting honors.

The white teenager and graduate student saw preference, power, appropriateness, and status in being an image manipulator. The black teenagers in all cases saw preference, power, appropriateness, and status in manipulating themselves as images.

Related to the clear pattern of preference for being in front or in back of the camera is an equally clear preference for participating in or avoiding the technical, mechanical aspects of filmmaking activity. The white teenagers competed for the use of the camera and editing apparatus, while the black teenagers had to be reminded frequently that since they were making a film, someone had to stay out of each scene to run the camera. They frequently wanted the teacher to run the camera for them so they could all be actors. White graduate students, of course, followed their teenage predecessors. Not only had they come to school to study communication, but they knew before they came that status was achieved by being an editor, director, cameraman, etc. The greater the amount of control they could acquire over the image making and image manipulating technology and social interaction, the greater was their inner feeling of status. The director controlled the actors, the writers, the editors; therefore the director had social status. In contrast to the black teenagers, control over their fellows as actors or images was rarely sought.

It is clear that making a film means different things to different groups in our society. Our findings on this point were beautifully expressed in the Hollywood film *Medium Cool* made in 1969. In one scene, two television news cameramen attempt to get an interview with some black activists, one of whom comments, "Man, when we appear on the tube, in front of all those people, that's when we live. That's life, man."

In relation to an adolescent's or young adult's strategic quest for recognition, the black preference for presenting self on camera and the white preference for asserting self behind it as an image manipulator, as the good filmmaker, illustrate two quite different behaviors.

The way a group or an individual performs an activity can be seen as a fundamental act of social communication—the communication of self, particularly if that manner of performance is patterned within the group and distinctive across groups. In the case of movie making activity, the individuals and groups engage in it not only to make movies, but also to make something of themselves, to show themselves as a certain kind of person, particularly as a person with a higher status than those others who cannot make movies, who do not have access to such an important technology.

In this sense, then, what is the status of filmmaking activity for the groups we have been discussing? For the white middle-class teenager and young adult the status is in capturing the symbolic form of the far away, the exotic, the novel, and in manipulating the symbols to produce messages, art forms, or entertainments. A white achieves status through filmmaking activity in direct proportion to his control over the images he manipulates.

For the black teenager the status in filmmaking activity is in presenting himself as image, as actor, entertainer, social activist or man of physical prowess. He does not see capturing symbols of others as a way to social status and social power. The more he himself is seen, the better.

For the Navajo the status in filmmaking activity seems to be in presenting moving images of his group in harmony with his environment. While the white filmmaker presents others and the black presents himself, the Navajo presents his context and his culture. The Navajo frequently says, "I want to show how *we* do things, how *we* live, how *we* look."

At present, it is difficult not to overemphasize black teenagers' enthusiasm for those parts of the filmmaking activity which promise the opportunity to act out a story and their disinterest in the technical-manipulative aspects of the craft.

Messaris, a white college student, reported a revealing incident as part of course work in the Annenberg School of Communications at the end of 1970. While doing community work in Princeton in 1969, he mentioned to two of his black roommates that he had access to a 16mm camera, and asked if they wanted to make a film. "They were very enthusiastic," he wrote. "They wanted to make a film called *The Black Invader* starring themselves as black aliens who would land in Princeton in a flying saucer and take over the world." He reports that they spent several weeks talking with each other about the story.

> They were going to star in the film. . . . They wanted all their friends to be in the film with them, and in the next few weeks more than 10 black youths, some of whom I had never met, came up to me, said that they heard [we] were making a film, and asked if they

could act in it. . . . They never asked my advice about anything. At no point did anyone ask to use the camera, learn how to use it, work on any sound or editing, or in any way involve himself with the technical aspects of the film. With these things they were all completely unconcerned. They were interested in having a good part, in playing members of the conquering army, and all questions were related to what the action was going to be like. . . . I often heard [them] discussing the story: they would always discuss action, conflict, the young blacks overcoming the local police and killing the mayor.

Unfortunately, the film was never made. It seems difficult to know how it could have been made unless Messaris himself would have been cameraman and editor.

There is a further distinction to be made about how people have been shown in films made by differing groups. Group members seem to have a feeling for how they want to be seen in film or how they want to show people in their footage. In the black projects the actors and actresses hammed and showed off playfully for the camera. There was a strong display of the self as a strong, tough, and cool (hip) individual. The camera would start and the hamming would begin. There was complete acceptance of their strong drive to show and see themselves.

The white filmmakers behaved differently. A person would not present himself for the camera; the camera would catch a person doing something as if he did not know the camera was being used, or, the cameraman would carefully direct people how to behave in the shot. As mentioned before, such direction occurred much more frequently with the white girls than boys. There is another strange quality concerning how the white filmmakers saw and filmed humans. In most cases, a person is used in a shot as an inanimate object, his status equal to that of a tree or rock. There is an intensely impersonal quality about the infrequent appearance of people pictured in the white male footage and an intensely personal quality about the human images in the black project.

One can think of obvious parallels in the new cinema forms of the 1960s. Cinéma verité, direct cinema, and the French *nouvelle vague* concentrated on the development and justification of an aesthetic based precisely on the notion of capturing real behavior on the screen—of developing acting and editing styles that give the impression of behavior caught rather than reenacted. The notion of "the story" is giving way to the notion of fragments of "real life" caught by the filmmaker.

The popularity of the ethnographic film—the film that objectively records the life of others—has also increased enormously in recent years and is now being included in the aesthetic of avant-garde white filmmakers. In all these movements, the overwhelming direction seems to be the enhancement of attitudes deeply rooted in white consciousness regarding appropriate filmmaking behavior along the lines we have described.

Topics and Themes

We can also compare film themes across different groups on several levels. First, similarities may be seen in the themes of the films made by several of the groups. Five out of the six Navajo films were about crafts and the Navajos' daily work. The films explained facets of Navajo life and work which revolved around the idea of productivity. We noted previously that one of the most common responses of Navajos to Navajo films was that such and such a film, actor, action, or sequence, shows "how well we do it [weaving, silversmithing, etc.]," how well so and so does it, or that a film shows how correctly a character performs his ritual activity—that is, how a character's performance fits the ritual demands of the culture.

The themes running through the black teenage films also have the quality of life-style explanation or exposition. However, the activities in the film all involve what we would consider play or playing around, fantasy, or wish fulfillment. They are rarely about "productive" as opposed to leisure activity.

Another thematic dimension separated white middle-class and black lower-class produced films. The black males and females wanted to film subject matter that was very familiar to them and to show it as it appeared in everyday reality. They seldom throught of distorting the image, either in the social circumstances (exchange one setting for another in editing), or by manipulating the filmmaking technology (slow motion, single framing, etc.) The white groups likewise wanted to film commonplace material, but they wanted to do something to it so that viewers would see it all in a new, fresh, and revealing way. Manipulations of camerawork and editing were often considered of primary importance, whereas the black filmmakers simply wanted to shoot and maintain on film the reality before them. The films made by black youth resemble the Navajo productions in that they both use film to convey information about how something looks. The films made by white teenagers, on the other hand, through various forms of manipulation, seek to convey a feeling for the novelty or originality with which the subject matter was shown.

The appearance and nature of a story line is another element of the film products that may be compared and contrasted. A story line is one technique a filmmaker may use to tie his film together, to give it a feeling of continuity and progression. However, it is not safe to assume that all filmmakers or filmmaking groups will value this method of achieving cohesion. They may develop an alternative strategy to determine what happens as the film passes through a projector from a beginning to an end. Thus the framework of story line, or lack thereof, is a variable which may be investigated for potential patterns.

Handling of this variable in each of the several Philadelphia groups under investigation is very similar. The majority of the films made by low socio-economic groups place importance on story line framework. Beyond the groups we have investigated, Achtenberg, Larson, and Robbin substantiate this observation. The films produced by groups taught by Worth's students were ci.ganized around the theme, "What we do." The films concentrated on the story possibilities of the boys' or girls' everyday lives. The Houston Center film, *What We Do in Our Spare Time on Saturday*, the DSS film, *Don't Make a Good Girl Go Bad*, as well as Tabernacle's *Not Much to Do* and Oxford's *The Jungle* illustrate this point.

As Worth and Adair observe, the organizing principle or strategy used by the Navajos was also consistent. Their story line (if one emphasizes the "story" aspect of the variable) is largely neglected. The Navajo films produced are held together by the process line rather than the story line. The "way to tell a story" of events necessary to the process, or the activity of making something, provided the unifying function. This is clearly seen in both weaving films (Susie Benally and Alta Kahn) and the silvermaking film (Johnny Nelson). Nelson's *Shallow Well* and the Tsosie sisters' medicine man film also use the natural ordered events of the process to order the events in the film, but they occasionally rearrange the order inside the natural beginning and end of the central process or activity.

In the examples provided so far by the white middle-class filmmaking groups, the rearrangement aspect and neglect of story line or natural progression of events is maximized. For instance, the male group, beginning their film with a sunrise, felt no need to end the film with a sunset. The films made by these teenagers tend to be collections of "neat" shots, segmented activities, and diverse subject matter. A viewer must work hard to put the pieces together. White graduate students show much the same tendencies. Although the course is called Documentary Film Laboratory, and the emphasis is on presenting a view of process, persons, or events, students rarely concentrate on the pure story line or on clear exposition of activity, process, or event. Rather, events are seen as providing the filmmaker with images which can be manipulated, rearranged, and controlled for political, social or artistic purposes. These students tend also to be concerned with effects, clever editing, and unusual juxtapositions, often preferring shocking cuts to merely unusual ones.

Even this brief review of the contextual background of filmmaking among several different groups clearly indicates that different forms of filmmaking activity exist for different groups. Analysis of similarities and differences between different groups seems to give insight into the breakdown of communication between groups of film viewers.

If filmmaking activity stands for different things for different groups, if status is achieved by being in front or in back of the camera, if it is appropriate for one group to show things far away and for another to show things nearby, there is a great likelihood that the film communications of one group will neither be "understood" or appreciated by the others.

Even if one was not concerned with this so-called communication breakdown or gap, another problem seems implicit in the data we are reporting. Our culture, preferences, and statuses are *the* values taught by schools, mass media, and life in a white-dominated society. "Making it" in our society means developing "our" notions of the appropriateness of filmmaking and other communication activity—including speech activity. We tend to undervalue the appropriateness of other motives for communication activity and hence to insist that members of other cultures see things (literally) our way.

Perhaps by seeing and understanding the fact that communications activity can have many and varied social purposes, we can recognize the value of encouraging others to develop their own form of communication and learn to understand and value them for what they are.

Chapter

16

Some Concluding Thoughts

The last chapter of a book reporting research in a new area is always a difficult one to write. Much of what we want to say in conclusion can be summed up in the typical scholar's phrase, "More research is needed." In all honesty much of this chapter is our attempt to make that cliche somewhat more specific. We shall refrain from saying it too often, but hope that some of our conclusions will be considered as possible areas for further study to clarify some of the issues we have raised, and to confirm or disconfirm our findings by testing them with other groups.

Most important among the many aspects of this report is that, for the first time, members of another culture radically different from ours in language, technological development, and use of images, have been taught to use the film medium and have produced expressions of themselves and their world as they see it. The films they made, the way they made them, and what they said about them are here reported so that all these activities can be compared with similar activities of different groups within our own society and elsewhere.

In this book we have shown some of the similarities and differences in films, filming, and filmmaking activity of different groups of people living in different ways. We have shown their attitudes toward filmmaking and their ways of organizing and patterning their view of their world. We have shown some of the things involved when different groups with different cultures reveal their own structure of reality through films they make.

We feel that this method may offer the fields of anthropology, communication, cognitive psychology, and the humanities a new research technique—another method for getting at the way people structure their own humanness. Our investigations seem to confirm that this method does help to reveal culture as determined and organized by the people within that culture. The other's view of his world is different from ours but not so different that we cannot understand it, and by it to see just how *we* pattern our own world through our own culture.

In many ways knowing how others structure reality is our only way to know about our own hidden structuring of the way we know our own reality. Culture is, after all, largely that part of our structuring process that we take so for granted that we can hardly conceive of it as being done any differently; we can hardly conceive that we are "doing" anything at all. Movies, we think, "only" reflect what is out there.

In a period when both social science and the mass media are increasingly showing us the world out there through film, it becomes extremely important for us to realize that we do structure reality through film, and that the structuring process embodies our notions of appropriateness, our notions of what is important, right, and good. Cultures are dying or being killed all around us. Anthropologists are organizing internationally in an effort to collect records of fast vanishing civilizations. Increasingly as technologies of filming and television develop, the record of man is being made on film. But who makes these films? "We" do. We do because that is the way we have done it since the motion picture camera was invented. We do because that is the way to be objective, scientific, and accurate. We do because we are anthropologists, scholars, researchers, or whatnot. We do because it never occurred to us that "they" ought to be doing it, that "they" can do it, and most importantly that when "we" do it we are showing a picture of our world and salvaging a culture not of others but of ourselves. Our record of them might very well be a record of us. (Worth 1972)

We are *not* advocating that anthropologists cease describing and analyzing other cultures. We are advocating that those who study others become aware that a major part of that study of others lies in studying precisely how they structure their reality compared to us and other "theys."

Much, of course, still has to be done to make a complex methodology a completely scientific tool for the study of man. The use of film in this way, however, offers a method whereby a few native people in a relatively short time can produce a visual statement of their own view of their culture which can be viewed and interpreted by many investigators in addition to those directly involved in the research.

The notion of teaching members of another culture to use the communication modes and technologies of our culture is a new one. We know little about the cultural effects of our method of teaching film, nor do we know if it is the best method for all cultures. There has been almost no research attempting to delineate different ways of teaching people to communicate, and none at all in different ways of teaching people to communicate through film. We hope that our method will provide a springboard from which other methods, such as Chalfen's socio-documentary approach, will be developed.

In this research we obviously had the advantage of working with a culture and with groups fully described in the ethnographic literature. The existing work afforded us a model of how the culture was perceived by the outsider, which we were able to use in guiding our research, and as a basis of comparison with the film model made by the members of the society themselves. The question remains, can this method be used in ethnographic exploration of little-known cultures, including those now rapidly disappearing?

Other cultures will have to be investigated by the same method to determine if cross-cultural comparisons can be made.

The success of this introductory study was enhanced by factors which may not exist in other cultures, and it would be necessary now to learn how many of the factors available to us by working with the Navajo are necessary for all cultures in order to produce films and other data similar in usefulness to that we have gathered. It must be remembered that (1) the Navajo are known as a people who value innovation and knowledge, and (2) the Navajo are a people for whom motion is central to language and to major areas of their cultural life. A medium which gives a person so attuned to motion such free access to manipulation of motion might be a stimulus that would not be present in a culture where motion plays a smaller or negative part in their lives. (3) The long association of Adair with the people in Pine Springs may have provided a background of trust and willingness which could not be replicated where such a long-standing relationship did not exist. (4) The role of the teacher in a new society may depend more on his personal characteristics than on his technical and scientific knowledge as an investigator.

It is our opinion that these four special attributes of both the investigators and the people being investigated were important interactions, the effect of which cannot be determined by this study alone. All field research depends on the ability of the investigators to do their job—to gain trust, to be able to teach their informants, and to learn from them. It will be necessary to discover whether this method is as rewarding under less favorable circumstances.

Since it is now established that films can made by people with other cultures, it might be worthwhile to explore the possibility that such films could be made for a variety of purposes differing from those in our project. Chalfen has shifted emphasis from filming and coding to filmmaking activity and social organization. Emphasis could shift from how the images were put together to content, what was shown by whom.

Another shift in emphasis might be to restrict the range of possible subject matter. Instead of asking people to make a film about anything they want, we might ask them to make a film about specific techniques, subjects, or concepts of interest to the investigator. What films would result from instructions like, "Show me how you build a house," or "Show me the important things in your village"? The instructions could be more specific —"Make a film about all the kinds of yams"—or less specific— "Make a film about health." As more groups are taught to use film, and as more films of other cultures are made and analyzed, we could begin to build up our meager store of knowledge about how people structure, not only a general view of their world, but a specific view of specific aspects of life such as health, housing, cooking, hunting, and so on. These aspects of life are shared by many groups and cultures but have different structures, patterns of use, and place in a society. Comparisons among such specific, requested views would help us to understand and to present a more complete picture of man.

We have shown that studying a culture such as the Navajo— a culture with a very different language and way of life—has helped us to study and work with segments of our own population where other modes of communication are severely restricted or have broken down. We have discussed some of the recent work done with black and white teenagers by methods comparable to those we used with the Navajo.

Other work of comparable nature is already being planned or underway. Children in various types of schools are being taught to make films in order to reveal cognitive data difficult to get at by other means. Adair is planning to work with alcoholics under the sponsorship of the National Institute of Mental Health to see if the bio-documentary technique can be useful in understanding the values and attitudes underlying a major health problem. The work of Chalfen at the Philadelphia Child Guidance Clinic and that of Hampe (a student of Worth) in the Marriage Counselling Service are further examples of the continued attempts to get people with special problems or worldviews to present themselves on film.

Worth is presently working with the Department of Community Medicine at Mt. Sinai Medical School in New York to develop a bio-documentary teaching unit which will teach doctors, medical students, patients, and members of the geographical community surrounding the medical school to present themselves and their world on film. Their films will be used to facilitate communication between the groups through cable networks in the community where films may be shown to provide data for research in the attitudes and values of the participants, and to provide teaching materials on specific health subjects made in the bio- and socio-documentary manner.

It has been our experience that while the Navajo were an ideal people to work with in this study, they are not necessarily unique in their willingness and ability to use filmmaking technology. We believe that filmmaking is a form of social activity and a mode of communication that will have an active and creative appeal for peoples in many areas of the non-Western as well as the Western world—for many of the same or similar reasons that the *viewing* of film and television has had so great an appeal to almost all people. To the best of our knowledge, wherever these media have been introduced people have been fascinated by them. The underlying reasons for moving pictures' universal appeal are little understood at the present time. We might guess, in the absence of evidence, that peoples less open to innovation (and contrasting to the Navajo in other respects) would also be willing to cooperate with investigators using this method for reasons going beyond cultural differences and into basic psychology. It may well be that film and television have their compelling quality because they most closely simulate dreaming. Everyone in every culture has had dreams and assumes that this flow of images in motion and sequence has meaning. We believe that people of varying cultures will be fascinated in actively participating in the film mode of communication because it can thus never be completely unfamiliar to them.

Why is this so? One may speculate that in the process of choosing images and image events and again in the process of editing them, the Navajo may have been projecting unconscious or innate systems of organization and of categorizing his world in ways that are little understood at present. While the Whorfian hypothesis deals only with verbal language and suggests a comparison between cultures whose languages are different, it might also be applied in a similar situation in which we could compare, not two different verbal languages and the way they act as constraints in describing a world, but two differing modes of communication, verbal language and visual "language" and the way the different modes act as constraints in describing the world that different people live in.

Since verbal language is arbitrary, the signs in use by different linguistic groups will differ greatly, making it obvious that groups communicate in different ways. Visual forms are much more deeply connected biologically (perceptually) with the outside stimulus they represent. The rules of social perception are learned early and contain similarities across the entire human species (although they are not identical). And yet, although the events we portray in film are basically recognizable to all—a picture of a man is after all an image common to man—we use them in different ways. Although there are such obvious perceptual universals involved in film communication, differences are real and have received very little attention.

While the systems of interpretation of dreams may differ across time and culture, the notion of taking meaning or sense from a flow of images might be deeply ingrained in human consciousness and might make filmmaking a uniquely easy and responsive methodology to learn. Although methods of dream interpretation have varied across cultures and over time, men always seemed to assume that their inner images and image events, organized unconsciously and remembered only in fleeting bursts, were worth reporting and understanding. Men from the earliest moments of recorded history have assumed that dreams have meaning, that the images selected for his dream were important and that the sequence in which they occurred played a part in their interpretation. Since the reporting of dreams was always verbal, it is impossible to say that the notion of the importance of sequence in the interpretation of image events occurred before language. It has certainly existed as far back as language and may indeed belong to that same innate ability which is man's language and symbolizing capacity.

At the moment we do not know if everyone can be taught to make a movie as everyone learns to use language. It might be worthwhile to see if man's symbolizing facility extends to making films, and if so how he goes about creating his systems and "language" of film symbols.

Although the relationship between dreams, language, culture, and communication is one we hardly dare do more than touch upon at this point, it might be useful here to quote Susanne Langer:

> Cinema is like dream in the mode of its presentation: it creates a virtual present, an order of direct apparition. That is the mode of dream. . . . The most noteworthy formal characteristic of dream is that the dreamer is always at the center of it. Places shift, persons act and speak, or change or fade—facts emerge, situations grow, objects come into view with strange importance. . . . But the dreamer is always "there," his relation is, so to speak, equidistant from all events. Things may occur around him or unroll before his eyes; he may act or want to act, or suffer or contemplate; but the immediacy of everything in a dream is the same for him. . . . The percipient of a moving picture sees with the camera; his standpoint moves with it, his mind is pervasively present. The camera is his eye. . . . He takes the place of the dreamer. *The work is the appearance of a dream, a unified, continuously passing, significant appari-*

tion of culture. . . . Motion pictures, are our thoughts made visible and audible. They flow in a swift succession of images, precisely as our thoughts do, and their speed, with their flashbacks—like sudden uprushes of memory—and their abrupt transition from one subject to another, approximates very closely the speed of our thinking. They have the rhythm of the thought-stream and the same uncanny ability to move forward or backward in space or time. . . . They project pure thought, pure dream, pure inner life. The work is the appearance of a dream . . . a significant apparition of culture . . . our thought made visible. (Langer 1953)

Other observations must also be made. While having viewed films before attempting their own possibly affected the nature of the films made by the Navajo filmmakers, it is our deep conviction that despite such contamination the patterns in both the films and in the behavior of the filmmakers reveal deep-lying cultural and psychological phenomena. Susie Benally, who had seen training films at school and some Hollywood films in movie theaters, made a film that is much the same in style, content, and syntax as the one made by her mother, Alta Kahn, who had been minimally exposed to films. It may be suggested that the similarity may be accounted for by the daughter's influence on the mother, just as any teacher influences a pupil. Nonetheless, the film made by the more acculturated daughter, despite contamination by seeing "our" films, is significantly different from film made in the usual Western tradition.

Ideally it would be well to have a "cleaner" test situation, not only to rule out the effect of Euro-American influence on the film style of non-Western primitive peoples, but also to see if a people who had never seen the results of filmmaking (or even any still photographs) would become motivated to use film as a method of expression and communication. Or, in other words, could a people who did not know that there is such a thing as motion pictures be motivated to make such pictures themselves without the stimulus of seeing the finished product made by someone else? Is it essential to see film of others or made by others in order to make the film at all?

There have been periodic reports in the anthropological literature over the last ten years suggesting that "primitive" people
learn to "read" photographs very quickly. We know nothing,
however, about their notions of making images that move. Given
a still camera many people who have never made a photo will
point it and accept the resulting "picture" with glee. Will these
same people, unexposed (literally and figuratively) to motion pictures, organize and order their cademes to make what we call
movies?

One practical fact should be noted. Peoples isolated from Western influence, such as those in interior New Guinea, are so far
from urban centers and film processing laboratories that it would
be difficult, if not impossible, to replicate our experiment with
the Navajo. Any greatly delayed feedback might prove crucial.
(The need for quick feedback must also, of course, be tested.)
Therefore, if this film method was developed for use with such
isolated people, processing equipment might have to be brought
to the field. This is by no means an unusual or novel idea. Robert
Flaherty in 1920 brought processing and projection equipment
with him when he made *Nanook of the North.* He used projectors
and processing machines in areas where electricity was almost
unknown. With the development of portable batteries, and the
miniaturized equipment available today, the student of culture
will find it infinitely easier to transport and to use in the field
cameras, processors, and projectors.

Quite aside from its scientific value and on some levels tran-
scending those values, filmmaking in the hands of native peoples
of diverse cultural traditions might also be considered as a contribution to the arts and humanities. *Intrepid Shadows,* for example,
demonstrates what a trained artist with cultural roots different
from our own can do with film reduced to its essential and basic
components. The white middle-class Western eye, conditioned
by its culture and the intricate technology and tradition of Hollywood and the television screen, is in danger of losing sight of the

beauty and vitality of the film produced simply and under the control of the filmmaker for personal expression. In commercial entertainment, ends become confused with means; sheer technical accomplishments in optical effects and sound recording aided by elaborate lighting and dolly shots carefully scripted and scheduled to meet the demands of a budget or a sponsor have diverted filmmakers from the force and beauty of simple human communication. This medium, taught by the bio-documentary method and used by an artist of another society, drawing on very different myth and musical styles, dramatic structures, and different concepts of event, time, and space, might well serve not only to present one culture to another but also to enrich that store of knowledge about man which our culture traditionally calls art, and which clearly is part of the scientific study of the culture of man.

It seems fitting to end this book in Navajo myth style by returning to the beginning before we come to the very end. In the beginning of the book we mentioned Malinowski's stricture, "The final goal of which an Ethnographer should never lose sight . . . is to grasp the native's point of view . . . to realize his vision of his world."

We therefore must not allow ourselves or our readers to forget how our Navajo friends might view the work we are doing. Johnny Nelson, in talking about his film, said:

> What I really want to see is something that can move in front of my eyes, that I took myself. . . . You make a movie about it, and then it's moving around where you can actually see what is being done—how it moves. . . . If you write a whole book about it then it's still. . . . You try to give it to somebody, and he reads it through, and he does not really get the picture in his mind.

Appendix

A Brief Summary of the Films Made by the Navajo

Practice Films

The first films made by the Navajos were made after two days of instruction in the technical use of the camera, exposure meter, and splicer. The Navajos were told: "Here is a hundred feet of film. Shoot anything you want with it." They were then asked what they were going to do, or subsequently what they had done. All the students decided to make little movies out of what was to us a practice assignment in the use of technology. The concept of "mere" practice seemed alien to the Navajo (either because of inherent dislike of waste, or because of inability to imagine useless practicing). At this point, it must be remembered there had been no instruction in editing or concepts of filmmaking.

MIKE ANDERSON: *The Piñon Tree.* 2 minutes.

This was the first subject that Mike thought of. He said, "I make a movie of a piñon tree. It grows from small to big." The film is a series of twelve edemes (shots) in which Mike started with a small bush (but shown full in the frame), going to bigger and bigger bushes, and finally trees. After this series of edemes (which Mike photographed in such a way that all the trees were the approximately same size in the frame) he continued with a dying piñon tree, then a fallen and dead piñon tree, then some old rotting branches of a tree, and finally a single piñon acorn.

Mike's only sequencing during editing was to transfer part of the acorn shot to the beginning of the film, keeping the other part for the ending.

JOHNNY NELSON: *The Summer Shower.* 2 minutes.

Johnny had to tell a story. It was "how the earth is dry and the Navajo waits for rain. Then comes the rain and everyone feels good." This was also Johnny's first idea for a film. He executed it with the confidence of a Hollywood director. He too shot it in the order in which the shots were to appear on the screen. He started with some moving shots of dry earth, cracked earth, dry grass, and cloudless skies. Then a Navajo boy walks in the dusty field and stoops down to crumble the dry earth in his hand. Suddenly the rain comes, a puddle forms, a small flower grows, the rain clouds are shown.

Here Johnny directed Worth to hold a water hose in such a way as to make rain (as it looked to him through the camera). He planted a flower and arranged the water so it puddled and flowed in the direction he wanted.

JOHNNY NELSON: *The Navajo Horse.* 3½ minutes. (Photos 6–11.)

This was Johnny's second film. Here he wanted to make a movie about "how important a horse is to the Navajo and how he knows all about him." The film started with ten or fifteen extreme close-ups of hoofs, nostrils, eyes, saddle, bridle, etc. Some of the shots were moving and some were still. At one point Johnny asked Worth, "If I take lots of shots of parts of a horse, and then take shots of many horses, and put the shots of parts of one horse in between all the horses, will people think the parts of one are parts of all?" He then tried to photograph another hundred feet of film showing many horses at the Squaw Dance (a ceremony held the next day). This was successful, and he made a film which started with several shots of complete and different horses, then cut back and forth from extreme close-ups of the one horse to shots of the horses as a group getting ready for a dash across the fields (part of the ceremony). In editing the film, he arranged his shots in an order different from that in which he took them in the camera, and cut shots into shorter pieces, using them in several different places in the film. The end of the film shows the dash of the horses across the field marking the start of the ceremony.

TSOSIE SISTERS: *John Adair Hangs Out the Laundry.* 2 minutes.

At this point the two sisters first decided to work as a team. They said they would make a film of John Adair and Dick Chalfen (our assistant) hanging out the laundry. This film followed a conventional plot structure, and merely had Adair hang out some laundry, aided by an assistant. It was shot in sequence and had the girls giggling for hours. It was edited almost the way it was shot.

MAXINE TSOSIE: *The Boys on the Seesaw.* 1½ minutes. (Photos 2–3).

Here Maxine photographed two boys on a seesaw. She took a series of shots from the same cademe showing the boys and the seesaw going up and down. When the film came back from the lab she decided to cut it up and "splice it for fun." She achieved the remarkable feat of cutting the action of a seesaw into parts, re-arranging them in a different order without changing the flow of action.

AL CLAH: *The Monkey Bars.* 2½ minutes.

Clah felt that he wanted to "experiment with the motion." He chose for his subject a set of climbing bars (monkey bars) which were in the school playground. He took a series of ten or twelve pans moving up, across, and down the various metal parts of the playground toy. Contrary to the others, he did not expect to photograph his little exercise in the sequence in which he would finally put it together. He said he merely wanted to try out "how it looks when the camera moves." It was in this first film that Clah began to show his extreme control over a variety of camera movements, and it was here that he first showed that he moved the camera in a circular rather than a linear fashion. When the film was returned he was pleased with the results and spent about four hours on the editing bench putting the sequence together. When asked what he was doing he said, "I want to see how the motion goes together."

SUSIE BENALLY: *The Swing.* 2 minutes.

Susie photographed the frame of the swings in the playground from various angles. Then she had several shots of the empty swings. The last shot showed a little Navajo girl swinging on a swing. It also was photographed in sequence, but Susie cut out parts of shots which she felt were "wrong."

MIKE ANDERSON: *The Ants.* 2½ minutes.

Mike wanted to photograph red ants in an ant hole. He crouched over the tiny hole and heap of sand and waited for ants to emerge. Since he shot with a wide angle lens, the ants were almost invisible and Mike did nothing further with this footage.

There were several other films made during the first practice day. All the students showed more or less the same skill in the use of the camera. All of them exposed their film accurately, loaded the cameras accurately, and were in general able to achieve just what they said they wanted to achieve.

Full Length Films

At the end of the first week the Navajos began working on their full length films which are described below.

SUSIE BENALLY: *A Navajo Weaver.* 20 minutes. (Photos 26–30).

Susie chose to depict her mother as she wove a rug. The film starts with a series of short shots showing a Navajo woman weaving at her loom. It then turns to the job of raising the sheep, shearing the wool, digging yucca roots for soap with which to wash the wool, carding and spinning, walking, digging and searching for roots with which to make dye, dying the wool, and putting the warp on the loom. Interspersed with these activities are large sections showing the mother walking and searching for the various materials necessary to make and to complete all these stages in the process of weaving. When towards the end of the film, *after 15 minutes have gone by,* the mother actually begins to weave the rug, we see interspersed shots of Susie's little brother mounting his horse and taking care of the sheep, the sheep grazing, and various other activities around the hogan. The film only shows about three inches of a six-foot rug being actually woven, and only about 4½ minutes of actual weaving. It jumps from the last shot which shows the mother handling the wool on the loom to the final shots which have the mother standing inside the hogan holding up a series of finished rugs. These are always shown in close-ups and long shots with the rugs held both horizontally and vertically. The same sequence is repeated with a different set of rugs with the mother standing outside the hogan. Of particular note in this film is the fact that there is only one close-up of a face—the "I am thinking about the design" shot which we mention in our analysis.

JOHNNY NELSON: *The Navajo Silversmith.* 20 minutes. (Photos 31–34.)

This film is structured in almost the same fashion as the weaving film. The film starts with a series of shots showing the Navajo silversmith completing the filing on some little Yeibechai figures which have already been cast and are on his work bench. We then cut away from this (as in *A Navajo Weaver*) to what is apparently the beginning of the story. We see the silversmith walking and wandering across the Navajo landscape and finally arriving at what appears to be a silver mine. The silversmith spends a great deal of time finding nuggets of silver embedded in the rock. He then spends another period of walking and wandering to look for the particular kind of sandstone from which he will make his mold. We see him working at sawing and grinding his mold, finally drawing his design in the sand, and then transferring it to the mold. At this point we have again the only face close-up (thinking of the design) in the film.

After the mold is made we see him melting the nuggets of silver and pouring the silver into the mold. He goes through the process of filing and polishing and the last shot in the film is the shot with which we began. At one point in the film, during the silversmith's wanderings to find silver, the film is interrupted to show us what appears to be an abandoned log cabin. In this sequence, the circular camera movements, moving clockwise like the sun, are most clearly apparent. This sequence was inserted to show that the mine was indeed very old, because the dwelling places around it are also old. Of note in this film, and mentioned in our analysis, is the fact that the Navajo have *never* mined silver on the reservation. Johnny was aware of that, but seemed unable to tell his story without starting at the beginning, and didn't worry about the "real truth."

MAXINE AND MARY JANE TSOSIE: *The Spirit of the Navajo.* 20 minutes. (Photos 35–40.)

Here the daughters of the chapter chairman of the community decided to make a film showing "the old ways." They chose their grandfather as subject. He was one of the best known "singers" (medicine men) in the area. The film opens with the old medicine man walking and wandering across the Navajo landscape, again digging and searching for roots and herbs which he is to use as part of a ceremony. We see him at one of the "camps" before a ceremony, eating and drinking. The sequence of the grandfather eating is the only one in which a face close-up is shown. It is apparent, however, that the shot was considered a humorous one, almost like a home movie in which one of the children sticks his tongue out at the camera. But even here the grandfather cannot have his eyes looking right at the camera, and we see an almost terrified sweeping back and forth of his black pupils as he tries to avoid looking straight at us.

We then see the making of a sand painting from beginning to end. We see the grandfather preparing the sand in his hogan, searching for the rocks with which to make the dried powder which is then dripped on the sand as paint, and we see part of the curing ceremony in which a "patient" appears. It was impossible for the Navajo to consider using a Navajo as a patient, so they chose our assistant, Chalfen, who agreed to reenact the part of a patient. The film ends with the grandfather walking from the hogan after his ceremony to his own camp.

JOHNNY NELSON: *The Shallow Well.* 20 minutes. (Photos 41–43.)

This is a film that Johnny undertook to make after he was reprimanded by the community for making the photographs of horses which are described in the text. It was at that time that he was asked to supervise the construction of a shallow well.

Johnny previously had experience as a foreman helping to

construct these wells in the community. He told the relative who suggested that he undertake the supervision of this construction that he couldn't do it because he was learning to make movies. But then he realized that perhaps he could make a film about it and thus regain some of his status.

This film is in many ways different from any of the other films made by the Navajo and is discussed in the analysis section. It opens, however, in much the same way, showing the old first—a series of shots of the old open ponds from which the Navajo used to draw water. We then see a series of close-ups of flies and insects on the water. After moving with the camera around the stagnant pool we cut quickly to a series of Navajo workmen beginning to build their shallow well. We follow, in almost educational film style, all the processes, in close-up, by which the various portions of the well are built. Intercut at moments are shots of the Navajo reading blueprints, measuring with yardsticks, and receiving instructions from the foreman who actually was in charge of this project. Johnny again shows the typical Navajo use of the circular pan in many of the shots of the cement work as the camera explores the various parts of the installation, always moving in a sunwise direction. When the job is finished we see a Navajo (Johnny used Worth to play the part of a Navajo) walking up to the well and drawing water and we see water coming from the various parts of the shallow well. The film ends not with shots of anybody walking, but with a series of shots of trucks driving away from the well.

Of interest here is that although there are no face close-ups, there are also no shots of Navajos walking to get anything. All the tools and all the equipment they need are right there. Instead of walking away from the job they ride away. This is the only time in any of the films in which Navajos are shown using their pickup trucks.

MIKE ANDERSON: *Old Antelope Lake.* 15 minutes. (Photos 56–60, 22–25.)

In this film Mike decided to make a movie about a lake. First he shows what turns out to be the source of the lake, or the mouth by which it is fed. He then proceeds to move sunwise (again) around the lake showing a variety of details of both animal and plant life. He also has a sequence of his younger brother washing clothes at the lake. The sequencing of shots in the film follows an almost exact natural order. That is, not only must the sequence be in a sunwise direction around the lake, but also certain shots must be followed by the appropriate animal and direction of action. The time element isn't very important in this film. Scenes that were shot in the morning appear later in the film than scenes that were shot in the afternoon. What was important to Mike was that we first saw the source and then moved all around the lake showing the unity between the natural things and the human beings in the environment.

AL CLAH: *Intrepid Shadows.* 15 minutes. (Photos 48–55.)

This is one of the most complex films made by the Navajo. It is the one least understood by the Navajo and most appreciated by "avant-garde" filmmakers in our society. The film opens with a long series of shots showing the varieties of landscape around our schoolhouse. We see rocks, earth, trees, sky, in a variety of shapes but mostly in still or static shots. The shadows are very small or short. When we have familiarized ourselves with the things that comprise the "world" we see a young Navajo come walking into the landscape. He picks up a stick, kneels down, and begins to poke at a huge spider web. At this point the tone of the film changes. Suddenly a hand appears rolling an old metal hoop. The hoop is cut in intermittently throughout the rest of the film, rolling as if propelled by unseen hands through the variations in the landscape. A Yeibechai mask appears in the film at this point,

wandering and walking through the landscape seemingly looking for something. The Yeibechai wanders behind trees, seen
always through bushes, looking at the sky, looking in all directions, and is intercut in an extremely complex manner with
continuing scenes of the landscape and of the legs and body of
a person dressed in white. As the Yeibechai mask wanders, the
camera work depicting the landscape begins to change from
static to complex circular, spiral, and almost indescribable movements. As the hoop, and then a rolling ball, and then the pages
of a notebook turn and move faster and faster, so do the movements of the camera as they seemingly search along trees and
rocks and bushes for whatever the Yeibechai is searching for.
Now the shadows in the film are long and some of the scenes are
deliberately dark. Suddenly we see what is very clearly the
shadow of the camera man walking through the landscape trying
to lengthen itself, and merging with the various parts of the
landscape, the rocks, the bushes, and the trees, until at the very
end the shadow of the man is almost a hundred feet long. There
follows the last shot in the film, a long shot showing the shadow
of the hoop whirling and twirling for almost fifteen seconds;
suddenly in the corner of the frame the hoop itself appears, and
as the spinning, which can now be seen as the hoop and its
shadow, grows slower, both come into the frame so that at the
very end we see the hoop spinning and the shadow that it makes.
The film is ended abruptly.

ALTA KAHN: *Untitled film.* 10 minutes. (Photos 44–47.)

Susie Benally undertook to teach her mother to make a movie.
Susie taught her to load and use the camera and exposure meter
in one day. The completed film was made in one week. The film
in many ways is very similar to Susie's film about her mother
weaving a rug. Alta Kahn starts by showing Susie picking herbs
for the dyes. She then has her daughter dying the wool and
spinning it. She spends a great deal of time on the spinning of

of the wool, whereas Susie, for example, spent a great deal of time on the finding of the herbs and several of the other processes. After Susie spins the wool she sets up her belt loom and weaves a belt. Some of the close-ups of hands and wool are extraordinary for one who has never used or seen a movie before. The film ends in somewhat the way that Susie's film ends: that is, Susie walks outside holding the belt up for the camera to look at, and the camera pans up and down very much as Susie did with her mother's rug.

What seems interesting is that there are no titles in this film. It is the only film made by the Navajo that does not have titles; and it is easy to speculate that titles never occurred to her mother because she had never seen a film. All the titles on the other films are extremely long—between twenty and forty-five seconds. Some of them contain several shots of the same title spliced together. Discussions with the students made it clear that they felt this was the proper time needed for reading the three or four words of each title.

Bibliography

ACHTENBERG, BEN
   1967. Making *Not Much To Do:* an experiment in the use of documentary filmmaking as a tool in communication research. Unpublished master's thesis, Annenberg School of Communications, University of Pennsylvania.
ADAIR, JOHN
   1944. The Navajo and Pueblo silversmiths. Norman: University of Oklahoma Press.
ADAIR, JOHN and EVON Z. VOGT
   1949. Navajo and Zuni veterans. American Anthropologist 51: 547–561.
ALBERT, ETHEL M.
   1956. The classification of values: a method and illustration. American Anthropologist 58: 221–248.
AMERICAN FILM INSTITUTE
   1969. AFI Newsletter 1(5 & 6).
ASTROV, MARGOT
   1950. The concept of motion as the psychological leitmotif of Navaho life and literature. Journal of American Folklore 63:45–56.
BARNETT, HOMER G.
   1953. Innovation: the basis of cultural change. New York: McGraw Hill.
BIRDWHISTELL, RAY L.
   1952. Introduction to kinesics. Louisville, Kentucky: University of Kentucky Press.
   1970. Communication and context. Philadelphia: University of Pennsylvania Press.

BOUMAN, JAN C.

1954. Bibliography on filmology as related to the social sciences. Reports and Papers on Mass Communication, No. 9. UNESCO.

BRITISH FILM INSTITUTE

1966. Film making in schools and colleges. P. Harcourt and P. Theobald, eds., BFI Education Department. London: Shenval Press.

CHALFEN, RICHARD

1969. It is the case that anyone can take a picture of anyone at any time, in any place for any reason, but one doesn't. Mimeo.

CHALFEN, RICHARD and JAY HALEY

1971. Reaction to socio-documentary filmmaking research in a mental health clinic. American Journal of Orthopsychiatry 41(1):91–100.
1969. Challenge for change. Montreal: Canadian Film Board.

CHOMSKY, NOAM

1965. Aspects of the theory of syntax. Cambridge: The MIT Press.
1968. Language and mind. New York: Harcourt, Brace & World.

COLLIER, JOHN, JR.

1967. Visual anthropology: photography as a research method. New York: Holt, Rinehart & Winston.

CULKIN, J. M.

1966. I was a teenage movie teacher. Saturday Review 49:51–53.

DEPARTMENT OF HEALTH, EDUCATION AND WELFARE

1968. The arts, youth and social change. Office of Juvenile Delinquency and Youth Development.

EISENSTEIN, SERGEI

1949. Film form: essays in film theory. J. Leyda, ed. and trans. New York: Harcourt, Brace & Company.

EKMAN, PAUL

1965. Communication through nonverbal behavior. *In* Affect, cognition, and personality. S.S. Tomkins and C.E. Izard, eds. New York: Springer Publishing Co.

FERGUSON, ROBERT

1969. Group filmmaking. London: Studio Vista.

GARDNER, ROBERT

1957. Anthropology and film. Daedalus 86:344–352.

GERBNER, GEORGE

1970. Cultural indicators: the case of violence in television drama. Annals of the American Academy of Political and Social Science 388:69–81.

GILBER, G.
1967. Asphalt documentary. U.S. Camera 30:70–71.

GOLDSCHMIDT, WALTER and ROBERT B. EDGERTON
1961. A picture technique for the study of values. American Anthropologist 63(1):26–47.

GOMBRICH, ERNEST H.
1961. Art and illusion. New York: Pantheon.

GOODENOUGH, WARD H.
1965. Cooperation in change; an anthropological approach to community development. New York: Russell Sage Foundation.

GOODMAN, NELSON
1968. Languages of art. Indianapolis: Bobbs-Merrill Company.

HARRISON, RANDALL P.
1964. Pictic analysis: toward a vocabulary and syntax for the pictorial code; with research on facial communication. Unpublished Ph.D. thesis, Department of Communication, Michigan State University.

HOIJER, HARRY
1951. Cultural implications of some Navaho linguistic categories. Language (Journal of the Linguistic Society of America) 27:111–120.
1954. The Sapir Whorf hypothesis. *In* Language in culture. H. Hoijer, ed. Chicago: University of Chicago Press.

HOLMBERG, ALLAN R.
1960. Changing community attitudes and values in Peru. *In* Social change in Latin America today. R.N. Adams *et al.*, eds. New York: Harper & Row.

HYMES, DELL
1964. Toward ethnographies of communication. *In* The ethnography of communication. J. J. Gumpert and D. Hymes, eds. Special publication, American Anthropologist 66 (6, pt. 2).
1967. Why linguistics needs the sociologist. Journal of Social Research 34(4).
1970. Linguistic models in archaeology. *In* Archeologie et calculateurs. Paris: Edition du Centre National de Recherche Scientifique.

KESSLER, HOPE
1970. The effect of varying the length of edemes related to meaning inferences from films. Unpublished master's thesis, University of Pennsylvania.

KLUCKHOHN, CLYDE and DOROTHEA LEIGHTON
1946. The Navajo. Cambridge: Harvard University Press.
LANGER, SUSANNE
1953. Feeling and form. New York: Scribner's.
LARSON, RODGER and ELLEN MEADE
1966. A guide for film teachers to filmmaking by teenagers. New York City Administration of Parks, Cultural Affairs Foundation, Department of Cultural Affairs.
LAYBOURNE, LAWRENCE CHRISTOPHER
1968. Filmmaking in secondary education. Unpublished master's thesis, University of California at Los Angeles.
LEIGHTON, ALEX H. and DOROTHEA C. LEIGHTON
1944. The Navajo door, an introduction to Navajo life. (Foreword by John Collier) Cambridge: Harvard University Press.
LÉVI-STRAUSS, CLAUDE
1964. Mythologique: le cru et le cruit. Paris: Plon.
LIDSTONE, JOHN and DON MCINTOSH
1970. Children as filmmakers. New York: Van Nostrand Reinhold Company.
LOMAX, ALAN
1968. Folk song style and culture. Washington, D.C.: American Association for the Advancement of Science, Publication No. 85.
MALINOWSKI, B.
1922. Argonauts of the western Pacific. London: George Routledge & Sons, Ltd.; New York: E.P. Dutton & Company.
MATTHEWS, WASHINGTON
1910. Navaho myths, prayers, and songs; with texts and translations. P.E. Goddard, ed. California University Publications in American Archeology and Ethnology 5(2), 1907–10. F.W. Putnam and A.L. Kroeber, eds. Berkeley: The University Press.
MCNEILL, DAVID
1966. Developmental psycholinguistics. *In* The genesis of language. F. Smith and G.A. Miller, eds. Cambridge: The MIT Press.
MEAD, MARGARET and RHODA METRAUX
1953. The study of culture at a distance. Chicago: The University of Chicago Press.
MEYER, LEONARD
1956. Emotion and meaning in music. Chicago: University of Chicago Press.

MILLS, GEORGE
 1959. Navajo art and culture. The Taylor Museum of the Colorado Springs Fine Arts Centre.
OSGOOD, CHARLES E.
 1966. Dimensionality for the semantic space for communication via facial expressions. Paper presented at Michigan State University.
PANOFSKY, ERWIN
 1939. Studies in iconology. London: Oxford University Press.
PEAVY, CHARLES
 1969. Cinema from the slums. Cineaste 3(2).
PORTER, EDWIN
 1914. The Moving Picture World. July 11.
REICHARD, GLADYS
 1950. Navaho religion: a study of symbolism. Bollingen Series 18. New York: Pantheon.
ROBBIN, DAN
 1966. Film making as a youth program tool. Richmond, California: Neighborhood House, mimeo.
ROUCH, JEAN
 1955. Cinéma d'exploration et ethnographe. Connaissance du Monde 1:69–78.
SAPIR, EDWARD
 1942. Navaho texts. (Supplementary texts by Harry Hoijer). H. Hoijer, ed. Linguistic Society of America. Iowa City: University of Iowa Press.
SCHOLTE, BOB
 1970. Toward a self-reflective anthropology: an introduction with some examples. Paper presented to the ISA Research Committee on the Sociology of Knowledge, 7th World Congress of Sociology, Varna, Bulgaria, September.
SKINNER, B. F.
 1957. Verbal behavior. New York: Appleton-Century Crofts.
SORENSON, E.R. and D. C. GAJDUSEK
 1966. The study of child behavior and development in primitive cultures. Pediatrics 37(1,pt. 2).
SPENCER, KATHERINE
 1957. Mythology and values; an analysis of Navaho chantway myths. Memoirs of the American Folklore Society, 48. Philadelphia: American Folklore Society.

SPICER, EDWARD H. (ed.)

1952. Human problems in technologial change. New York: Russell Sage Foundation.

1961. Perspectives in American Indian culture change. Chicago: University of Chicago Press.

SPINDLER, GEORGE D.

1955. Sociocultural and psychological processes in Menomini acculturation. Berkeley: University of California Press.

STEWART, DOUGLAS C.

1965. Movies students make. Harpers 231:66–72.

STODDARD, ROBERT

1967. Not much to do. Concern May–June.

VOGT, EVON Z.

1961. Navajo. *In* Perspectives in American Indian culture change. E.H. Spicer, ed. Chicago: University of Chicago Press. 278–336.

WHORF, B.L.

1952. Collected papers on metalinguistics. Washington, D.C.: Department of State, Foreign Service Institute.

WOLFENSTEIN, MARTHA and NATHAN LEITES

1957. Movies. Glencoe, Illinois: Glencoe Free Press.

WORTH, SOL

1963. Student film workshop. Film Comment (Summer).

1965. Film communications—a study of the reactions to some student films. Screen Education July–August.

1968. Cognitive Aspects of Sequence in Visual Communication. Audio Visual Communication Review 16(2):1–25.

1969. The Development of a Semiotic of Film. Semiotica 1(3):282–321.

1969. The Navaho as filmmaker: a brief report on some recent research in the cross-cultural aspects of film communication. American Anthropologist 69:76–78.

1970. Navajo filmmakers. American Anthropologist 72(1):9–34.

1972. Toward an Anthropological Politics of Symbolic Form. *In* Reinventing Anthropology. D. Hymes, ed. New York City: Pantheon.

Index

---

teaching Navajos to use film, 74–127

teenagers' films, 47–48, 101, 169–71, 189, 228–51

themes: of group films, 241–44, 248–51; of Navajo films, 139, 181–89; restricted range of, 256

"Tracking Bear," 148

Tsosie, Juan, 41, 56–60, 63, 65, 72

Tsosie, Mary Jane, 56, 58, 63–68, 80–82, 86, 103–4, 172, 265, 269: *see also* Tsosie sisters

Tsosie, Maxine, 56, 58, 63–68, 80–82, 93–94, 98–100, 103–4, 171, 199, 226, 265–66, 269; *see also* Tsosie sisters

Tsosie sisters, 128, 130, 144–45, 156–65, 172, 183, 250

12th and Oxford Filmmaking Cooperative, 235, 250

universal appeal of film, 257–58

"universals" in film communication, 134–35

University Settlement Film Club, 230

value systems: Navajo, 57–58, 131; as revealed in film, 28–29

verbal vs. visual communication, 258

vidistics, 27

visual communication: and codes in context theory, 137–41; coding of, 17–20; and cognitive processes, 28; cross-cultural, 12–13; and ethnography of film, 231–33; image selection in, 258; research on, 6, 13–14, 43–47

Vogt, Evon Z., 30, 74

walking, in Navajo films, 144–52, 204, 205

What We Do . . . on Saturday . . ., 234, 250

white vs. black teenage filmmakers, 239–51

Whorf, B.L., 28, 199

Whorf Sapir hypothesis, 28, 177, 180, 207, 258

Wilder, Mitchell, 150

Wolfenstein, Martha, 47

workshops, film, 228–51

"world premiere," 128–31

Worth, Mrs. Sol, 124–25

Yazzie, Florence, 71

Yazzie, Sam, 3–5, 50, 58, 65, 69, 103–5, 129, 156–65, 172, 183

Zillmann, 18